GOD, GERMANY,
AND BRITAIN IN THE
GREAT WAR

GOD, GERMANY, AND BRITAIN IN THE GREAT WAR

A Study in Clerical Nationalism

A. J. Hoover

PRAEGER

New York
Westport, Connecticut
London

Copyright Acknowledgments

Selections from the following sources are reprinted with permission:

F.R. Barry, *Religion and the War*, Methuen & Co.

James Black, *Around the Guns*, James Clarke & Co.

W.H. Drummond, *The Soul of the Nation*, Lindsey Press.

R.T. Davidson, *The Testing of the Nation*; and H.H. Henson, *War-Time Sermons*, MacMillan & Co.

J. Oman, *The War and Its Issues*, Cambridge University Press.

B. Mathews, *Three Years' War for Peace*; J. Paterson-Smyth, *God and the War*; and G.A. Studdert-Kennedy, *Rough Talks by a Padre*, Hodder & Stoughton.

G.K.A. Bell, *Randall Davidson*, 3rd edition (1952); P. Dearmer, *Patriotism* (1915); and B.H. Streeter, *War, This War, and the Sermon on the Mount* (1915), Oxford University Press.

Every reasonable effort has been made to trace the owners of copyright materials in this book, but in some instances this has proven impossible. The publishers will be glad to receive information leading to more complete acknowledgments in subsequent printings of the book, and in the meantime extend their apologies for any omissions.

Library of Congress Cataloging-in-Publication Data

Hoover, Arlie J.
    God, Germany, and Britain in the great war : a study in clerical nationalism / A.J. Hoover.
        p.   cm.
    Bibliography: p.
    Includes index.
    ISBN 0-275-93169-2 (alk. paper)
    1. World War, 1914-1918—Religious aspects. 2. Nationalism—Religious aspects—Christianity—History—20th century.
    3. Nationalism—Germany—History—20th century. 4. Nationalism—Great Britain—History—20th century. 5. Sermons, English—History and criticism. 6. Sermons, German—History and criticism.
    7. Germany—Church history—20th century. 8. Great Britain—Church history—20th century. I. Title.
    D639.R4H64   1989
    940.4'78—dc19   88-34246

Library of Congress Catalog Card Number: 88-34246
ISBN: 0-275-93169-2

First published in 1989

Praeger Publishers, One Madison Avenue, New York, NY 10010
A division of Greenwood Press, Inc.

Printed in the United States of America

The paper used in this book complies with the
Permanent Paper Standard issued by the National
Information Standards Organization (Z39.48-1984).

10 9 8 7 6 5 4 3 2 1

To
Dr. William J. Teague,
President
Abilene Christian University

The highest compact we can make with our fellows is—Let there be truth between us two forevermore. . . . It is sublime to feel and say of another, I never need meet, or speak, or write to him; we need not reinforce ourselves or send tokens of remembrance; I rely on him as on myself; if he did thus or thus, I know it was right.

Emerson

Contents

Abbreviations

AELK	*Allgemeine Evangelisch-Lutherische Kirchenzeitung*
AK	*Allgemeines Kirchenblatt für das evangelische Deutschland*
C	*The Churchman*
CF	*Christliche Freiheit*
CW	*Die Christliche Welt*
CQR	*Church Quarterly Review*
DEV	*Deutsch-Evangelische Monatsblätter für das evangelische Deutschland*
ED	*Das Evangelische Deutschland*
EF	*Evangelische Freiheit*
EK	*Evangelische Kirchenzeitung*
HJ	*The Hibbert Journal*
MP	*Monatschrift für Pastoraltheologie*
P	*Protestantenblatt*

Preface

Because I dislike boring introductions I have refrained from beginning this book with careful definitions of religion and nationalism, two notions that are difficult to define. I prefer to let the meaning of these concepts come out in actual combat, as it were, while we unfold the story of the Great War in the sermons of the British and German Protestant clergymen. After a time the subtle connotations surrounding religion and nationalism and the meaning of "Christian nationalism" should become clear.

The core of material for this study comes from war sermons of the British and German clergy of 1914-18. But it includes more than this; on the periphery is a ring of material from other thinkers, which makes this an investigation of the Protestant religious community in general. Most of the preachers involved are Anglicans and Lutherans, but a few are Reformed, Methodist, Baptist, and Presbyterian. We look not only at pastors, vicars, and chaplains, but also at deans, canons, bishops, archbishops, and university theologians. From time to time we shall even call in a layman, even a secular layman, to show that the thinking of the Protestant religious community was close to that of the rest of the nation.

The Protestant churchmen played a significant role in the First World War, a role not fully appreciated by historians. The church's influence was diminishing at the beginning of the century, to be sure, but was still significant. Furthermore, the war brought with it a religious revival of sorts, and people flocked to churches by the millions and purchased books of patriotic sermons by the thousands. "A Mighty Fortress Is Our God" became the favorite song of German soldiers marching into battle. Clerical admonitions appeared in major newspapers. Chaplains wrote gripping accounts of life in the trenches. Religion became a key ingredient in the "war fever" of the Great War. I hope that this study will make a modest contribution to understanding that fever.

I have been studying clerical nationalism, off and on, for three decades, since the early 1960s when I was a graduate student at the University of Texas, Austin. I did a paper on Friedrich Schleiermacher, which I enlarged into a Masters Thesis, which in turn became a doctoral dissertation on the nationalism of the clergy in the era of Napoleon (1806-15). Later I enlarged that study into an analysis of German clerical nationalism from Napoleon to Versailles, which became a book, *The Gospel of Nationalism* (Stuttgart: Steiner, 1986). Since I have read thousands of sermons from the Great War, I feel that I have earned the right to generalize. When I say the Germans on the whole did this and the British in the main did that, I have the data to back up these generalizations.

My research has taken me to Berlin, Heidelberg, Marburg, Oxford, and Cambridge. I owe a deep debt of gratitude to all those library workers who don't get mentioned often enough in prefaces like this. The Research Council of Abilene Christian University has graciously funded my research for three consecutive summers (1985-87). Mention should also be made of the National Endowment for the Arts and Humanities for a grant to work at the University of Heidelberg in 1968. Valuable critical assistance in understanding clerical nationalism has been rendered over the years by my colleagues in the Abilene Christian University history department, Dr. Richard Hughes and Dr. Fred Bailey. My wife, Gloria, my best critic, has been the greatest help of all, supporting my research all these years and proofreading thousands of pages from rough draft to final draft to galley sheets.

GOD, GERMANY, AND BRITAIN IN THE GREAT WAR

1

The Guns and Sermons of August

In August, 1914, Europe stumbled into war. Millions of pages have been written about the summer that brought us World War I but nearly all historians would now agree that the blame for starting the Great War must be shared by several powers. No one nation was deliberately planning for a conflict that would engulf the world, kill ten million people, cost $337 billion, and wreck western civilization. Article 231 of the Treaty of Versailles, which placed the blame exclusively on Germany, was a milestone in diplomatic asininity.[1]

The spark that touched off the European powder keg was the assassination on June 28 in Sarajevo, Bosnia, of Austrian Archduke Francis Ferdinand, heir to the thrones of Austria and Hungary and nephew of the aging kaiser, Francis Joseph. Gavrilo Princip, a trained assassin for the Black Hand, a secret Serbian organization, jumped on the running board of the archduke's touring car and emptied his pistol into Francis Ferdinand and his wife. The Austro-Hungarian regime suspected immediately that government officials in Serbia were involved in the murder plot and launched an investigation to confirm its suspicions. Meanwhile, Vienna obtained a promise from Berlin that Germany would support the Dual Monarchy in case it should move against Serbia. With Francis Joseph consenting, Vienna sent a harsh ten-point ultimatum to Serbia, July 23, so harsh that it was obviously designed to be rejected.

When Serbia's reply to the ultimatum proved unsatisfactory, on July 28 Austria-Hungary declared war on Serbia and initiated hostilities. At this juncture the Russians announced plans to mobilize their vast army and assist Serbia, a move that caused the fearsome alliance system that had been developing since 1879 to crank into action. All the great powers and many of the small powers of Europe were locked into a complicated system of mutual

promises called the Triple Alliance and the Triple Entente. Germany warned
Russia that her mobilization would lead to war but Russia refused to back
down. Germany declared war on Russia on August 1. When the French
gave an evasive reply to Germany's request for neutrality, Germany declared
war on France, August 3. On August 2, German troops moved into Luxembourg and on August 4 they invaded Belgium, whereupon Britain promptly
declared war on Germany. Britain's entry meant that her empire and commonwealth would be involved in the conflict, so by August 4 it was truly a
world war.

Historians generally agree that World War I was probably the most catastrophic event in modern European history, worse than the fall of Rome or
the Thirty Years War. When it was finally over, four empires lay in ruins
and the map of Europe had been drastically altered. It was obvious to everyone that history had taken a sharp turn in the road. As we turn now to the
clergy of Britain and Germany we will notice an interesting fact: most people
in Europe perceived this turn very early in the war.

THE SHAKING OF THE FOUNDATIONS

"Who lifted the lid off of hell?" asked Elbert Hubbard in a popular tract
of 1914. The question typified the alarm and astonishment most people felt
on both sides of the English Channel at the scope and destructiveness of the
war. In less than a month more soldiers had died than in all the Napoleonic
Wars a century earlier. In the wink of an eye that smug Victorian optimism
of the nineteenth century had vanished. How hollow now sounded Mathew
Arnold's prediction that, "We, the elect of culture, are making for righteousness on a stream of tendency." More appropriate seemed his somber lines
from "Dover Beach" that we humans live

> here as on a darkling plain,
> Swept with confused alarms of struggle and flight,
> Where ignorant armies clash by night.

Several British sermons contained the funereal lines of Rudyard Kipling:

> Our world has passed away,
> In wantonness o'erthrown;
> There's nothing left to-day
> But steel and fire and stone.

The world music had entered into the tragic grandeur of the minor mood.
Humanity was passing through an international Good Friday; mankind was
being crucified on the cross of war. But would there be an Easter following
the great slaughter? Europe was in birth pangs but would anything be born?
This was the question that troubled many pastors and vicars. God was sift-
ing mankind like wheat but would there be any genuine response to the crisis?

The destiny of the race was in the melting pot—what would be the response of the clergy? Everything depended on reading correctly the "signs of the times."

L. P. Jacks warned Englishmen: "The war is the most significant object-lesson that has ever challenged the attention of mankind, and the fate of civilization may hang on our ability to read the lesson aright."[2] "Never," said Joseph Dawson, vicar of Ilkey, "was there greater need for congregations to pray that preachers should have understanding of the times, for, failing in that at present, they will miss the finest opportunity Providence has offered to the pulpit for a hundred years, perhaps in all history."[3] "Seldom," said pastor Cordes of Leipzig, "has a generation been granted the opportunity to divine so clearly the progressive movement of world history."[4] Archbishop of Canterbury Randall Thomas Davidson summed up the general feeling succinctly: "The well-being of the world in centuries unborn may turn, *turn*, upon our right use everywhere and in all ways of this momentous, this decisive hour."[5] Dawson agreed:

The colours, the attitudes, the relations of our mental life, are undergoing a revolution; nothing stands now, nothing will ever stand again precisely as it stood before the first shot was fired. It is a time of revaluation. . . . It is a time of transvaluation. The world is passing out of one thing into another; much that we set high is being lowered, much that we placed low is being lifted up. Are you not conscious of the vibration, the change, the new gleams flashing out from under the old eyelids?[6]

But what exactly was passing away? Many things are mentioned in the war sermons of the times, but clergymen seemed to relish pointing out that the war was destroying internationalism. Pastor Georg Löber of Leipzig gloated: "The war is the grave of internationalism. . . . The war produced a strong national consciousness. A *Volk* that cannot find this national consciousness in the war has played out its roll."[7] It was like the Tower of Babel all over again—God was scattering mankind! The war was ringing down the curtain on all manner of "internationals."

For example, the war destroyed international *socialism*. The working classes in both countries called a truce in their struggle with capital and supported their national governments in 1914. Especially noteworthy was the defection of the German Social Democratic party from the banner of international socialism, an event that greatly distressed Lenin. On August 4, 1914, there occurred in the Reichstag what pastors considered one of the greatest "revelation-hours" of all German history. On that day the Reichstag approved by a unanimous vote an initial war credit of five billion marks for the war effort. In an earlier caucus the delegates of the SPD, the largest party and the one expected to oppose war credits, voted 96 to 14 in favor of them. Later, in the final vote, all 110 Socialist deputies voted for credits. Without a single dissenting deputy, the Reichstag stood behind the government of the kaiser. William II gloated: "I see no more parties; I see only Germans!"[8]

The war destroyed international *pacifism*. All those who dreamed of a brotherhood of man, a universal republic, seemed now to have been pursuing an illusion. All the arguments of Tolstoy, William Penn, Quakers, and Mennonites could not stay the hand of Mars when the fateful hour struck, the hour of moral decision, the hour of the fatherland's need.[9] Nationalism destroyed the hopes of Tennyson, expressed so beautifully in his "Ode Sung at the Opening of the International Exhibition":

> And let the fair white-wing's peacemaker fly
> To happy havens under all the sky,
> Till each man find his own in all men's good,
> And all men work in noble brotherhood,
> Breaking their mailed fleets and armed towers.

The war destroyed international *commercialism*. Richard Cobden of the Manchester School, the "apostle of free trade," has assured mankind that commerce was "God's international law" and that international business would make war obsolete. In 1910 Norman Angell wrote *The Great Illusion*, an attack on war, arguing that nations were so tied together economically that a major war would paralyze them and they would be forced to conclude peace in a few months. David Lloyd George had insisted that free trade guaranteed peace; if the Germans sell us tons of sugar beets, would they kill their own market?[10] After the guns of August went off Ernst Troeltsch mused: "The world economy did not prevent the world war and our war is no economic war. It is a war for the freedom of hearth and home, for the right of the German spirit and German labor."[11]

The war destroyed international *feminism*. This movement, of course, was not very strong in the Victorian period, but in the land where it was strongest, England, the ladies forgot their grievances and their charges about sexism in order to defend their country.[12]

The war destroyed international *science*. It brought a humanistic *Götzendämmerung*, a "twilight of the idols." It felled the false gods of knowledge, scholarship, education, rationalism, and intellectualism. Many people were asking if the war had shaken religion but Whitaker put the shoe on the other foot and asked: "Is our faith in science shaken?" After all, science is a rival creed that places all hopes for future happiness on the increase of our knowledge of the physical world. Why didn't science prevent this terrible war?[13]

Henry Wace, Dean of Canterbury, wasn't the only cleric who asked: "If we westerners are so smart, what happened to the Germans?" Germany is the most highly educated country in Europe yet "the nation, as a whole, has formed a judgment so false and inhuman, on the very elements of moral duty, that we are forced to recognize that in fighting it we are fighting not merely a political foe, but a moral outlaw from Christian civilization."[14] The war forced people to conclude that information does not produce good judgment, that knowledge is not the same as wisdom. As Holland said, "The educated and civilized man is wounded in his best and innermost self. The dart has struck him in the heart and he must pull it out or bleed to death."[15] E. A. Burroughs, Chaplain to the King, concluded, "The resources of man are at an end: civilization, science, progress—all the things we trusted in—have failed the world in its greatest need."[16]

It was obvious to most careful observers that the Victorian "generation of materialism" had overlooked something.

THE NECESSITY OF THEODICY

When Europe lifted the lid off of hell people discovered evil again. On both sides of the North Sea preachers testified that the war caused the scales to fall from their eyes, eyes that had been blinded for a century or two by hedonism and pseudoenlightenment. A British observer of an English field hospital at Antwerp confessed: "One felt that one was in the presence of wickedness such as the world has rarely seen, that the powers of darkness were very near, and that behind those blackened walls there lurked evil forms. . . . One could almost hear the devil laughing at the handiwork of his children."[17] In "Locksley Hall," Tennyson, said some, must have been clairvoyant:

> Chaos, Cosmos, Cosmos, Chaos, who can tell how all will end?
> Read the world's wide annals, you, and take wisdom for your friend.
> Aye, if dynamite and revolver leave you courage to be wise,
> When was age so crammed with menace, madness, written, spoken lies?

The carnage of the battlefield was enough to destroy all one's ideals. Wrote historian M. A. Hamilton, who lived through the war: "Life was less than cheap, it was thrown away. The religious teaching that the body was the temple of the Holy Spirit could mean little or nothing to those who saw it mutilated and destroyed in millions by Christian nations engaged in war. All moral standards were held for a short moment and irretrievably lost."[18] William Drummond spoke of soldiers returning from the trenches with "soul-shock," having been brought face to face with an evil of which they had never dreamed.[19] Kipling reported that a certain Frenchman told him, "The Boche is saving us by showing us again what evil is." Many asked: why did we need reminding?[20]

The rediscovery of evil coincided with a recovery of the traditional, biblical God. C. S. Lewis once quipped that most people don't want a father in heaven, they want a grandfather in heaven, a kind, permissive old man who will say, "Oh, just let the children play!" The Great War restored many Christians to a father in heaven. Pastors Kern and Kirchner stressed the fact that the phrase, *die liebe Gott* ("the good Lord") is nowhere found in scripture and the notion of a soft, effeminate deity is an affront to the religious consciousness. The biblical Jehovah is a masculine deity with juice and daring, a god who combines both love and anger, an almighty Lord of heaven and earth who causes war and who uses war in his plan for history (Isa. 45:7).[21]

But the recovery of evil brought with it one of the oldest of philosophical problems—the problem of evil. Why did God allow such a terrible war as this? More to the point, how could such a war break out among God's special people, the Christians?

How, indeed could the most terrible war in history break out among Christian nations? William Temple deplored the fact that "members of the body of Christ are tearing one another, and His body is bleeding as it once bled on Calvary, but this time the wounds are dealt by His friends. It is as though Peter were driving home the nails and John were piercing the side."[22] Three days before the war began Archbishop Davidson wrote to German theologian, Ernst Dryander: "War between the two great Christian nations of kindred race and sympathies is, or ought to be, unthinkable in the twentieth century of the Gospel of the Prince of Peace."[23]

But the unthinkable happened and Christians had to face the problem. One English lady declared, "I cannot read the New Testament now, for I find it very difficult to think Christianly. I must turn to the Old Testament—and only to parts of that." It was reported that Chinese Christians were offering daily prayers for the forgiveness of Christian clergymen in the belligerent nations. The heathens could now answer the missionary call: "Physician, heal thyself!" Warned Jacks: "Unless the moral forces of Europe can show themselves able to meet the challenge, not only will Christianity lose the respect of the non-Christian races, but it will cease to believe in itself."[24]

British Labor leader Ramsey Macdonald delivered a scathing denunciation of formal religion and of the hypocritical absurdity of both Britain and Germany invoking the same God, concluding that he would rather worship some racial deity than the "universal" Jehovah. Henry Scott Holland, professor of divinity at Oxford and canon of Christ Church, picked up this gauntlet and counterattacked. He said there was nothing puzzling or contradictory about the fact that both sides prayed to the same God for victory. We would think less of the Germans if they did not believe in their cause. Herein lies our only hope—that both sides believe in a simple law of righteousness; a universal conscience. Praying to the same God proves that we are not relativists. We British pray that God will help Britain, not because she is Britain, but because she is righteous:

We are one in Conscience; in the Law we serve; in the God whom we worship. Herein we find a brotherhood, which we have never lost. Our methods of vindicating the honour of this one Supreme Law of Right are hideous, and cruel, and absurd. Pour out all your indignation upon them! But in the common consent to appear before one Bar of Judgment, and lay our Cause before the one Eternal Righteousness, lies our solitary hope of strength and of salvation.[25]

Many clergymen handled this question by simply denying that Christianity had anything to do with causing the war. "It is a *monstrous misuse of language*," thundered the Lord Bishop of London, Arthur Winnington-Ingram, "to talk of the breakdown of Christianity when what has produced the war is the *exact contrary to Christianity*."[26] Many preachers pointed out that "Christendom" was a giant abstraction and that most people in Europe were either pagans or only nominal Christians. It would be ridiculous to speak of a "Christian nation" since a nation is not the kind of entity that could become Christian. There is and always will be a good deal of paganism in western culture. "The sooner the non-Christian world realizes that Christendom is not yet Christian," claimed Edwyn Bevan, "the better for the prospects of Christianity."[27]

Most churchmen on both sides had something to say about the problem of evil in general. How could one believe in God anymore, now that such a catastrophic war had occurred? The answers usually followed the historic Christian position on the problem of evil. First, it would be naïve to think that the Great War was a new kind of evil, or even a new degree of evil. It was a terrible concentration of evil in a small time and space, true, but evil is not morally worse nor less of a problem because there is more of it. Evil occurs every day, all over the world, and therefore one could just as easily ask why Christianity hasn't yet abolished crime, police, courts, and laws. Evil will continue in all its forms until the end of time because evil men will continue to violate the will of God.[28]

P. T. Forsyth, principal of Hackney College, Hampstead, wrote the best theodicy of the war called *The Justification of God* (1916). He noted that the war was a sharp blow to a certain kind of faith, "a faith that grew up in a long peace, a high culture, a shallow notion of history, society, or morality, and a view of religion as but a divine blessing upon life instead of a fundamental judgment and regeneration of it." Evil will always destroy a shallow faith, a Pollyanna worldview. "We are here to fight the good fight," concluded Forsyth, "rather than to have a good time."[29]

God could have made a world without evil, reasoned most clerics, but it would also have been a world without free, moral creatures like man. God is responsible for evil only in an indirect sense, that is, he made the creatures that could choose evil, but he did not make their evil choices. If this makes God responsible, then parents are responsible for the crimes of their children. Creation is always a risky business but to get rid of evil by getting rid of free creatures would be like cutting off your entire foot to cure a sore toe. Since God made man free, he does not intervene to deliver an individual or a nation or a civilization from the consequences of their own mistakes. To do so would be to treat them as slaves and not children, puppets and not men. God would then be a grandfather, not a father. People deserve the governments they get and the wars they get. "God will never drive men to obey him," insisted Chaplain Studdert-Kennedy, "nor compel them to do right. God wills to be the Father of free sons, and not the driver of dumb slaves. God is not a German. He will never take away from us our power to choose. It would be easier for us if he would."[30]

Furthermore, pain and suffering have great value in the school of moral education. If disasters like the war really destroyed God then mankind would have renounced its faith in the supernatural centuries ago. People still believe in God in spite of wars because, down deep, they perceive the profound truth that pain brings special insight into the nature of things, especially into the nature of the noumenal world. Christ taught us that God prunes his vines so they will produce more fruit (John 15:1-8). God's basic rule has always been no suffering, no fruit; no cross, no crown; no dying, no life.[31] German pastors especially labored to convince their parishioners about the pedagogical value of suffering. For example, Bruno Doehring, court preacher in Berlin, told his congregation in May, 1915, that God was blessing Germany just as much in days of hardship as in the earlier days of victory. By hardship God was welding together a great "community of suffering" (*Leidensgemeinschaft*). He concluded, "That is the Gospel for these difficult days: times of suffering are God's times!"[32]

In the final analysis, one simply does not know why God allows evils like war to occur. One must just adopt a humble faith like that of Job and declare that one has no right to speak on such sublime matters (Job 40:5). To demand an explanation for everything would be kin to fleshly hedonism, a hedonism of the mind, as it were. We learn to live with thorns in the flesh and evil is just a "thorn in the mind" with which we must learn to live. Forsyth suggested that God vindicates his justice by saving men from the doubt of it, rather than by demonstrating to them the truth of it.[33]

This does not mean that God stands aloof from man in his struggles with evil. On the contrary, when he became man in Jesus Christ God entered the realm of evil and suffering and participated in all man's perplexities. God knows all about the horrors of war because he was man and was tempted in all possible ways (Heb. 4:15). God somehow causes wars and directs wars to the realization of his plans in history; he is not the author of the evil but he uses the evil once it starts. The prophet Isaiah asked God: "Why is thy apparel red, and thy garments like his that treads the wine press?" God answered, "I trod down the peoples in my anger . . . and I poured out their lifeblood on the earth" (Isa. 63:2,6). The Bible is not afraid to make God a participant in wars and revolutions and human suffering. God takes his stand with man, wherever man happens to be. He shares man's strange and mixed and terrible situation. It is all a glorious yet incoherent picture but it is vain for the rationalist to tidy it up and make it all logical. The believer must walk by faith and live with the incoherence.[34] When God shook the foundations in 1914 he also rattled that old idol, rationalism.

THE COLLAPSE OF MATERIALISM

"Perhaps God has allowed us to pull down the temple of modern civilization over our heads in order that the survivors may be cured of the modern habit of regarding man as a calculating machine."[35] Percy Dearmer thus captured the feelings of hundreds of clergymen in Britain and Germany who believed that World War I was a divine judgment on the error of materialism.

Materialism asserts that all reality is matter, that the real world is corporeal, empirical, sensible, and concrete. Negatively, this theory implies that all events in the universe have natural or material causes, that no events are caused by idealistic or spiritual processes. Mind, soul, spirit, nous, reason, *Geist*, or whatever else one might think to be immaterial—these are all explained as simply functions of matter, as cases of complex organizations of matter. Consequently, the material universe is not affected by any transcendent intelligence, purpose, free will, or final cause, but rather by brute material forces, forces that are amoral and ateleological. Practically and ethically, materialism connotes an axiology that affirms wealth, money, gadgets, bodily satisfactions, and sensual pleasures to be the greatest values in life.

British culture had for several centuries tilted toward materialism with its illustrious string of empirical thinkers—Hobbes, Locke, Hume, Bentham, Mill, and Spencer. Germany had produced two powerful thinkers in the middle of the nineteenth century—Ludwig Feuerbach and Karl Marx—who explained all religion and philosophy in terms of material and natural categories.[36] Then practical materialism comes along to buttress the theoretical; science and industry grow so rapidly that even the common people begin to see its truth. Bismarck's *Realpolitik* seemed to prove that the "realistic" mentality was the only possible approach to politics. Materialism mingled with ideals of rationalism and progress; Carlton J. H. Hayes wrote of the Victorian era, "The Generation of Materialism was the supreme one of Enlightenment."[37]

Then came 1914. Most people instinctively use the principle of sufficient reason—from a big effect they infer a big cause. The Great War was an effect so big that it required the indictment of an entire century or more to explain it. A searching critique of the nineteenth-century *Zeitgeist* was necessary to lay bare the roots of the catastrophe. Classical scholar Gilbert Murray noted that from Waterloo to the present "there has passed one of the greatest and most swiftly progressive centuries in all human history."[38] French philosopher Henri Bergson noted that more tools had been developed in the last fifty years than in the previous one thousand years.[39] Many churchmen took a perverse pride in pointing out the paradox: "The Age of Progress ends in a barbarism such as shocks a savage. The Age of Reason ends in a delirium of madness."[40]

The Bible provided an excellent text here: "It is good for me that I was afflicted, that I might learn thy statutes" (Ps. 119:71). During good times the eyes become blinded with fatness but war clears the vision and allows us to discover the soul again and reorder our priorities. We discover that man does not live by bread alone (Matt. 4:4), that the unseen things are really the eternal things (2 Cor. 4:18), that man was not created just to make money or to be "an ass beneath a burden of gold." When a nation becomes limp and lax and fearful God sends a great crisis to stir it up, to restore its good qualities. When it loves life too much or fears death too much, God sends war and we can rejoice with Tennyson's Rizpah, "I have been with God in the dark."

When God sweeps away our material luxuries we discover the things that really matter: truth, honor, love, discipline, sacrifice, simplicity of life. German preachers seemed particularly pleased that God had terminated the enervating affluence that had spread over the Reich since the great victory over France in 1870. They seemed to have discovered Nietzsche's truth, that in great victory there is great danger. Dawson spoke for both sides when he said, "It is a memorable day for a man when he realizes that he has a soul as well as a body, and that while his body belongs to the dust his soul aspires to a home beyond the stars."[41]

British churchmen saw an unusually precious illustration of the collapse of materialism in the behavior of brave little Belgium in 1914. It was as if Satan had fallen like lightning from heaven when Belgium made the costly but inspired decision to stand against the mighty German army. She could have allowed the Germans to march through her territory but then Germany would have crushed France in just a few weeks. And then—who knows?— Germany might have invaded England. Several preachers referred to a cartoon in the magazine *Punch*, which pictured William II talking to King Albert of Belgium amid a scene of great destruction. The kaiser remarked, "So, you've lost everything?" Albert replied, "Everything except my soul!" To most people it brought to mind the words of Christ, "Do not fear those who kill the body but cannot kill the soul; rather fear him who can destroy both soul and body in hell" (Matt. 10:28). "If you saw that picture," claimed Winnington-Ingram, "you would understand what it meant to 'have nothing and yet possess all things' in the admiration of the whole civilized world."[42]

A materialist could not possibly understand the mind that would risk material goods for spiritual or ideal treasures. Belgium now lives in our hearts as Athens lived after Marathon, said Walter Mursell, and she behaved in a way that "baffles the enemy, and defies defeat, and mocks at misfortune, and even laughs at death. This power is latent in the heart of man, and it is indeed a witness of man's kinship with God."[43] J. M. L. Thomas said that Belgium could have sold out to Germany but "she preferred the chastity of her soul to the price of shame and the wages of a harlot."[44] James Black compared Belgium to Leonidas and his 300 brave Spartans, noting that Belgium had "taught the world that the Germans are men and not gods, and their horses are flesh and not spirit."[45]

Germany resembled the wicked King Ahab of Israel, who coveted a vineyard adjacent to his royal property. He offered to purchase it but the owner, Naboth, replied, "The Lord forbid that I should give you the inheritance of my fathers" (1 Kings 21:3). Ahab killed Naboth and took the vineyard, but God took vengeance on him and slew all his sons in due time. The parallel was obvious to Frederic Macnutt, Canon of Southwark: "Belgium's bitter cry is the protest to God and man of humanity outraged by the unrestrained practice of the devil's creed that might is right."[46]

"Belgium has shown us," said Lyttelton, "that though fortresses may fall, though bravery may end in failure, in and through her unspeakable woe she is powerful as the quickener of Europe's moral sense."[47] H. H. Henson agreed: "Belgium waked the civilized conscience; and by sustaining the extreme miseries which have since befallen her land and people, Belgium has kindled the sleeping passions for Justice and Freedom, which not even the deadening effects of modern commercialism and luxury have been able wholly to destroy."[48] Many others testified that Belgium's bravery inspired the British to take up arms and sustain their commitment to the war.[49]

THE GERMAN PENTECOST

German clerics were even more excited than their British counterparts at the collapse of materialism and the recovery of spiritual realities in 1914. The world-historical Reichstag meeting of August 4, 1914, amazed them with its display of unity among the German people. It must have been the coming of the Holy Spirit upon the German people, just like the first Pentecost that witnessed the very beginnings of the Christian church (Acts 2:1-4). In a sermon on Pentecost, 1915, Gustav Freybe of Hanover described the "mobilization day" of August 4 in words that paralleled almost exactly the passage in Acts 2:

When the day of mobilization had fully come, there were Germans all together in unity—villagers and city dwellers, conservatives and freethinkers, Social Democrats and Alsatians, Welfs and Poles, Protestants and Catholics. Then suddenly there occurred a rushing from heaven. Like a powerful wind it swept away all party strife and fraternal bickering. . . . The apostles of the Reich stood together united on the fourth of August, and the Kaiser gave this unanimity the most appropriate expression: "I see no more parties, I see only Germans!"[50]

Chaplain Fritz Philippi got so carried away with this theme that he became a universalist. "Have we not recovered a common sanctuary for all our parties,'' he asked; ''Do we not have a home again in which we can pray to the same God? Catholic, Protestant, and Jew, yes, even more, Christians and freethinkers can feel the same Holy Spirit for the fatherland.''[51]

For many churchmen, God's Holy Spirit had become merely a German *Volksgeist*, as one can see from this ecstatic sermon by Walter Lehmann:

The God of the Germans had come to life! This God is perhaps not entirely orthodox Christian. He belongs to no particular confession, he swears to no special dogma, and he does not always hold to the Second Article. He is rather an inwardly spiritual, undogmatic, interconfessional piety. Catholics and Protestants, Liberals and Orthodox stand together. In the German religion everything dogmatic and confessional becomes of secondary importance while the most valuable things in Christianity remain. To recognize and describe these things in all their depth and power is not easy. The most valuable features of Christianity have been strongly and firmly united with the unique character of the German nationality.[52]

All over Germany pastors emphasized not only the Holy Spirit but spirit (*Geist*) in general. They told their parishioners that even though materialism had eaten its way into German culture from the West, God had snuffed it out in the crisis of 1914 and forced the German people to return to the roots of their strength—*Geist*. Encircled by a world of enemies, the German *Volk* had to look inward, into the world of the unseen, for those idealistic qualities that would bring victory: will, faith, conscience, spirit, determination.

Indeed, according to a crass physical calculation it seemed foolish for Germany to take up arms against the Triple Entente in 1914. She was outnumbered about four to one. With the Russian steamroller in the East and the British navy in the West the odds makers of the world predicted that Germany would not last long. But the odds makers all through history have been materialists, realists, and pragmatists, like the British, petty men who calculate the percentages and play the averages. They never reckon with the spirit, or the will, or faith, or the unseen factors in a struggle. They calculate by the slogan of Napoleon who said that ''God is on the side of the strongest battalions.'' They reason like Stalin who asked of the pope, ''How many divisions does he have?''

But then, against the odds, Germany began to win victories in August, 1914. The fortresses of Belgium gradually yielded to German arms; the Schlieffen plan pressed to within a few miles of Paris; the Russians scattered at Tannenberg. German soldiers pressing forward and singing ''A Mighty Fortress Is Our God'' seemed invincible. Chaplain Reetz boasted, ''Nations are not numbers and God is not bound by the laws of mathematics.''[53] In a sermon on the power of faith, Otto Dibelius made the point well:

According to mathematical necessity Germany should have been crushed in 1914 by superior power—and she is still alive! By mathematical necessity our munitions should have been exhausted by the beginning of 1915 for the lack of raw materials—and we are still shooting! By mathematical necessity we all should have starved in the summer of 1915—and we are still eating and drinking! There is a reality that evades sober calculation. And the strongest part of this reality is the power of faith.[54]

Preachers found many examples in history where *Geist* got more mileage out of its matter and defeated "mere matter." There was the case of the ancient Greeks, who, animated by a love of country, defeated a Persian force many times their number. The patriotic Dutch finally won their independence from the numerically superior troops of Catholic Spain. Frederick the Great, with tiny Prussia behind him, withstood the four nations of Austria, France, Russia, and Sweden for seven years. Naturally the greatest German of all history would be a prime example of the heroic idealist:

Luther was a monk against a Pope, a theologian against a Church, a man against an era, an individual against a world. His monastic brethren said to him, "That won't work." Staupitz told him, "That won't work." Occasionally Luther even said to himself, "That won't work." "It must work," said his conscience, his faith, his love, his spirit, his entire better self. "It must work!"[55]

From the Bible German preachers took even more impressive examples. The story of Gideon (Judges 7) told of a man of God who cut his army from 32,000 down to 300 so that God would receive the glory for the victory. The tiny state of Judah was saved from the rapacious Assyrians because God was on her side and her good king, Hezekiah, like the German kaiser, was a devout, prayerful sovereign (Isa. 7:37). But by far the favorite biblical example of *Geist* over bulk was that of David and Goliath (1 Sam. 17). A small Jewish shepherd boy with God on his side killed the heavily armed giant of the Philistines with a small stone fired from a humble weapon, the slingshot. Many preachers compared David to Germany and Goliath to England, a clear case of faith versus mass. They also likened the slingshot to the U-boat, the "secret weapon" of the fatherland, whereby 20 men could send 2,000 men down to their death. With this instrument Germany would bring the British giant crashing down to his well-deserved destruction. Truly, as John Knox said, "One plus God is a majority." Or, as the old German proverb has it: *viel Feind, viel Ehr*—"many enemies, much honor."[56]

In many ways, World War I was a great culmination, an Omega Point, for German idealism, a consummation that had been developing for centuries through great thinkers like Eckhart, Leibniz, Kant, Fichte, Schelling, and Hegel.[57] Many thinkers in the Great War such as Troeltsch, König, Deissman, Rittelmeyer, Tolzien, and Seeberg interpreted the conflict as the judgment day of idealism over materialism, with God carrying on his judgment from Germany. Drawing on the spiritual resources she had been developing for centuries, Germany was going to demonstrate through military victory that *Geist* could conquer matter, that *Innerlichkeit* (inwardness) was superior to externality and superficiality, that the spirit, far from being an epiphenomenon, could master technology, science, mass, and matter for idealistic purposes. Troeltsch affirmed that it was the spirit of Kant, Hegel, and Schleiermacher who sought and found the way out of our religious and philosophical confusion with their reshaping of the Occidental-Christian religion into the idealism of freedom. They unfurl its flag today to lead the nation to victory over the dumb resignation to the conformity of nature, over the vulgarity of the thoughtless craving for pleasure and the superstitious deification of money, over crippling scepticism and cavalier wittiness.[58]

In the thinking of Bruno Doehring, God had arranged modern history so that only Germany had the right answer to the error of materialism. How, he asked, can we fight the evil of mammon?

There is only one power that can do it. That power is neither international Rome, nor international Social Democracy, nor international Judaism. It is certainly not Anglo-American hypocrisy that serves God and mammon together and casts the name of Jesus in the dust. I will tell you right now personally that it is purely and simply— the German, Martin Luther, the man of the gospel, who found the courage through the power of the gospel and the sword of the spirit to assault the whole world and its money politics.[59]

Thus in both Germany and Britain the Great War seemed to bring a collapse of materialism and a renewal of religion. Both nations supposedly experienced a revival of belief in the supernatural and an achievement of national unity so unusual that many called it a miracle, or, in the case of Germany, a visitation of the Holy Spirit. The feeling was almost universal in both camps that, to borrow the words of Reverend Kilgour: "There is amongst us all a new sense of dependence on God which is in itself worth many victories."[60]

The scripture teaches us that the Spirit of God brings unity to the body of Christ, the church (Eph. 4:3; 1 Cor. 12:13). We shall see, however, that the "Spirit of 1914"—whatever it was—did not bring unity to the Protestant churches of Britain and Germany. On the contrary.

NOTES

1. On the causes of the war, see A. J. P. Taylor, *The Struggle for Mastery in Europe, 1848-1918* (Oxford, 1954); Luigi Albertini, *The Origins of the War of 1914* (London, 1952-57); S. B. Fay, *The Coming of the World War* (New York, 1928). For studies in British and German clerical nationalism during the war see Albert Marrin, *The Last Crusade: The Church of England in the First World War* (Durham, NC, 1974); C. E. Bailey, "British Protestant Theologians in the First World War: Germanophobia Unleashed," *Harvard Theological Review*, 77:2 (1984), 195-221; P. C. Metheson, "Scottish War Sermons, 1914-1919," *Records of the Scottish Church History Society*, XVII (1969-71), 203-13; Wilhelm Pressel, *Die Kriegspredigt 1914-1918 in der evangelischen Kirche Deutschlands* (Göttingen, 1967); Gottfried Mehnert, *Evangelische Kirche und Politik, 1917-1919: Die politische Strömungen im deutschen Protestantismus von der Julikrise 1917 bis zum Herbst 1919* (Düsseldorf, 1959); Karl Hammer, *Deutsche Kriegstheologie, 1870-1918* (Munich, 1971); Günter Brakelmann, *Der deutsche Protestantismus im Epochenjahr 1917* (Witten, 1974); *Protestantische Kriegstheologie im Ersten Weltkrieg: Reinhold Seeberg als Theologe*

des deutschen Imperialismus (Bielefeld, 1974); Gerhard Besier, *Die protestantischen Kirchen Europas im Ersten Weltkrieg* (Göttingen, 1984); Wolf-Dieter Marsch, "Politische Predigt zum Kriegsbeginn, 1914/15," *Evangelische Theologie,* XXIV (1964), 513-38; Wilhelm Niemöller, "Evangelische Verkündigung in zwei Weltkriegen," *Junge Kirche,* XXV (1964); Arlie J. Hoover, *The Gospel of Nationalism: German Patriotic Preaching from Napoleon to Versailles* (Stuttgart, 1986).

2. "The Tyranny of Mere Things," *HJ,* XIII:3, 488.

3. *Christ and the Sword* (London, 1916), 63.

4. *Kriegsbrot* (Leipzig, 1916), 100.

5. *The Testing of a Nation* (London, 1919), 30.

6. *Christ and the Sword,* 40; see also Karl König, *Kriegspredigten* (Jena, 1915), 59; F. R. Barry, *Religion and the War* (London, 1915), 23; John Oman, *The War and Its Issues* (Cambridge, 1915), 4; Henry Holland, *So as by Fire* (London, 1915), 68; William Sanday, *The Meaning of the War for Germany and Great Britain* (Oxford, 1915), 105; J. M. L. Thomas, *The Immorality of Non-Resistance* (Birmingham, 1915), 74; Wilhelm Meyer, *Vom erhlichen Krieg* (Marburg, n.d.), 3; P. Humburg, *Drei Kriegsandachten* (Cassel, n.d.), 4; Charles Gore, *The War and the Church* (London, 1914), 80; Basil Mathews, *Christ and the World at War* (London, 1919), 80.

7. *Christentum und Krieg?* (Leipzig, 1915), 24; also Holland, *So as by Fire,* 3.

8. See Hoover, "God and Germany in the Great War: The View of the Protestant Pastors," *Canadian Review of Studies in Nationalism,* XIV:1 (Spring, 1987), 65.

9. For details see chapters 7 and 8 of Hoover, *Gospel of Nationalism.*

10. See Barry, *Religion and the War,* 1; Marrin, *Last Crusade,* 66.

11. *Deutscher Glaube und Deutsche Sitte in unserem grossen Kriege* (Berlin, n.d.), 14.

12. Arthur Marwick, *The Deluge: British Society and the First World War* (London, 1965).

13. "Is Our Faith Shaken?" in *Ethical and Religious Problems of the War* (ed. Carpenter, London, 1916), 142.

14. Henry Wace, *The War and the Gospel* (London, 1917), 57.

15. *So as by Fire,* 7.

16. *The Fight for the Future* (London, 1916), 69; see also F. H. Dudden, *The Delayed Victory and Other Sermons* (London, 1918), 92; Gerhard Tolzien, *Kriegspredigten* (7 vols., Schwerin, 1914-19), I, 82; Christian Bürckstümmer, *Ein feste Burg ist unser Gott* (Munich, 1915), 8; W. Kuhaupt, *Gibt es eine sittliche Weltordnung?* (Stuttgart, 1920), 23; D. Dunkmann-Greifswald, *Krieg und Weltanschauung* (Dresden, 1914), 30; König, *Kriegspredigten,* 16; Walter Mursell, *The Bruising of Belgium* (Paisley, 1915), 66-68.

17. *Paganism or Christ?* (Letchworth, 1915), 10.

18. Cited in Marwick, *The Deluge,* 108-09.

19. *The Soul of a Nation* (London, 1917), 67.

20. Ibid., 73; see also John Muir, *War and Christian Duty* (Paisley, 1916), 268; Burroughs, *The Patience of God* (London, 1916), 13; H. G. Woods, *Christianity and War* (London, 1916), 41; D. Schoell, *Kriegspredigten* (Wurster), 62; Adolf Deissmann, *Inneres Aufgebot* (Berlin, 1915), 79; Reinhold Dietrich, *Gott mit uns* (Ulm, 1914), 75; Gerhard Hilbert, *Weltkrieg und Gottes Weltregierung* (Schwerin, 1916), 13.

21. P. Kern, *Warum dieser Weltkrieg?* (Zwickau, 1916), 12-13; P. Kirchner, *Kriegszweifel* (Kaiserslautern, n.d.), 4-7; also Meyer, *Vom ehrlichen Krieg*, 42; Drummond, *Soul of a Nation*, 74; J. R. P. Sclater, *The Eve of Battle* (London, 1915), 11-12.

22. *Christianity and War* (London, 1914), 3.

23. G. K. A. Bell, *Randall Davidson: Archbishop of Canterbury* (Oxford, 1952), 733.

24. "Mechanism and the War," *HJ*, XIII:1 (October, 1914), 46. See also Sclater, *Eve of Battle*, 19; Barry, *Religion and the War*, 70; Mathews, *Christ and the World at War*, 28; Wace, *War and the Gospel*, 139; Harold Begbie, *On the Side of the Angels* (London, 1915), 41; E. A. Preston, *War and the Task of the Church* (London, 1914), 17; Ernst Dryander, *Evangelische Reden in schwerer Zeit* (24 vols., Berlin, 1915-21), XI, 20.

25. *So as by Fire*, 107-9.

26. *The Potter and the Clay* (London, 1917), 230.

27. *Brothers All: The War and the Race Question* (London, 1914), 15; see also F. B. Macnutt, *The Reproach of War* (London, 1914), 21; Mathews, *Christ and the World at War*, 68; Frank Ballard, *Britain Justified: The War from the Christian Standpoint* (London, 1914), 12; James Plowden-Wardlaw, *The Test of War* (London, 1916), 136; Kirchner, *Kriegszweifel*, 21; Gerhard Hilbert, *Krieg und Kreuz* (Schwerin, 1915), 6; Adolf von Harnack, *Erforschtes und Erlebtes: Reden und Aufsätze* (4 vols., Giessen, 1923), 307; Christian Geyer, *Die Stimme des Christus im Krieg* (Munich, 1917), 60; Ludwig Ihmels, *Das Evangelium von Jesus Christus in schwerer Zeit* (Leipzig, 1916), 70; Walther Buder, *In Gottes Heerdienst* (Stuttgart, 1918), 68.

28. See Carpenter, *Ethical and Religious Problems*, 68; J. B. Mozley, *War: A Sermon Preached Before the University of Oxford* (London, 1915), 20.

29. *The Justification of God: Lectures for War-Time on a Christian Theodicy* (London, 1916), 99.

30. G. A. Studdert-Kennedy, *Rough Talks by a Padre* (London, n.d.), 127; see also R. Ussher, *Christianity and the War* (Buckingham, n.d.), 3.

31. Buder, *Gottes Heerdienst*, 18; A. T. Coldman, "Some Moral Problems of the War," *CQR*, LXXXII (August, 1916), 74.

32. *Gott und wir Deutsche* (Berlin, 1916), 12; see also Meyer, *Vom ehrlichen Krieg*, 11; Ihmels, *Evangelium in schwerer Zeit*, 123; Christian Römer, *Des Christen Weg* (Stuttgart, 1914), 266; Hans von Schubert, *Die Erziehung unseres Volkes zum Weltvolk* (Berlin, 1916), 19; Hilbert, *Weltkrieg und Weltregierung*, 31.

33. *Justification of God*, vi; see especially the excellent article by Jacks, "A Question that Should Not Be Asked," *Ethical and Religious Problems* (Carpenter), 124ff.; Meyer, *Vom erhlichen Krieg*, 53.

34. Holland, *So as by Fire*, 51-55; for additional sermons on this topic see Dawson, *Christ and the Sword*, 54; Dudden, *Delayed Victory*, 8; Plowden-Wardlaw, *Test of War*, 57; Wace, *War and the Gospel*, 206; John Bernard, *In War Time* (London, 1917), 71; Barry, *Religion and the War*, 85; Mathew, *Christ and the World at War*, 85.

35. Percy Dearmer, *Patriotism* (London, 1915), 4.

36. See Sidney Hook, *From Hegel to Marx* (New York, 1950); Z. A. Jordan, *The Evolution of Dialectical Materialism* (London, 1976); William Barrett, *Death of the Soul: From Descartes to the Computer* (Garden City, 1986).

37. *A Generation of Materialism: 1871-1900* (New York, 1941), 328.

38. "Thoughts on the War," *HJ*, XIII:1, 76.

39. "Life and Matter at War," *HJ*, XIII:3, 473.

40. Paul Bull, *Christianity and War* (London, 1918), 63.

41. *Christ and the Sword*, 89; see also Dudden, *The Problem of Human Suffering and the War* (London, 1919), 27; Bernard, *In War Time*, 18-20; Muir, *War and Christian Duty*, 192; A. H. Gray, *The Only Alternative to War* (London, 1914), 11; Woods, *Christianity and War*, 97; Macnutt, *Reproach of War*, 78; John Kelman, *Salted with Fire* (London, 1915), 4; G. N. Whittingham, *Who is to Blame?* (London, 1916), 22; Winnington-Ingram, *Victory and After* (London, 1919), 36; Studdert-Kennedy, *Rough Talks*, 130; John M'Fadyen, *The Bible and the War* (London, 1916), 24; Hilbert, *Krieg und Kreuz*, 22; Fritz Philippi, *An der Front: Feldpredigten* (Wiesbaden, 1916), 55; Ernst Rolffs, ed., *Evangelien-Predigten aus der Kriegszeit* (Göttingen, 1916); Otto Zurhellen, *Kriegspredigten* (Tübingen, 1915), 55-57; Reinhold Seeberg, *Geschichte, Krieg, und Seele* (Leipzig, 1916), 267; Römer, *Des Christen Weg*, 321; Reetz, *An meine Soldaten*, 35-37; König, *Kriegspredigten*, 15-17; Paul Klein, *Du bist mein Hammer meine Kriegswaffe* (Mannheim, 1914), 48; Paul Kirmss, *Fürchte dich nicht, denn ich bin mit dir* (Berlin, 1915), 7-13; Else Hasse, *Der grosse Krieg und die deutsche Seele* (Munich, 1917), 39; Dryander, *Evangelische Reden*, IV, 20; Bürckstümmer, *Ein feste Burg*, 44; Dietrich, *Gott mit uns*, 12.

42. *The Church in Time of War* (London, 1915), 174.

43. *Bruising of Belgium*, 200.

44. *Immorality of Non-resistance*, 68.

45. James Black, *Around the Guns: Sundays in Camp* (London, 1915), 62.

46. *Reproach of War*, 53-54.

47. "What Next?" *HJ*, XIII:2, 267.

48. *War-Time Sermons* (London, 1915), 173.

49. See Burroughs, *Fight for the Future*, 32; J. H. Potter, *The Discipline of War* (London, 1915), 67-68; Muir, *War and Christian Duty*, 61-63; John Sinker, *The War: Its Deeds and Lessons* (London, 1916), 78.

50. Pressel, *Kriegspredigt*, 17-18; see also Buder, *In Gottes Heerdienst*, 21-22; Paul Althaus-Göttingen, *Kommt, lasst uns anbeten!* (Berlin, 1915); D. Sardemann, *Das Reich Gottes und der Krieg* (Cassel, n.d.), 25; G. Nowak, *Stark und getrost im Herrn* (Berlin, 1917), 94; Gottfried Naumann, *Stark in Gott* (Leipzig, 1915), 30-31; J. Rump, *Berliner Kriegs-Betstunden* (Leipzig, 1915), 41; Johannes Kritzinger, *Mit Schmerzen gesucht* (Berlin, n.d.), 9; König, *Kriegspredigten*, 38; Kirmss, *Fürchte dich nicht*, 38; Ludwig Ihmels, *Darum auch wir: 7 Predigten während der Kriegszeit* (Leipzig, 1914), 77; Hasse, *Der grosse Krieg*, 99; Dryander, *Evangelische Reden*, I, 6-7; Otto Dibelius, *Gottes Ruf in Deutschlands Schicksalstunde* (Berlin-Lichterfelde, 1915), 59; Deissmann, *Inneres Aufgebot*, 120; Brakelmann, *Kriegstheologie*, 37.

51. *An der Front*, 54.

52. Walter Lehmann, *Vom deutschen Gott* (Ulm, 1914), 106, 113.

53. *An meine Soldaten*, 168.

54. Cited in Pressel, *Kriegspredigt*, 275.

55. Tolzien, *Kriegspredigten*, VII, 29.

56. See Rüling, *Ein feste Burg* (Doehring), I, 323; König, *Neue Kriegspredigten* (Jena, 1915), 24; Dryander, *Evangelische Reden*, X, 36-38; Tolzien, *Kriegspredigten*, V, 68-69; Samuel Keller, *Ist Gott Neutral?* (Freiburg, n.d.), 9; Bachmeister, *Kriegspredigten*

(Wurster), 220, 224; Dietrich, *Gott mit uns*, 64; Rump, *Kriegs-Betstunden*, 82-84; Zurhellen, *Kriegspredigten*, 53-55; Baumgarten, *EF*, XIV, 330; Klein, *Du bist mein Hammer*, 15.

57. For good studies of idealism see K. Löwith, *From Hegel to Nietzsche* (London, 1964); A. C. Ewing, *Idealism: a Critical Survey* (London, 1933); N. K. Smith, *Prolegomena to an Idealist Theory of Knowledge* (London, 1924); Josiah Royce, *Lectures on Modern Idealism* (New Haven, CT, 1919).

58. *Deutscher Geist und Westeuropa* (Tübingen, 1925), 39.

59. *Und wenn die Welt voll Taufel wär!* (Berlin, 1916), 74-75.

60. *Sermons for the Times*, I, 19. For additional testimony to the revival of religion see Winnington-Ingram, *Potter and Clay*, 53; C. L. Ives, *Intercession During: Two Plain Sermons* (London, 1914), 14; Holland, *So as by Fire*, 73; Barry, *Religion and the War*, 57; Burroughs, *Fight for the Future*, 50; T. W. Crafer, *Soldiers of Holy Writ* (London, 1915), 74; Cordes, *Kriegsbrot*, 167; Rump, *Kriegs-Betstunden*, 82-83; Martin Rade, *Dieser Krieg und das Christentum* (Stuttgart, 1915), 15; Emil Ott, *Religion, Krieg und Vaterland* (Munich, 1915), 2-4; König, *Kriegspredigten*, 29-30; Otto Hättenschwiller, *Aus blutgetränkter Erde* (Regensburg, 1916), 21-22; Hammer, *Kriegstheologie*, 98.

2

The Sins of Germany—According to Britain

Great Britain went to war with a heavy heart in August, 1914. Reading the sermons preached in this period one feels a strong need to explain the war with Germany, indeed, almost to apologize for it. The British people obviously had a profound admiration for German culture in all its facets: art, music, philosophy, religion, education, scholarship, industry, and especially in the military. One had a strong premonition that Germany would soon replace France as *la grande nation*, the role-model nation for all the world to emulate.

Going to war with Germany seemed like fratricide. England and Germany were alike in so many ways. Both were European and Teutonic; both were Christian and Protestant; both were missionary nations; both were civilizing, colonizing powers; both were leading industrial powers; both were part and parcel of western Christian civilization. As John Oman confessed, we are at war with a civilization "linked by ties of intercourse, friendship, knowledge, ties of race, religion, and temper."[1]

British clergymen seemed to go out of their way to remind their listeners that they were fighting a great enemy, an honorable foe. H. H. Henson called Germany "one of the greatest and most richly endowed of all civilized nations."[2] M.E. Sadler, Vice-Chancellor of the University of Leeds, said, "Let us remind ourselves of the debt of the modern world to German patience, discipline, organisation, and ideas. While the first act of the tragedy is still unfinished, let us keep in mind what is noble and inspiring in German character and in German achievement."[3] W. H. Carnegie, canon of Westminster, insisted that "a race that has produced Hegel and Goethe and Bach and Beethoven, and a host of others not less distinguished, cannot be reprobated in unqualified terms, and treated as moral outcasts or intellectual monstrosities."[4] Eleanor McDougall told her readers that "in music, philosophy, and scholarship the modern world owes more to Germany that to all the rest of Europe put together."[5]

Charles Gore, Bishop of Oxford, was typical of those who felt that Germany had fallen into temporary madness: "We who know the incalculable debt which we owed to Germany in the past must desire to see her with her unparalleled gifts only emancipated from what hinders her from the peaceful service of humanity."[6] Percy Gardner was typical of those who pointed to the ambiguous traditions in German history; to those who were distressed over German militarism he recalled that "Scharnhorst, Blücher, and Moltke were not the founders of the real greatness of Germany, but Kant and Schleiermacher, Goethe and Schiller, Humboldt and Helmholtz, Niebuhr and Ranke."[7]

H. A. L. Fisher, eminent historian and vice-chancellor of Sheffield University, warned his compatriots not to belittle the Germans. This enemy, he insisted, is greater than the Spain of Philip II or the France of Louis XIV and Napoleon:

I am thinking of social and moral factors . . . of the burning patriotism of the Germans, of their devotion to duty, of their wholesome family life, of the undeviating and concentrated purpose which informs their political action, of their exact aptitude for business, of the great imaginative and artistic powers which for three centuries have given them the unchallenged mastery in the domain of European music, of the disinterested love of knowledge which has earned for German universities the respect of the whole learned world.[8]

William Sanday of Oxford, chaplain to the king, summed up in rare style the paradox of having to fight Germany: "As Germany loved us, we are grieved; as she was fortunate, we rejoiced at it; as she was valiant, we honour her; but as she was ambitious, we are fighting her. There are tears for her love, joy for her fortune, honour for her valour, and war for her ambition."[9]

What should the good Englishman do when forced to fight such a great people only lately gone wrong? Listen to some good German music, advised James Plowden-Wardlaw of Cambridge, and you will find the true Germany again. "You will feel the blessing as of an old mother stirring about your head, and you are a child again, nestling inside the folds of Granny's gown. How foolish and far-away now the rabid talk of your Treitschke's and Bernhardi's. Away from them into the pit of forgetfulness! You have recovered your lost Allemagne."[10] F. R. Barry of Oxford gave similar advice: "It is well, when Zeppelins are hovering overhead, to read some great piece of German writing. One realizes then the heart-rending superficiality of the present struggle and the essential unity that lies beneath. It enables us, on the following Sunday, to go in peace to our Communion."[11]

But now the eulogies must end and the criticism must begin, because something strange and terrible had happened to this great people.

THE DOCTRINE OF THE AMORAL STATE

The British discovered many faults in the Germans but by far the greatest error was a doctrine—the belief in the amoral state. Preachers referred to this tenet by many names: kaiserism, Bismarckism, Prussianism, Bernhardism, *Realpolitik*, the Gospel of Force, or simply Might Makes Right. Whatever its name, however, it referred to the notion that morality did not apply to the state, that great *Gemeinschaft* that Hegel had taught the Germans to revere. Personal morality is binding on the individual because the group will enforce it, but the state has nothing above it and thus must be the judge in its own cause. Since there is no tribunal above the state, war is the only possible court of appeal.[12]

Clergymen expressed deep shock that a great cultured nation in the modern, civilized world would have the temerity to seriously suggest the barbaric idea that mere power determined the right between nations. Sir Henry Jones complained that the Germans had taken the normally low level of international morality and made it into a virtue.[13] Edward Wilmore exclaimed, "We thought Socrates had refuted Thrasymachus forever!" The Germans seemed to be asserting that "there is no righteousness save what Krupp makes."[14] Winnington-Ingram called the idea "the Pagan Doctrine of the State" and claimed that "the entire theory is a legal, philosophical, metaphysical falsehood, the most disastrous piece of false thinking still surviving on earth."[15] Jones said the Germans had "taken the sacred things of the moral law, the vessels of the temple, and drunk wine in them."[16] Plowden-Wardlaw poked fun at the idea with the observation that the Germans believed "Thou shalt not kill" applied to the pickpocket but not to the emperor.[17] The following lines appeared in many sermons:

> For right is right, since God is God;
> And right the day must win;
> To doubt would be disloyalty,
> To falter would be sin.[18]

One need only refer to the behavior of the German imperial government during the first few weeks of war to illustrate the pernicious effects of this baneful teaching. First, Germany invaded Luxembourg, an action that was in direct contravention of the Treaty of London, concluded May 11, 1867, signed by Great Britain, France, Russia, Belgium, Italy, Prussia, Austria-Hungary, and the Netherlands. Next, she invaded Belgium, whose neutrality was guaranteed by a treaty of 1839 signed by Prussia, England, Russia, Austria, and France. In August, 1870, before the Franco-Prussian War, fresh guarantees of the neutrality of that small nation were obtained from the French and German governments by Lord Granville, England being at that time prepared to resist by force of arms any infringement of that neutrality.

When the German chancellor, Theobald von Bethmann-Holweg, heard that Britain had gone to war with Germany, August 4, 1914, merely to protect Belgian neutrality, he exploded at the British ambassador, Sir William Edward Goschen. He protested that Britain had gone to war just for a word—neutrality. He called the Belgian treaty a "scrap of paper." The ambassador replied that to Britain it was a matter of life or death to keep her compact. The chancellor asked, "But at what price will that compact have been kept? Has the British government thought of that?" Goschen hinted to Bethmann-Holweg that "fear of consequences could hardly be regarded as an excuse for breaking solemn engagements."[19]

However, it was German behavior *inside* of Belgium that horrified clergymen the most. They called it "scientific animalism" and "savagery reduced to a science." German atrocities mentioned in hundreds of sermons included such actions as the following: murder of innocent civilians on the slightest pretext, sexual assaults on young women and girls, shelling unarmed cities, shelling clearly marked ambulances and hospitals, shelling churches and cathedrals, cruel treatment of the wounded, murder of the wounded, poisoning water wells, using Red Cross wagons as carriages for machine guns, using the white flag as a trick to cover an attack, placing women and children in the front of an advancing column, blowing up miners underground in their mines, and much more.[20] After the Bryce Commission had done its careful work, there seemed no more doubt that German atrocities in Belgium had actually occurred. They were not just Allied propaganda. The best evidence was captured diaries of German soldiers whose consciences were troubled over these outrages.

John Henry Bernard, archbishop of Dublin, found the perfect passage to express British moral indignation toward Germany: "My companion stretched out his hand against his friends, he violated his covenant. His speech was smoother than butter, yet war was in his heart; his words were softer than oil, yet they were drawn swords" (Ps. 55:20-21).[21]

As the Germans cut their way through Belgium into northern France they left two ruins that stood out sharply in the world's memory—the library of Louvain and the cathedral of Rheims. How a university library and a Gothic cathedral could be considered military targets mystified most Britons; they saw it as an act of blind, wanton cruelty, what the Germans frankly called *Schrecklichkeit*—"frightfulness." Rheims cathedral had rightly been called "the Parthenon of France." It was one of the finest examples of Gothic architecture in all the world. William Drummond, editor of *The Inquirer*, felt poignantly its loss: "Every shell that has crashed down upon it, shattering its glass and splintering its stone, was helping to destroy one of the priceless treasures of the soul. . . . One of the living scriptures of God has been defaced, and no one can put the soul back into the shattered fragments."[22] James Moulton lamented the fact that such deeds proved that "official Germany has shown that there is no longer a conscience to appeal to."[23]

The British were firmly convinced that the doctrine of the amoral state was a throwback to barbarism and thus a threat to the very foundations of civilization. Archbishop of Canterbury, Randall Thomas Davidson, staked out the moral high ground for the Allies: "We believe, with an intensity beyond words, that there does exist exactly what our opponents deny, a higher law than the law of the state, a deeper allegiance than can be claimed by any earthly Sovereign, and that in personal and national conduct alike we have to follow higher and more sacred principles of honour than any State law can enforce."[24] Sanday disputed the German claim by arguing: "It does not follow that there is no such thing as international morals because there is no superior drill-sergeant to keep discipline and order amongst nations."[25]

Joseph Dawson, vicar of Ilkey, pointed out that the German theory made the human conscience into a piece of camp furniture, carted from place to place and "liable to be prostituted to ignoble service."[26] Henson asserted that "the diplomatic doctrine of Berlin implies the categorical repudiation of the prime conditions of civilised life—international good faith."[27] On September 19, 1914, David Lloyd George delivered at the Queen's Hall a speech called "Honour and Dishonour" in which he drove home the dangers of *Realpolitik*:

German merchants, German traders had the reputation of being as upright and straightforward as any traders in the world. But if the currency of German commerce is to be debased to the level of her statesmanship, no trader from Shanghai to Valparaiso will ever look at a German signature again. This doctrine of the scrap of paper . . . goes to the root of public law. . . . The whole machinery of civilisation will break down if this doctrine wins in this war.[28]

Clergymen took every opportunity to stress that *Realpolitik* contradicted the clear teaching of scripture. Nothing is more clearly taught in the Bible than that nations are responsible to God for ethical conduct. The Old Testament has God dealing with nations just like individuals. For example, Achan's trespass after the Battle of Jericho caused Israel to lose the next battle, the Battle of Ai (Josh. 7:11).[29] "The Divine Right of the State to do wrong and to escape punishment," said Whitaker, "forms part of no sacred text."[30] "States," agreed Smith, "are as responsible to God as individuals for the moral use of the power He permits them. They have a character and honour to maintain, and may deny this only on peril of their existence."[31] If Christ were asked about Germany, said Dawson, he would have to reply in the words of the parable, "Depart from me, I never knew you!"[32] If Britain had let Germany crush Belgium, said Mathews, it would have been comparable to the priest and the Levite in the Parable of the Good Samaritan, who, instead of helping, just "passed by on the other side." "We might have done that, and have gone down to ruin amid the crash and fall of all western civilization that must have followed the inevitable triumph of Germany."[33]

What must a person do when the state asks him to do something contrary to the moral law of God? In a book entitled, *An Answer to Bernhardi*, D. S.

Cairns gave the typical answer: he must obey God and disobey his country! "If our country is going to do such things [Belgian atrocities] and make us complicit in them, then we shall renounce our country and seek admission to some nobler State."[34]

So shocking was Germany's crime that many preachers and writers devoted several pages to the moral argument for God, which, ironically, goes back to the German philosopher, Immanuel Kant. If the Germans denied morality on the national level, then the British must affirm the evident presence of morality in all the earth, even throughout the universe. Muirhead quoted with approval the ancient words of Antigone, who spoke of the eternal precepts of the Tao: "They are the unwritten and unfailing statutes of heaven. Their life is not of to-day or yesterday, but from all time, and no man knows when they were first put forth."[35]

If all these Germanic faults were true, then the British have a moral obligation to war against such a nation. The famous chaplain, G. A. Studdert-Kennedy, known as "Woodbine Willy" because of his practice of giving out a certain brand of cigarettes, minced no words in encouraging the British soldiers to fight Germans with a clear conscience. "A traitor friend betrayed the Christ," he claimed, and "a traitor nation has crucified the world!" The most precious virtues "Germany has damned as vices—love is nonsense, loyalty is fear, honour is weakness, honesty is hypocrisy. It is this demand for perpetual war that is reactionary; it bids us look back to savagery instead of forward to civilization. It is mad." Christ had worked hard to build up certain virtues in man, but "now this brute-force Empire comes and tries to break down all that He has built. Their thinkers laugh at Faith, despise Honour, and scorn Truth. They fling back His hope of Peace into His face with contempt and say that it is bad, and that war must last for ever in the world. They are, I say, the enemies of God." German leaders worshipped a false god: "The god the German leaders worship is an idol of the earth—a crude and cruel monster who lives on human blood. . . . He is the god of discord and all that separates and severs men."[36]

Archbishop Davidson asserted boldly that "we are out to denounce and for ever to destroy, the wicked contention that in a nation's life and prowess and conduct, 'might is right.' " The British motto, therefore, must be, "Fight now, fight to the uttermost, resisting it may be even unto death, or peace shall never visit thee any more."[37] T. W. Crafer predicted that "the mailed fist" would be broken by "the nailed hand."[38] "An end, and a complete end," must be made to the German system, said Worsey, and if it is not, "our children and our children's children may have reason to curse our memories in the days to come."[39] Mathews agreed: "The world can never be safe until this new cancer is cut clean out of the body of humanity."[40] The Lord Bishop of London assured his charges that "this is a *Holy War*."

We are on the side of Christianity against anti-Christ. We are on the side of the New Testament which respects the weak, and honours treaties, and dies for its friends, and looks upon war as a regrettable necessity, and we are against the spirit that war is a good thing in itself, that the weak must go to the wall, and that might is right. It is a Holy War, and to fight in a Holy War is an honour. It uplifts life to be asked to do so.[41]

THE DEATH OF GERMAN CHIVALRY

One would think that since Germany's sociopolitical institutions were semi-feudalistic, her men of God would emphasize the old code of chivalry more than the British. This was not the case. British preachers emphasized the ideals of chivalry much more than German pastors. They accused the Germans of forsaking the values of the "Christian knight," swapping them for the foul soup of Bernhardi's Social Darwinism, which justified *Schrecklichkeit*.

Churchmen affirmed that the British love of sports, often maligned by the Germans, was just a sublimated code of chivalry. British talk about "playing the game," but this is just religious parlance for what might well be called a "desire for righteousness," a recognition of a transcendent morality. Even the British kings must play fair, claimed Paterson-Smyth: "No despot or war-Lord should dominate the national conscience."[42] Chaplain Studdert-Kennedy felt that the British were the pioneers of freedom for the same reason they were the pioneers of sport:

The sportsman puts right before might. He hits, and hits hard, but never hits below the belt. However great the gain may be, however strong temptation is, he plays the game to rule, and will not take advantage of the weak. The sportsman regards the man who will foul to win as the most contemptible person on earth, and he is in that absolutely Christian.[43]

Preachers reminded their people that in previous centuries the Christian knight was required to place his sword on the altar to signify his devotion to the church and a holy life. Then he took an oath to protect the weak, to maintain right against might, and never by word or deed to stain his character as a knight and a Christian. Then, before he put on his armor, he kept a night-long vigil with his weapons beside him before the altar of God. Black encouraged his recruits with the assurance that "there is a sense, as with the ancient knights, in which these roaring guns of yours may be baptised for the service of goodness and truth. . . . Let us lay our rifles on the altar of God, and vow that we shall use them for truth and liberty."[44] Streeter explained to the soldiers that "no act is more essentially Christlike than the deliverance of the oppressed. . . . The knight-errant riding the world in search of distressed damsals to succour is as good a Christian as the Quaker literally turning the other cheek."[45] Sclater contrasted this chivalry with German behavior:

There is the spirit that shatters Louvain; and there is the spirit that rescues drowning enemies from the angry sea. There is the spirit that makes women and children cower;

and there is the spirit that shelters and defends them. There is the spirit of blood and iron; and there is the spirit of knightliness. Choose well betwixt the two. . . . A nation that keeps its ideals is a nation that no force can destroy.[46]

The loss of the chivalric ideal was just one more proof that Germany had abandoned the Christian ethic for *Realpolitik*, with its inherent denial of universal morality.

THE MENACE OF MILITARISM

British clergymen often referred to "Prussianism" as the thing Britain was fighting, and by this they meant militarism, the inordinate glorification of the army and the military class. They usually knew enough German history to inform their listeners that the highly militarized state of Prussia had unified Germany just a few decades before the war and had penetrated most of German culture and society. They depicted militarism as pagan, antichristian, undemocratic, illiberal, brutalizing, and culturally stifling. They saw the history of Prussia in terms of a cultural lag.

H. H. Henson, for example, lamented the fact that "the lower standards of semi-heathen Prussia" had been accepted by Germany as a whole. Prussia really never "went through the school of Christian civilization" because she missed the benign influence of both the Roman Empire and the medieval church, the two great agents through which western Europe received its advanced culture. The Teutonic Knights carried on a bloody crusade for 50 years before the Prussian people, a mixture of German and Slav, were even superficially Christian. Prussia was actually a military wolf in civilized sheep's clothing, a "mighty parade" of external symbols and intruments of civilization coexisting with "an interior and essential barbarism."[47]

Jesus Christ had long ago laid down the principle that "all who take the sword will perish by the sword" (Matt. 26:52). Prussian-German militarism illustrated that fundamental truth in the Great War. Most states have an army, but with Germany the tail was wagging the dog. Germans had brought odium on the adage, *se vis pacem, para bellum*—"if you want peace, prepare for war." They carried the saying to its absurd conclusion, so that peace, rather than being the norm, was nothing but preparation for war. As Oman noted, it wasn't so much that Germany was prepared for war but that she was prepared for war in such a way as to spell bankruptcy for peace: "A war in such circumstances is as suspicious as a fire in a house the owner has over-insured to the verge of ruin."[48]

The Prussian tradition had an unfortunate strain of moral relativism in it. It was in Potsdam that the doctrine of the amoral state reached its apex under Frederick II, the greatest king of Prussia. When Frederick the Great attacked Silesia in 1740 he had already brought his troops into the province while he was still paying tribute to Empress Maria Theresa of Austria. Thus did the hero of Prussia, the idol of the Hohenzollerns, cynically violate his pledged word to a fellow sovereign.[49] Fisher recalled discussing this subject with his fellow students at the University of Göttingen, men who were privately very moral but who argued that Frederick's increase of the Prussian state excused any violence, that a nation could disregard a treaty once the treaty became inconvenient.[50]

When militarism penetrates a society it produces a "strut" mentality. It leads to brutality, inflicted by arrogant soldiers on both animals and humans. German soldiers were notorious for beating their horses unmercifully. Army men had been known to shoot people for accidentally stepping on their boots. German civilians lived in fear of soldiers. An Englishman will take orders from a policeman but not from a soldier, whereas in Germany the opposite is true, or rather, a German will take orders from both. In Germany you dare not call a policeman by an intimate name, whereas in England you can call any policeman "Bobby" and get away with it. Germans fear this toleration and egalitarianism but the English have learned that it is no weakness in a state.[51]

A military civilization will produce cultural stagnation with its attendant "blighting control of predatory pedants, officialism, and dynasties," where the drill sergeant gets into the school libraries.[52] Such a civilization will produce a race of "political donkeys."[53] Dawson found it curious that the Germans would allow wild thoughts about Christ and the Bible but not about the state: "As a scholar you may cut the Bible into shreds, but as a citizen you must not snip a button from the Kaiser's uniform."[54] Cook solved the problem of how the Germans could destroy Rheims cathedral or the cloth hall of Ypres or the library of Louvain with as little compunction as they would blow up a canteen: "The architecture of Berlin is a measure of their appreciation of art."[55] Hicks summed up:

The truth is that Prussian militarism has meant for the German populace the stifling and stagnation of humanistic culture. Hemmed in by the official supervision and control which surrounds him, the individual citizen is bereft of the freedom and initiative needful for the development of individual reflection. His individuality is crushed out of him by police and soldiery.[56]

L. P. Jacks, Unitarian clergyman, professor of philosophy, editor of the *Hibbert Journal*, and principal of Manchester College, Oxford, felt that Prussian militarism offered a striking illustration of *mechanization*, a phenomenon he considered the great error of the nineteenth century. The Germans designed the destiny of a nation as though they were laying down the lines of a battleship, which was a grave error. "No greater illusion was ever suffered to obsess the human mind. At every point it [mechanism] falsifies essential truth, leads to grossest miscalculations, and comes into conflict with the fundamental needs, instincts, and intuitions of humanity."[57] If you create a vast fighting machine, it will sooner or later compel you to fight, whether you want to or not. Such machines are made to be used! The military machine will finally overpower the minds that have called it into being. You can't even choose the time of the war; the time comes when the mechanism reaches a certain degree of perfection. The machine creates its own momentum.[58]

Henri Bergson, world-famous French philosopher, attacked Prussianism in similar terms. He insisted that artificiality marked the essence of Prussian culture from the very beginning. Her administration was mechanical, "as if everything within her went by clockwork, from the gesture of her kings to the steps of her soldiers." Even German unification under Bismarck came from without, from Prussia, by mechanical force rather than by internal organic growth. Bismarck left an evil legacy—the sanction of mechanistic militarism. Germany "told herself that if force had wrought this miracle, if force had given her riches and honour, it was because force had within it a hidden virtue, mysterious—nay divine." Bergson compared the militarist to the witch who trained her broom to go to the river and fill buckets of water, but, having no formula to check the work, watched her cave fill with water until she drowned.[59] One is reminded of the observation of another Frenchman, Talleyrand, that you can do almost anything with bayonets except sit on them.

Prussian militarism was such a threat that it must be completed destroyed. Thompson referred to it as "gangrene" that must be ruthlessly cut out.[60] Ballard depicted Prussian pride and lust for conquest as cholera or typhoid germs that had entered the bloodstream of German culture.[61] Cram insisted that the Allies must have unconditional surrender and it would be "treason against civilization" to speak of any other policy.[62] Winnington-Ingram said, "We believe that when Prussian militarism has been annihilated the German people will learn to bless those whom they now curse. We shall be liberating the hard-working, industrious people of Germany from a cursed tyranny, which is opposing them and seeking to oppress the whole world."[63]

BASHING THE KAISER

British ministers personally blamed Kaiser William II for many of the evils emanating from imperial Germany. If he was not the cause of German errors, he was at least the prime embodiment of them. They referred to him as "William the Wicked" or "Willy the Hun" or "Attila II."[64] They blamed him for the massacres in Armenia committed by the Turks.[65] They blamed him for *Schrecklichkeit* in Belgium, for, after all, did he not send his troops to China in 1905 with the admonition to act like Huns?[66]

Austin Harrison traced the downfall of German culture to the Kaiser. "In fifteen years all the German virtues of centuries disappeared from the land at the will of the military tyrant at Potsdam masquerading in the boots of Bismarck, misusing and demoralizing his people." His problem was "inherent littleness" and "overpowering vanity." "In reality, he is the creature of his age—the age of advertisement, false values, press sensation, talk, and shallowness. Everything he touched he vulgarized, like the *nouveau riche* of his time.''[67] Samuel Hemphill felt that ''if Frederick the Noble [Frederick III, who died in 1888] had lived, this calamity would not have come. We all wanted to see Germany powerful; and the last thing that ever entered our minds was to envy her her greatness.''[68] Gough reminded his listeners that William's great uncle, Frederick William IV, was mentally unsound; he said the kaiser combined ''physical infirmity with the inordinate passion for exciting admiration so commonly found in degenerates.''[69] Cook spoke for many when he concluded that ''we have to destroy the Kaiser, his dynasty, and his kingdom as if he were a mad dog.''[70]

British clerics were especially irritated by the kaiser's frequent references to God in his public addresses to the German people. He talked as if he had a personal pipeline to the Almighty.[71] In one speech to soldiers at the front, for example, he proclaimed: ''Remember that the German people are the chosen of God. On me, on me as German Emperor, the Spirit of God has descended. I am his weapon. His sword and his vizard. Woe to the disobedient! Death to cowards and unbelievers!''[72]

What could one say to such blasphemies? Whittingham recalled the observation of Caesar that the Germans honored only the gods that were useful to them.[73] Renshaw said the kaiser's god was brute force since ''men act in emergencies according to the kind of god they really trust in.''[74] Maclean said God would answer the kaiser's prayers in the words of scripture: ''Even though you make many prayers, I will not listen; your hands are full of blood'' (Isa. 1:15).[75] Plowden-Wardlaw insisted that the ''god'' on the kaiser's lips was a false god, made in Germany, in fact ''the crowning product of modern Germany, which has achieved not merely the newest guns . . . but the newest God.'' The kaiser ''with the rulers of his army, worships Satan under the alias of the Prussian tribal god. . . . How angels must weep to see the tragedy of the fall, the moral fall, of Germany.''[76] Woods called attention to the ''moral conditions'' that God requires of men before there can be any communion between their spirit and his.[77] Mursell advised the kaiser to be more like Lincoln, who worried not if God was on his side but if he was on God's side. It was profane to ask the true God to lay his benediction upon ''the laying of mines, the throwing of bombs, the breaking of treaties, the burning of towns, and the slaughter of the innocent.'' That would be to worship the ''tribal deity of the darkest Old Testament times'' not the Father or our Lord Jesus Christ.[78]

GERMAN *HUBRIS*

Classical scholar Gilbert Murray reached back into ancient history to find the proper word to describe Germany's sin—*hubris*, pride, arrogance, insolence, presumption. ''By that sin fell the angels,'' he said, quoting an ancient text.[79] Chaplain Studdert-Kennedy expressed it in simpler terms: Germany had a ''severe swelled head.''[80] Smith applied to Germany a judgment

used on Victor Hugo, a great but arrogant writer: "A quality of self-suffi-
ciency so inordinate as scarce to be distinguished now and then from an immense stupidity."[81] Dawson said that Germans were driven by "a crazy ambition to dominate not only the states of Europe, but the fortunes of the
world."[82]

James Plowden-Wardlaw, chaplain of St. Edward the King of Cambridge,
informed his listeners that the great philosopher Hegel had considered himself almost divine. Hegel began a lecture one day by saying, "I may say with
Christ, that not only do I teach truly, but that I am myself truth." Great
men often have this problem, but, asked the chaplain, "is it not a curious
parallel . . . to see in modern times a whole race, the Teutons of Northern
Germany, admittedly in the front rank of national intellectual achievements,
full of domestic virtues, foremost in scholarship and science, should be afflicted by wholesale megalomania?"[83]

Megalomania caused the Germans to think of themselves, charged Dawson, "as the apostles of a heaven-born culture, as the divinely appointed
leaders of mankind, as the nation over whose intellectual development and
military prowess and commercial advancement the angels are expected to
purr with delight."[84] Harrison called pangermanism a case of "political ele-
phantiasis" and charged that the kaiser had been preaching it as a new religion.[85] Jacks claimed that the Germans treated humanity "as though it were
mere *prey* to that section of the race which can prove itself the most violent
and the most astute." He called this "the mind of Mephistopheles."[86] Germany wanted her "place in the sun," noted Mursell, but she was more likely
to get her place in "the outer darkness."[87]

According to many clergymen the German word *Kultur* became a hiss
and a byword during the first few weeks of the Great War. It was almost as
if something had been lost in the translation or as if Germans were speaking
a non-European language, to believe that Belgian atrocities could be called
"culture." The kaiser often dramatized the "Yellow Peril" threatening Christian civilization, but his "Prussian Peril" was a much greater danger to the
Occident.[88] Ballard noted the irony of the fact that Germans boasted of their
cultural mission to the world but when Britain liberated their colonies in
Africa the natives rejoiced.[89] "It is morally impossible," said Winnington-
Ingram, "that to a hand red with the blood of so many victims should be
finally entrusted the domination of the world."[90]

German arrogance, said the British, expressed itself in a haughty, condescending attitude toward the smaller nations of Europe, like Belgium,
Poland, and Serbia. Lloyd George said that the Germans believed only the
6'2" nations mattered in the world, whereas the truth is that the world owes
much to the little 5'5" nations.[91] Dearmer agreed, pointing out that civilization owed a tremendous debt to small nations like Greece, Florence, and
Palestine.[92] Historian Hugh Seton-Watson condemned the Germans for de-
siring totalitarian cultural uniformity, whereas the Allies were fighting for

diversity, variety, and pluralism.[93] "It was Christ Himself," said Archbishop Davidson, "who taught us that greatness is quite different from mere bigness, mere material force and strength, or, for a Nation, mere numbers or armament."[94] Holland stated the ideal of pluralism in these words: "Nationality can never be used as a principle, unless it sanctions all nations alike. This is the extraordinary blunder of the German claim that their Ideal of Culture is so specially precious that it must cancel all other ideals."[95]

British churchmen felt confident that their cause was just and that Germany was in the wrong when they observed the world-wide coalition that ranged itself against the Central Powers. They noted with approval the refusal of Italy to come into the conflict in 1914, proof that Germany was not fighting a defensive war as the original Triple Alliance envisioned.[96] The entry of the United States, the "great neutral Republic of the West," settled the matter for it ratified the world's verdict, said Mathews, on Germany's "moral leprosy."[97] Seton-Watson concluded, "All good Europeans are now ranged against the renegade foe."[98] Cook said that Germany was "fighting against the general conscience of mankind."[99] Box pointed out that the German military autocrats had succeeded in uniting against their race the other three races of Europe: Anglo-Saxons, Latins, and Slavs.[100]

German insolence, of course, invited many biblical parallels. One of the favorites was Assyria, that cruel, aggressor nation that boasted that it collected nations like eggs (Isa. 10:14).[101] Isaiah's description of Babylon sounded much like German national egoism: "You felt secure in your wickedness; you said, 'No ones sees me'; your wisdom and your knowledge led you astray, and you said in your heart, 'I am, and there is no one beside me.' " (47:10).[102] Germany had succumbed to Satan's third temptation; she was worshiping the Devil himself in order to gain all the kingdoms of the world (Matt. 4:9).[103]

The German mind was obviously in bad shape. But where had all these wrong notions come from? What was the origin of German moral relativism, militarism, brutality, materialism, mechanism, intolerance, and national egoism? What were the roots of German madness?

NOTES

1. *The War and Its Issues*, 102.
2. *War-Time Sermons*, 117.
3. *Modern Germany and the Modern World* (London, 1914), 3.
4. *Sermons on Subjects Suggested by the War* (London, 1915), 17-18.
5. *Germany and Germans* (London, 1915), 14.
6. *Patriotism in the Bible* (London, 1915), 18.
7. "Two Studies of German 'Kultur,' " *HJ*, XIII:3 (April, 1915), 517.
8. *The War: Its Causes and Issues* (London, 1914), 7.
9. *The Meaning of the War*, 114.
10. *The Test of War*, 59.
11. *Religion and the War*, 73.

12. Sanday traced the official beginning of the idea back to A. L. von Rochau, whose book, *Realpolitik*, appeared in 1853. See his *Meaning of the War*, 59ff.

13. "Morality and Its Relation to the War," *Ethical and Religious Problems of the War: Fourteen Addresses*, ed. J. E. Carpenter (London, 1916), 35.

14. "Why Are We Fighting?" *HJ*, XIII:2 (January, 1915), 333-34.

15. *Christ and the World at War*, ed. Basil Mathews (London, 1916), 157.

16. "Why We Are Fighting," *HJ*, XIII:1 (October, 1914), 67.

17. *Test of War*, 42.

18. See e.g., Dudden, *Delayed Victory*, 14.

19. Goschen to Grey, 8 August 1914, *Why We Are At War* (Oxford, 1914), 200.

20. For a contemporary account see Joseph Bedier, *German Atrocities from German Evidence*, trans. B. Harrison (Paris, 1915).

21. *In War Time*, 88.

22. *Soul of a Nation*, 61-63.

23. *British and German Scholarship* (London, 1915), 16. See also George Whittingham, *Who Is to Blame?* (London, 1916), 57; R. T. Davidson, *The Testing of a Nation* (London, 1919), 85; T. A. Cook, *Kaiser, Krupp, and Culture* (London, 1915), 84.

24. *Testing of a Nation*, 87.

25. *Meaning of the War*, 120.

26. *Christ and the Sword*, 137.

27. *War-Time Sermons*, 172.

28. *Honour and Dishonour: A Speech at the Queen's Hall* (London, 1914), 4. For more sermons on this see Henry Denison, *Some Spiritual Lessons of the War: Five Sermons* (London, 1915), 18; A. L. Smith, *The Christian Attitude to War* (London, 1915), 11; Macnutt, *Reproach of War*, 38; Henson, *War-Time Sermons*, 98.

29. Muir, *War and Christian Duty*, 79.

30. "Is Our Faith Shaken," 141.

31. *The War, the Nation, and the Church*, 17.

32. *Christ and the Sword*, 101.

33. *Three Years' War for Peace* (London, 1917), 75.

34. (London, 1914), 9. For additional examples of the same answer see Crafer, *Soldiers of Holy Writ*, 22; Sanday, *The Deeper Causes of the War* (London, 1914), 5; Macnutt, *Reproach of War*, 73; Wace, *War and the Gospel*, 185.

35. "God and the World," *Ethical and Religious Problems* (Carpenter), 108.

36. *Rough Talks*, 136, 185, 194-95.

37. *Testing of a Nation*, 57-59.

38. *A Prophet's Vision and the War* (London, 1916), 72.

39. *Under the War-Cloud: Being Nine Sermons on the War Preached in a Country Church* (London, 1914), xi.

40. *Three Years' War*, 23.

41. *Sermons for the Times*, IV, 8-9.

42. *God and the War: Some Lessons on the Present Crisis* (London, 1915), 55. For a good description of the Code of Chivalry, see Ramon Lull, *The Book of the Ordre of Chyualry*, trans. W. Caxton (London, 1926).

43. *Rough Talks*, 27.

44. *Around the Guns*, 21.

45. *War, This War and the Sermon on the Mount* (London, 1915), 5.

46. *Eve of Battle*, 70. For more sermons on this idea see Henson, *War-Time Sermons*, 98; Denison, *Spiritual Lessons*, 23; Ingram, *Potter and the Clay*, 62; Crafer, *Soldiers of Holy Writ*, 41.

47. *War-Time Sermons*, 99, 204-5. In his *Black Slaves of Prussia* (London, 1918), Frank Weston, Bishop of Zanzibar, attempted to show how Prussian militarism expressed itself in brutal, inhumane treatment of the natives of German East Africa.

48. *War and Its Issues*, 77-78.

49. J. W. Headham, *England, Germany, and Europe* (London, 1914), 11; Cook, *Kaiser, Krupp, and Culture*, 2; Selwyn Image, *Art, Morals, and the War* (London, 1914), 10.

50. *The War*, 11.

51. See Austin Harrison, *The Kaiser's War* (London, 1914), 127; Oman, *War and Its Issues*, 88-89; McDougall, *Germany and the Germans*, 13.

52. Wilmore, "Why We Are Fighting," 336, 338.

53. Sadler, *Modern Germany and the Modern World*, 5.

54. *Christ and the Sword*, 135.

55. *Kaiser, Krupp, and Culture*, 8.

56. "German Philosophy and the Present Crisis," *HJ*, XIII:1 (October, 1914), 100.

57. "Mechanism and the War," 32-33.

58. "The Tyranny of Mere Things," 478-80.

59. "Life and Matter at War," *HJ*, XIII:3 (April, 1915), 466-67, 470. This article was a translation of Bergson's address as president of the Academy of Moral and Political Science. See also his book, *The Meaning of the War: Life and Matter in Conflict* (London, 1915), 29-30.

60. *Prussia's Devilish Creed* (London, n.d.), 14.

61. *Britian Justified*, 67.

62. *The Significance of the Great War* (Boston, 1914), 16.

63. *Church in the Time of War*, 42.

64. Henson, *War-Time Sermons*, 9, 177; Thompson, *Prussia's Devilish Creed*, 4; Plowden-Wardlaw, *Test of War*, 77.

65. Holland, *So as by Fire*, 109.

66. Mathews, *Three Years' War*, 24; Harrison, *Kaiser's War*, 130.

67. *Kaiser's War*, 99, 127.

68. *Sermons for the Times*, IV, 22.

69. *God's Strong People* (London, 1915), 78; see also E. E. Holmes, *The Colours of the King: Red, White, and Blue* (London, 1914), 58; E. A. Burroughs, *The Eternal Goal* (London, 1915), 17.

70. *Kaiser, Krupp, and Culture*, 87.

71. Mursell, *Bruising of Belgium*, 79-80.

72. Cited in Lloyd George, *Honour and Dishonour*, 9.

73. *Who Is to Blame?* (London, 1916), 35.

74. *Christ and the War: Very Simple Talks* (London, 1916), 16.

75. *God and the Soldier* (London, 1917), 165.

76. *Test of War*, 23, 77-79.

77. *Christianity and War*, 33.

78. *Bruising of Belgium*, 79.

79. "Ethical Problems," *Ethical and Religious Problems* (Carpenter), 12-13.

80. *Rough Talks*, 76.

81. *The War, the Nation and the Church*, 15.

82. *Christ and the Sword*, 98.

83. *Test of War*, 3-4.

84. *Christ and the Sword*, 122.

85. *Kaiser's War*, 140.

86. "Mechanism, Diabolism, and the War," 45.

87. *Bruising of Belgium*, 141.

88. See Richard Roberts, *Are We Worth Fighting For?* (London, 1914), 10; Plowden-Wardlaw, *Test of War*, 38-39; Macnutt, *Reproach of War*, 55; Worsey, *Under the War-Cloud*, 56.

89. *Mistakes of Pacifism* (London, 1915), 14.

90. *Victory and After*, 7; see also John Sinker, *The War, Its Deeds and Lessons* (London, 1916), 91-94; Sanday, *Meaning of the War*, 107; Charles Gore, *The War and the Church and Other Addresses* (London, 1914), 7; Wace, *The War and the Gospel*, 57; Streeter, *This War and the Sermon on the Mount*, 9.

91. "Through Terror to Triumph," A Speech delivered at Queen's Hall, London, 19 September, 1914, 10.

92. *Patriotism*, 12.

93. *What Is at Stake in the War* (London, 1915), 6.

94. *Testing of a Nation*, 88.

95. *So as by Fire*, 30.

96. See *To the Christian Scholars of Europe and America: A Reply from Oxford to the German Address to Evangelical Christians* (London, 1914), 9.

97. *Three Years' War*, 46, 88; see also Davidson, *Testing of a Nation*, 131.

98. *What Is at Stake*, 6.

99. *Kaiser, Krupp, and Culture*, 99.

100. Smith, *The War, the Nation and the Church*, 15.

101. Oman, *War and Its Issues*, 28; Kelman, *Salted with Fire*, 19.

102. Smith, *The War, the Nation and the Church*, 15; Charles Mackarness, *Faith and Duty in Time of War* (London, 1916), 32.

103. G. C. Morgan, *God, Humanity, and the War* (London, 1915), 63; Dudden, *Problem of Human Suffering*, 55-56.

3

Roots of German Madness

There was a broad general agreement among the British clergy that the German people were in a strange state of mind during the Great War. It was said that they were suffering collective temporary insanity, passing through an evil dream, or enduring a state of demon-possession.

What was the cause of this malady? There was no absolute agreement on this question, but most clergy pointed to defects in the traditional German religion as the basic cause, defects that had issued in a weak Bible and a weak church. These, in turn, had allowed the rise of materialism and *Realpolitik* as well as the recovery of ancient pagan beliefs that Christianity had once destroyed.

DEFECTS IN GERMAN RELIGION

What was wrong with German Christianity? Were not the Germans Christians? Were not most of them members of that great community, Protestant Christendom? Not really, answered the British; they had slipped from this position in recent times. They had allowed a critical rationalism to weaken their faith in the Bible as God's authoritative revelation. Dr. Edward Lyttelton charged that the prevailing tone in Germany was "rather critical than submissive; more condescending than reverent; marked by a courteous interest rather than by a feeling of awe," all leading to a "general tendency to treat Christianity as a set of propositions offered to each man for his approval or rejection."[1] Wace concurred that the educated classes in Germany had lately been imbued with a complete distrust of Christ and the scriptures.[2]

You need only turn to the pages of the *Encyclopedia Biblica*, said McCurdy, and you will find great German theologians telling you with much learning that the Bible story of Christ's birth is a fable invented in the reign of the

Emperor Nero and that the accounts of the Resurrection are hallucinations.[3] However, noted Dawson wryly, these same savants think it a sin to criticize the state! "As a scholar you may cut the Bible to shreds, but as a citizen you must not snip a button from the Kaiser's uniform."[4] Potter maintained that Germany "as a nation has largely renounced Christianity, fallen back upon a shadowy theism, and adopted a new Gospel, might is right."[5]

The Great War had cleared the air. It had showed the British that their idol—German scholarship—had feet of clay. Whittingham quipped that this sudden loss reminded him of the verse, "They have taken away my Lord and I know not where they have laid him."[6] Selbie noted that to many Britons, "it has been the most painful experience of their lives to find men, whose names they have long been accustomed to revere, showing themselves so blindly and bitterly partisan in their judgments regarding the causes of the war."[7] Worsey expressed the general feeling:

German religious teaching for many years has had an anti-Christian tendency. From Germany have been directed the most violent assaults on Scriptural truth, dogma, and ethics. The Germans, as a race, have become, for the most part, rationalists, not Christians, by profession, and we British have been inclined to give this German teaching a too favourable hearing, just as we have encouraged German trade and German employment in our midst.[8]

In addition to a weak Bible the Germans had a weak church. Some asserted it had been weak ever since the Reformation, when Luther put it under the state for safe-keeping. The early Luther was a great individualist who spoke his mind fearlessly, who claimed that when God spoke popes and kaisers mattered for nothing. But the elder Luther had to "call in the police" to save his movement from radicalism, a tragic turn that eventually led to the subjugation of both individual and church to the state.[9] The result was that by the twentieth century the church in Germany was almost wholly swallowed up in the state. It had become merely a department of state, incapable of raising any independent moral voice in the community. The reason the German clergy raised no protest over Belgium was simple—the German church had become a state church. Gone were the days when a prophet like Amos could call kings to account or a bishop like Ambrose could deny Mass to the Emperor Theodosius. The kaiser's shameful use of God as his own personal Nordic war god was proof of this great fall of the German church. Such a distortion would have been impossible if the church had been free. The motto of the Germans stood enshrined in the words of Bismarck: "We will not go to Canossa!"[10]

British preachers liked to compare Germany and England to illustrate this weak church hypothesis. Lyttelton found it significant that the church in England was three hundred years older than the state. He contended that in Germany Protestant individualism had destroyed the organic church, the only institution that could have acted as a counterweight to the worship of the state when it arose in the nineteenth century. The secular individualist, the creature of modern mentality, has no regard for the church because he is convinced that it is as distinctly human in origin as the state. Lyttelton concluded with a strong warning to the British: "If you behold here a mighty moral declination which seems to be due to the individualistic presentation of Christianity, take heed in your island home before it is too late, and hold fast to your heritage as members of the indestructible Church of Christ."[11]

THE UNHOLY TRINITY

A weak Bible and a weak church leave a society vulnerable to the rise of dangerous ideas—like *Realpolitik*. Of all the guilty parties identified by British preachers to explain Germany's problems, three occupy more attention than any others: Bernhardi, Treitschke, and Nietzsche—called the Unholy Trinity. These three, but the greatest of these was Bernhardi.

General Friedrich von Bernhardi (1849-1930) wrote a book in 1912 entitled *Deutschland und der nächste Krieg* (*Germany and the Next War*). It ran through five editions by the end of the year. British clergymen seized upon it as an official expression of German Darwinian *Realpolitik*. Some went too far and exaggerated its influence; for example, Paget said it had been "adopted as a national classic" and the Lord Bishop of London said it was "read with admiration by the whole of Prussia."[12] However, Cairns was close to the truth when he said that the book expressed the thinking of the party that controlled the German government.[13] The German historian, Fritz Fischer agreed:

This book is generally dismissed by German historians as the eccentric outpourings of an undisciplined pan-German with little relationship to the plans either of the general staff or of the government, but the author's summing up of his arguments and conclusions under the heading "World Power or Decline" epitomised the intentions of official Germany with great precision.[14]

General Bernhardi argued that three things were necessary for Germany to advance to the position of world power, as her destiny merited. First, she must completely eliminate France as an obstructing power. Second, she must found a Central European Federation under German leadership, wherein the smaller states would seek protection of German arms. Third, she must develop into a world power by the acquisition of new colonies and the inauguration of a new world arrangement of nations. These grandiose ambitions would naturally and inevitably bring Germany into conflict with the British empire, as well as with the other races of the continent, such as the Latins and the Slavs.

Bernhardi was taken to task for his Darwinian *Realpolitik*, his crude glorification of war, and his obvious moral relativism. Clutton-Brock said that his defense of national expansion sounded vaguely like a plea for kleptomania, collective kleptomania. Cairns showed him to be inconsistent because he condemned other nations for treachery and violence in the international sphere yet denied there was any international law of right. Fischer took offense at his position that Germany's destiny was a matter of *Weltmacht oder Niedergang*—"world power or decline." He indicated that this was a faulty dilemma and predicted, "If Germany persists in calling *Weltmacht*, then England is regretfully bound to answer *Niedergang*."[15]

The second member of the demonic godhead was Heinrich von Treitschke (1834-1896), one of the greatest German historians of the nineteenth century, a fiery patriotic lecturer, an implacable foe of Britain, and an ardent teacher of German nationalism to an entire generation. It was said that in England he would be like a combination of Carlyle and Macaulay. The clergy attacked him for much the same reasons as Bernhardi. Sanday scored his inconsistency for attacking Britain in falling short of an ideal yet insisting elsewhere that states were not bound by ideals.[16] Harrison accused him of preaching the "Doctrine of the Successful State" to educated Germans after Bismarck.[17] Plowden-Wardlaw said he was a fine example of the jealousy that arose out of Germany's missing an empire.[18] Wilmore called him, "the Machiavelli of a debased Protestantism" while Prussianism was merely "the teutonic analogue of Jesuitism."[19]

The third member of the "mad, false prophets" was the most enigmatic of all—Friedrich Nietzsche (1844-1900). It was no great defect in the British clergy to misunderstand Nietzsche, since he is one of the most difficult philosophers in all of human history. In spite of this, however, it would be impossible to consider Nietzsche as a forerunner of modern German nationalism. He was not a pangerman nationalist or an anti-Semite. In fact, in many ways he despised Germany, German beer, German cooking, current German philosophy, and especially the Bismarckian Reich.[20] To lump him with Bernhardi and Treitschke is strange since the state was the devil of Nietzsche's ethical system. No harbinger of Pangermanism could have written the following statement:

A little fresh air! This absurd condition of Europe shall not go on much longer! Is there any idea at all behind this bovine nationalism? What value can there be now, when everything points to wider and more common interests, in encouraging this boorish self-conceit? And this in a state of affairs in which spiritual dependency and disnationalization meet the eye and in which the value and meaning of contemporary culture lie in mutual blending and fertilization![21]

The trouble with Nietzsche was that he loved to get one's attention with shocking one-liners like, "The last Christian died on the cross," or, "Nothing is true, everything is permitted to the strong," or, "War has achieved more than was ever achieved by love of neighbor," or, "Man, after all, does not really desire happiness, only the Englishman does that." The mad philosopher had a low view of the English:

The English are the nation of consummate cant. In England every man who indulges in any trifling emancipation from theology must retrieve his honour in the most terrifying manner by becoming a moral fanatic. The English are a fundamentally mediocre species, ponderous, conscience-stricken, herding animals. The plebeianism of modern ideas is England's work and invention.[22]

But then, on the other hand, most British had a low view of Nietzsche. For example, E. Griffith-Jones, principal of Yorkshire United College, Brandford, expatiated on the dangers of Nietzschism in an essay called, "The Cult of Nietzsche and What It Has Led To." He declared that "the German attitude in this war is the translation into action of the theories of that bold and unscrupulous thinker; and it is against Nietzsche that the rest of the world is instinctively under arms." Most thinkers would never go so far as Nietzsche, he observed, but this demented sage finally crossed the axiological Rubicon and repudiated energetically the ethic of Jesus. He called Christ "a charlatan and a knave." At least Nietzsche had the courage to put the real alternative to the Christian creed, which is a pure Darwinism: "Pure Darwinism spells pure *egoism*; the race is to the swift . . . and the battle to the strong." Nietzschism is "the philosophical justification of privilege and power and pushiness." To permit the victory of this "Gospel of the Bully" would be to "reverse the course of history for 2000 years and to unlearn all the higher lessons of human experience."[23]

Since Nietzsche seemed to delight in dark sayings, the British clergy repaid him by placing much of the blame for Germany's mental abberation on him. "The Superman has arrived," exclaimed Clifford, "all brawn and brain and without conscience."[24] Jacks noted that many of Nietzsche's doctrines were well known in the Neolithic Age, and, he added, "there is no nuisance more ancient than the superman." "It is but a short step," he charged, "from the 'morality of Nietzsche' to the massacre of Louvain."[25] "That men should exalt the superman as the ideal of humanity," mused Muir, "is perhaps the most striking evidence of the corruption of human nature."[26] Nietzsche has been misunderstood, conceded Image, but the fact remains that "a vast number of his countrymen have sucked in poison from the man and have translated his teaching into specious philosophic and scientific justification for their own unregenerate arrogance, irreverence, and selfish brutality."[27] Morgan lumped Nietzsche with Schopenhauer and called both of them "The Immoralists"; he said this teaching led directly to the kaiser's rationalization of the violation of Belgium.[28] Mathews identified Nietzsche as the Antichrist and declared him to be the fulfillment of the "man of sin" prophecy in 2 Thessalonians 2.[29] Plowden-Wardlaw worked Nietzsche into a sermon for the soldiers: "In the name of Heaven I call upon you to consecrate yourselves as did the Hebrews of old, to consecrate yourselves as soldiers of God's host, to battle with, and to conquer this anti-Christian philosophy of Nietzsche, which has now made the Germany military caste its world-protagonist.''[30] Many other clerics made similar charges against Nietzsche.[31]

A few scholars made an effort to understand Nietzsche and defend him against the attacks of the misinformed patriots. Chief of these was F. R. Barry, Fellow and Lecturer in Theology, Oriel College, Oxford. Barry maintained that Nietzsche's Superman (*Übermensch*) bore witness to the human soul's indelible need for adoration and to the conviction that the world's course must have a purpose, that man's life reaches out into the infinite. Nietzsche also understood the beauty of hardship, the discipline of suffering, the energy of effort for great ends; he came close to understanding what is meant by "the Christian warfare." He was right to attack the priest, the man who tries to eliminate suffering. He was right to say that we must "live dangerously." It is wrong to just "grin and bear it," to think, like the Stoics, that we should "wish that to happen which is happening." In his understanding of struggle, concluded Barry, Nietzsche came closer to the truth than the pacifist Tolstoy.[32]

NEOPAGANISM

Many of the British clergy got their material on German history and German thinkers from a book entitled *Germany and England*, written by J. A. Cramb, Professor of Modern History, Queens College, London. Cramb's thesis was that Germany was not only preparing for world empire but was developing a new religion to go with it—the religion of valor.[33] Nietzsche had been a significant part of this development, said Cramb, because he had cleared away the accumulated rubbish of twelve hundred years and attempted to "set the German imagination back where it was with Alaric and Theodoric."[34] It was the martial spirit of Napoleon versus the gentle spirit of Christ. "Corsica, in a word, has conquered Galilee."[35] To illustrate this new religion, Cramb composed a mock beatitude that got quoted in many war sermons:

Ye have heard how in old times it was said, Blessed are the meek, for they shall inherit the earth; but I say to you, Blessed are the valiant, for they shall make the earth their throne. And ye have heard men say, Blessed are the poor in spirit; but I say unto you, Blessed are the great in soul and free in spirit, for they shall enter into Valhalla. And ye have heard men say, Blessed are the peacemakers; but I say unto you, Blessed are the war-makers, for they shall be called, if not the children of Jahve, the children of Odin, who is greater than Jahve.[36]

There had been in existence for several decades a significant document on German neopaganism, a striking prophecy from the poet Heinrich Heine, who predicted the coming clash between the Christian ethos and German neopaganism. In 1834 Heine wrote:

Christianity—and this is its greatest merit, has occasionally calmed the brutal German lust for battle, but it cannot destroy that savage joy. And when once that restraining

talisman, the cross, is broken, then the old combatants will rage with the fury celebrated by the Norse poets. The wooden talisman is fast decaying; the day will come
when it will break pathetically to pieces. Then the old stone gods will rise from un-
remembered ruins and rub the dust of a thousand years from their eyes, and Thor
will leap to life at last and bring down his gigantic hammer on the Gothic cathedrals.
. . . Do not smile; it is no mere fantasy. . . . German thunder is truly German; it
takes its time. But it will come, and when it crashes it will crash as nothing in history
crashed before. . . . A drama will be performed which will make the French Revolution seem like a pretty idyll.[37]

Several preachers quoted this famous passage and elaborated on Heine's
thesis that the Germans were "reverting to type," going back to their original
pagan beliefs and abandoning Christianity. One might say that Christian
baptism did not "take." Paterson-Smyth suggested that the new Germany
after Bismarck reverted to paganism because Christianity was "too gentle
for its dream of world-empire."[38] Gough asserted that power had "become
the religion of this people, that long ago called Christ down from His Cross,
and now has utterly thrown over Christianity. . . . It is not too much to say
that the whole content of supernatural Christianity is looked upon as an un-
manly superstition."[39] Woods said that "the new German philosophy of life
condemns sympathy as weakness."[40] Snell assured his listeners that "The will
and conscience of mankind are against the return to Odinism with Berlin for
its Mecca and the Kaiser for its prophet."[41]

SOCIAL DARWINISM

In searching out the roots of German madness, a few British mentioned
the theory of evolution, or, more accurately, the notion of Darwinism, as a
cause. A crude Social Darwinism ran like a red thread all through Bernhardi's
Germany and the Next War. Preachers often noted that the new Darwinism,
with its emphasis on struggle and survival, resembled closely the old paganism, the rage of the Nordic warriors Heine mentioned. Archbishop Davidson
affirmed that Darwinism was "fundamentally false and mischievous" and
"positively damnable in its harmfulness to mankind."[42] Chaplain Studdert-
Kennedy and Muirhead accused the Germans of a false interpretation of
Darwin and an exaggeration of the principles of "struggle for existence"
and "survival of the fittest" and both pointed favorably to T. H. Huxley,
who celebrated the virtues of mutual cooperation that characterized the human community. Anyone who justified robbery or crime on the grounds
that the strongest must survive would be like the foolish gardener who justified weeds in his garden because they were hardier than cabbages.[43]

Sir Peter Chalmers Mitchell, a famous British zoologist, wrote an entire
book, *Evolution and the War*, explaining the German misuse of the principle
of "struggle for existence." He called Bernhardi's use of evolution to justify
war "a dangerous mishandling of science." The scientific world is agreed
on evolution, he noted, but not on natural selection as a mechanism to explain

it. Natural selection is still a hypothesis and it may be wrong to shift it from animals to humans. He accused the Germans of the misuse of analogy when they applied the principle to humans. Modern nations are not units of the same order as the units of the animal kingdom from which the law of struggle is a supposed inference. "Looking through the animal kingdom as a whole," he concluded, "I find no grounds for interpreting Darwin's metaphorical phrase, 'the struggle for existence,' in any sense that would make it a justification for war between nations."[44]

Baron von Hügel, in his book *The German Soul*, warned about jumping from the animal to the human sphere. He pointed to the worldview of materialism, naturalistic monism, as exemplified in Ernst Haeckel's *Die Welträtsel* (*The Riddle of the World*, 1899), as the cause of a growing "pedantic barbarism" in Germany, a coarsening of human feeling, thinking, and theory. He chided German thinkers for trying to treat politics as if it were an exact science and called on them to "respect the delicate, profound differences between the Organic, especially the Human, and the simply Physical." To understand the state one must transcend physics and introduce the category of value:

It [the state] is understandable, judgeable, improvable, indeed tolerable, only when thus apprehended and operative in its true nature, not as a ruthless machine, a tornado, a fate, a physical law, a pack of wolves, a monkey horde, but as essentially human, springing from man, operating through man, leading to man—man who is man only, everywhere, only as a creature of flesh *and* spirit, of force *and* justice, and even of love.[45]

Reading some general history texts one would get the impression that Social Darwinism did not greatly affect German thinking until the Third Reich, but according to many of the British critics in the Great War it was a primary ideological aberration long before Hitler and the Nazis.

GERMANY'S TEMPORARY INSANITY

Archbishop Davidson set the tone for the British clergy in its evaluation of Germany's mental errors in the Great War. He quoted the simple words of Jesus from the Cross: "Father, forgive them, for they know not what they do."[46] Most observers of the German mind agreed that the Germans were passing through a tragic phase in their national history. This temporary national insanity was described in many ways, but the central idea was *loss of control.* Some compared it to childhood. Clutton-Brock said, "Germany must be mastered and held down, like a child that has lost all control."[47] Paterson-Smyth contrasted Germany with England in terms of age:

Britain is an old nation; like an oak tree, disciplined by the blasts of 1,000 years. There was a time when she was capable of doing the evil that Germany is doing today. Germany is a young nation, only a century old, and with all the recklessness and conceit and perversity of undisciplined youth. We trust God is more patient with young nations. We trust that by His grace Germany will one day look back with penitent shame on the year 1914 in her history.[48]

Some referred to Germany's problem as a case of demon-possession. McCurdy said that "the world can never be safe for democracy or for Christianity or for peaceful decent people, until the German people have cast out the devil that has entered into them and renounced militarism and all its works."[49] Winnington-Ingram used the same metaphor, pointing out that when exorcism occurs it often tears the patient to pieces.[50]

Some likened Germany's problem to a dream. Woods called it an "evil dream," from which the Germans would eventually awaken.[51] Cairns called Bernhardi's book "a madman's dream, from which soon or late there must be an appalling awakening, an awakening to the reality of the Righteous God."[52]

Most British critics affirmed, in some fashion, that Germany was going through a period of passing lunacy. Sanday said that "the German mind has gone seriously wrong" and was "far removed from reality." He suggested that the British think of the Germans as "a noble nation for a time gone wrong," or "out to lunch," as the Americans say, or, to use the words of Hamlet, "jangled, out of tune and harsh."[53] Paget claimed that Germany was like "a skilled giant, but with an evil will."[54] Snell said that the German problem resembled "the wreck of a noble intellect gone down in darkness."[55] Dawson referred to it as a form of drunkenness and a "passing madness."[56] Oman called it "a strange sense of loss of contact with reality, almost a sense of mental alienation."[57] Gough said the Germans were "guided by minds that are mad indeed, and yet marvellously organized to work destruction" and they were subject "for alienist treatment."[58] Henson said the Germans had suffered a "fearful loss of mental and moral sanity."[59] If the Germans could justify the sinking of the *Lusitania*, said Muir, then they have become "victims of delusion and moral insanity."[60] Mathews referred to the same act as a case of a "perverted moral view."[61] Carnegie called the Germans "patients suffering from some horrible form of mental and moral obsession."[62]

Frank Ballard charged that the Germans were "a deluded and infuriated nation" and a "mad nation . . . raging in desperate fury against the Allies," a "mad nation warring against the well-being of humanity." He compared them to Nebuchadnezzar, the ruler of ancient Babylon, who was stripped of his human reason and driven into the field like an animal because of his insolence and pride (Dan. 4:25). God told him he would remain in this subhuman state until he knew that "the Most High rules in the kingdom of men, and gives it to whom he will." Ballard concluded that pacifism was an egregious error because it gave free rein to such madmen; the best way to "love" a fanatic, he said, is to throw him into the padded room.[63]

Yet most British churchmen expressed a strong hope that the Germans would come out of their passing madness. Typical was Henson who said, "The time will come . . . when the scales will fall from the eyes of the German people, and they will once more see themselves and their actions in normal and healthy perspectives. Then they will themselves pass judgment on the crimes and follies which are deluging Europe with innocent blood."[64] Sanday said, "I do not doubt for a moment that in the end Germany will see her mistake. . . . We shall hail the penitent's return. . . . Someday the clouds of war will roll away, like an evil dream."[65]

THE FIRST BLIND MAN THESIS

The historian must pause at this point and pay tribute to a generous strain in the British clergy. Most of them, in one way or another, subscribed to what I shall call "the first blind man thesis." This idea is taken from the proverb, "If the blind lead the blind, they will both fall into the ditch." It suggests that Germany was not necessarily more guilty than the other European nations in practicing the way of life that led to the Great War. Rather, Germany was just the most dedicated practitioner of that lifestyle, the leader of the pack, as it were. Being the leader, she was the first to go over the edge when the errors of the *Zeitgeist* reached the fullness of time in 1914. Once the Germans plunged over, the other European nations suddenly realized the general error that all nations had been following.

What was this general error? In a word: selfishness. In several words: materialism, mechanism, hedonism, love of pleasure, worship of money, worship of power, rationalization of greed and ruthless competition, admiration of mere success. Richard Roberts put it well: "This war only makes manifest and concrete a state of latent and potential war which is chronic in the world."[66] Woods agreed: "The end of selfishness on a large scale is always war."[67] Barry warned his compatriots that they had almost lost their capacity for Christian criticism of contemporary culture, having so long "equated Christian ideals with the current standards of European civilization and called on Christ to supply religious sanction for what is really the code of Mrs. Grundy." "War," he concluded, "is a result of a perverted attitude of will, the deadly fruit of a long development of moral wrong."[68]

In 1915 the German philosopher Hermann Keyserling was asked to do an article for the *Hibbert Journal* entitled, "On the Meaning of the War." Keyserling argued that Germany was indeed responsible for the war but not "guilty" in the sense assumed by British public opinion. Conceding that Germany could have acted with more tact and humanity, Keyserling said that Germany took the course taken by all European nations under similar conditions, so that if we condemn Germany we are really condemning pan-European traditions. All western races, in spite of their Christian ideals, are intrinsically aggressive. All have constantly disregarded the rights of others.

None has ever respected treaties if it seemed against national interests. All have tacitly assumed throughout their history that might is right. It is no accident that the Chinese refer to all westerners indiscriminately as "pirates."[69]

L. P. Jacks insisted that *mechanism* was the villain of the piece. Materialistic mechanism was the most common philosophical conviction of all advanced, industrialized European nations before the outbreak of the Great War. Once installed as a guiding principle in the culture of nations, mechanism is bound to issue at last in the crass appeal to force, based on the vulgar doctrine that might is right. Mechanism offers you a truncated view of man. What the world needs is love and community but mechanism gives you an economic animal. "Of all principles, mechanism is the most directly opposed to the recognition of a common interest in the races who people the earth. Its spirit divides but cannot unite, and the more skillful the intellect becomes in reasoning under its direction, the further will thought diverge from the moral instincts of mankind."[70]

By this thesis, the Great War was really not a holy war with the elect nation of Britain battling the reprobate nation of Germany. It was, rather, a tragic struggle of two nations that had both been pursuing the same illusion. Germany was more guilty than England, of course, but England bore a large share of the blame. If the Germans worshiped the idol of militarism, observed Clutton-Brock, "we have been worshipping an idol of money and have talked as much nonsense about our idol as they about theirs."[71] Maclean noted that "It is more dangerous to be a child in the slums of London or Glasgow than to be a soldier in the trenches of Flanders."[72] Temple asserted that British commercialism had "let loose the spirit of grab and push, the oppression of the weak and the admiration of mere success."[73] Gray said that the kaiser was only the political counterpart of the British millionaire who built his industrial empire on "the broken lives of uncounted workers."[74]

Sir William Robertson Nicoll, Scottish clergyman and man of letters, pointed out that German writers who praised *Realpolitik* and militarism were no different from Carlyle and Ruskin who were both professional apologists for despots, militarism, slavery, and slaveholders.[75] Foakes-Jackson insisted that we must abolish the British "tyranny of great wealth" as well as the German "tyranny of the sword."[76] Moberly warned the British lest they pray the prayer of the hypocrite: "God, we thank Thee that we are not as other men, hypocrites, breakers of treaties, slayers of women and children, or even as this Kaiser."[77] Clutton-Brock confessed, "We may not have loved war, but we have not hated it, or loved peace strongly enough to make some man of genius the mouthpiece of our common love."[78] Burroughs echoed the common sentiment when he said that the only remedy for Europe lay in "a concerted and conspicuous repudiation of the money standard as the determinant of life."[79]

Great Britain claimed to be the extirpator of evil in Europe, but what of the evil in Britain? Why can't the British crusade against evils in their own society like they crusade against kaiserism? Lyttelton concluded that the Great War had shown the crying need for "a new spirit in the people" of Europe. If we fail in this complete general moral renewal, he said, "it will mean that humanity will be turning over a new leaf only to begin another long and dismal chapter of international competition, jealousy, and greed; because if we fail to discern the higher law, these are the only principles left to us to follow."[80]

But why were the Germans the first to go over the edge? Were they the most notorious materialists and mechanists? No, answered many clerics, the Germans went over the edge first because of a special national trait. Of all Europe's nations, the Germans possessed *par excellence* that dogged seriousness, that tenacious ability to believe, really believe, in a system of thought and to press it to its logical conclusion. If you wish to see the practical results of an idea—true or false—give it to the Germans; they will reduce it to absurdity. All of Europe was heading toward the abyss along the same highway of materialism, but the Germans were heading with system and intensity. When the Germans go wrong, said Sanday, "in proportion to their intrinsic greatness and the coherence of their parts, they go wrong with system and method and on a great scale. . . . The disaster is more complete when it is based on principle, when behind it there is a whole theory of conduct."[81] As Clutton-Brock expressed it: "These Prussians are men like ourselves, perverted by a more resolute idolatry than ours, more actively foolish and dangerous because they have thought and willed more clearly in a wrong direction."[82] Only Germany, said Wilmore, had affirmed the gross doctrine of struggle "logically, brazenly, openly, and as a law of the Universe."[83]

Baron von Hügel seemed to have an unusually acute appreciation of the German soul. Hedonism, he noted, was preached more expertly by two Englishmen, Bentham and Spencer, yet when it traveled to Germany it "found lodging within an incredibly vehement and concentrated, systematic and visionary soul." Unlike the Englishman, who is averse to anything deliberately systematic, intellectual, or doctrinaire, the German has a thirst for theory, system, and *Weltanschauung.* "It is this innate need of system that renders him steady, but also obstinate; virile and brutal; profound and pedantic; comprehensive and right in outlook, and rationalist and doctrinaire." The Englishman is not cruel by nature, but even if he were, his freedom from theoretical obsession would save him from a great incitement to cruelty; conversely, even if the German were not more cruel by nature, his visionary obsessions would make him harsher than the Englishman. This is why a pitiless doctrine like *Realpolitik* is more dangerous in the hands of a German than in the hands of an Englishman.[84]

Ironically, this same German trait was the hope for the future. "Without knowing it," said Oldham, Germany "may be the means of recalling the world to a better mind. With her unique gift of systematic thoroughness and scientific precision she has carried a certain view of life to its logical conclusion, until the conscience of the whole world has risen in revolt."[85] Sanday said he had no doubt that "when the Germans see their duty clearly marked out before them, they will face it with all their natural tenacity, conscientiousness, and courage."[86]

The only problem now was to beat them and exorcise the demon, stop the evil dream, and cure the insanity. No amount of sympathy and understanding should deter Britain from her hard military task.

Thus "the first blind man thesis" gave many British preachers and thinkers the opportunity to express sympathy for the unique German problem while at the same time resisting to the death German aggression. It was, truly, a case of "forgive them for they know not what they do."

NOTES

1. *Christian's War Book* (Murray), 49.
2. *War and the Gospel*, 9, 60.
3. *Freedom's Call*, 12.
4. *Christ and the Sword*, 135.
5. *Judgment of War*, 72.
6. *Who Is to Blame?*, 72.
7. *War and Theology*, 8.
8. *Under the War Cloud*, 42.
9. Temple, *Our Need for a Catholic Church*, 16; Oman, *War and Its Issues*, 89.
10. See Henson, *War-Time Sermons*, 100; Thomas, *Immorality of Nonresistance*, 96; Oman, *War and Its Issues*, 113.
11. "What Next?" *HJ*, XIII:2, 269.
12. Paget, *In the Day of Battle*, 44; Winnington-Ingram, *Sermons for the Times*, IV, 4.
13. Cairns, *Answer to Bernhardi*, 3; Winnington-Ingram, *Potter and Clay*, 229.
14. Fritz Fischer, *Germany's Aims in the First World War* (New York, 1959), 34.
15. Clutton-Brock, *Bernhardism in England*, 6; Cairns, *Answer to Bernhardi*, 11; Fisher, *The War*, 12. See also Holland, *So as by Fire*, 18; Morgan, *God, Humanity, War*, 64; Sanday, *Meaning of the War*, 65; Macnutt, *Reproach of War*, 38.
16. *Meaning of the War*, 77.
17. *Kaiser's War*, 53.
18. *Test of War*, 47.
19. "Why Are We Fighting?," 335. See also Thomas, *Immorality of Nonresistance*, 40; Paterson-Smyth, *God and the War*, 47; *To the Christian Scholars*, 7.
20. *Religion and the War*, 6-10. For a good analysis of Nietzsche's idea of will to power see W. M. Salter, "The Philosopher of 'The Will to Power,' " *HJ*, XIII:1 (October, 1914), 32ff. For an excellent critical biography of Nietzsche see Ronald Hayman, *Nietzsche: A Critical Life* (Oxford, 1982).
21. *The Will to Power*, trans. Walter Kaufman and R. J. Hollindale (London, 1968), 395.
22. Translated by Ballard in *Britain Justified*, 22.
23. *Kaiser or Christ?*, 30-33.
24. *The War and the Churches*, 9.

25. "Mechanism and the War," 42; "Tyranny of Mere Things," 490.

26. *War and Christian Duty*, 272.

27. *Art, Morals, and the War*, 13.

28. *God, Humanity, and War*, 21.

29. *Christ and the World at War*, 84.

30. *Test of War*, 6.

31. See e.g., Ballard, *Britain Justified*, 67, 141; Thompson, *Prussia's Devilish Creed*, 3; Bennet, *England's Mission*, 12; Gough, *God's Strong People*; Paterson-Smyth, *God and the War*, 47; Sanday, *Meaning of the War*, 59.

32. *Religion and the War*, 6-10.

33. *Germany and England* (London, 1914), 118.

34. Ibid., 116.

35. Ibid., 119.

36. Ibid., 117.

37. Cited in Louis Untermeyer, *Heinrich Heine: Paradox and Poet* (New York, 1937), I, 229. Sermons quoting this prophecy are in Murray, *Christian's War Book*, 46; Burroughs, *Eternal Goal*, 18; Mackarness, *Faith and Duty*, 51.

38. *God and the War*, 46, 150.

39. *God's Strong People*, 72, 97.

40. *Christianity and War*, 41.

41. *Supreme Duty*, 4. For more see Dawson, *Christ and the Sword*, 106; Winnington-Ingram, *Day of God*, 29; *Potter and Clay*, 224; Henson, *War-Time Sermons*, 251.

42. *Testing of a Nation*, 82.

43. Studdert-Kennedy, *Rough Talks*, 55; Muir, *Ethical and Religious Problems* (Carpenter), 103-4. See also F. S. Martin, "The Unity of Civilization," *HJ*, XIII:2, 342-46.

44. *Evolution and the War* (London, 1915), 2, 4, 9, 19, 41, 108.

45. *The German Soul*, 66, 179-80.

46. *Testing of a Nation*, 85.

47. *Are We to Punish Germany?*, 15.

48. *God and the War*, 54.

49. *Freedom's Call and Duty*, 20.

50. *Church in Time of War*, 239.

51. *Christianity and War*, 8.

52. *Answer to Bernhardi*, 12.

53. *Meaning of the War*, 66, 122.

54. *In the Day of Battle*, 62.

55. *How Are We to Love Our Enemies?*, 8.

56. *Ethical and Religious Problems* (Carpenter), 185.

57. *War and Its Answer*, 62.

58. *God's Strong People*, 64.

59. *War-Time Sermons*, 207.

60. *War and Christian Duty*, 163.

61. *Three Years' War*, 83.

62. *Sermons on Subjects*, 4.

63. *Mistakes of Pacifism*, 7, 14; *Plain Truths*, 136.

64. *War-Time Sermons*, 207.

65. *Meaning of the War*, 122-23.

66. *Are We Worth Fighting For?*, 33.

67. *War Watchwords*, 95.

68. *Religion and the War*, 5, 28.

69. *HJ*, XIII:3 (April, 1915), 534-36.

70. "Mechanism, Diabolism, and the War," *HJ*, XIII:1 (October, 1914), 30-32.

71. *Cure for War*, 13.

72. *God and the Soldier*, 72.

73. *Christianity and War*, 9.

74. *War Spirit in Our National Life*, 13.

75. *Christian's War Book* (Murray), 63.

76. *Sermons for the Times*, II, 11.

77. *Christian Conduct in War Time*, 16.

78. *Cure for War*, 5.

79. *Fight for the Future*, 99.

80. "What Next?" *HJ*, XIII:2 (January, 1915), 264-65. For additional sermons on this topic see Fry, *Christ and Peace*, 19; Clifford, *The War and The Churches*, 12-14; Henson, *War-Time Sermons*, 102; Macnutt, *Reproach of War*, 53-54; Woods, *War Watchwords*, 13-15; Lenwood, *Chariots of Fire*, 9; Moulton, *British and German Scholarship*, 13-15; Orchard, *The Real War*, 7; Wace, *War and the Gospel*, 59-60; Gore, *League of Nations*, 10; Oldham, *The Church the Hope*, 4; Whittingham, *Who Is to Blame?*, 64-70; Holland, *So as by Fire*, II, 80.

81. *Meaning of the War*, 109.

82. *Cure for War*, 11.

83. "Why Are We Fighting?", 336.

84. *The German Soul*, 143, 156, 188. The Baron was 63 years old when he wrote this book. He had spent over 40 of his 63 years in England. His parents were pure German, but west German, from Coblenz and Mainz. He says he had been deeply influenced by German scholars but had never really understood the spirit of Prussianism.

85. *The Church the Hope*, 6.

86. *Meaning of the War*, 122.

4

The Sins of Britain—According to Germany

The religious leaders of Germany were deeply convinced that God had favored the Germans in modern European history, especially from the time of the Reformation. How, then, did Germany get into such a precarious situation in 1914, with most of the great powers of Europe against her? German pastors were stunned by the attack of the Entente Powers—although Germany had attacked first—but they had a ready answer: God's chosen vessels often excite jealousy in evil people. To be chosen of God does not mean that a nation is exempt from hardship.

Preachers took to their pulpits in August, 1914, to declare vigorously that the fatherland was guiltless in starting the war. Several of them quoted Christ to illustrate Germany's innocence: "They hated me without a cause" (John 15:25). Dr. Paul Wurster of Stuttgart saw a parallel in the biblical story of King Jehoshaphat, who found himself surrounded by three hostile nations. God's promise to him was the same as his pledge to innocent Germany in 1914: "Fear not and be not dismayed at this great multitude; for the battle is not yours but God's. . . . Take your position, stand still and see the victory of the Lord on your behalf" (2 Chron. 15:17).[1]

The truth was that foolish diplomacy had gotten Germany into the dangerous situation of August, 1914, but the German leaders could not admit this because it would be a terrible blow to their national self-image. So they searched for a scapegoat. Who was most responsible for the fatherland's deplorable situation? England. The clergy followed their kaiser in laying all the blame at the feet of Albion, who was proving to be "perfidious" indeed. After explaining that Germans do not hate France and Russia, Pastor August Pott of Königsberg said, "We hate Italy because they broke their treaty with us. But we hate England the most because we were bound together in culture and heart and blood. A brotherly love that has been betrayed will become a burning hate. Our other enemies would never have dared to go to war without England's policy of encirclement. With all our enemies, we really have only one enemy—England."[2]

This sounds dangerously close to the famous "Hymn of Hate" written by Ernst Lissauer:

> Hate by water and hate by land;
> Hate of heart and hate of the hand;
> We love as one and hate as one;
> We have but one foe alone—England.[3]

It is gratifying to note that not all German clerics participated in this hate campaign against England.[4] Many pastors warned that it was clearly contrary to the gospel of love or that it was, at best, ineffective and counterproductive. The German soldier did not need to hate to be a good soldier; he could be motivated by more ethical means.[5]

What, now, were the sins of Great Britain? First and foremost was the sin of imperialism. Pastors mentioned the British empire more often than anything else in their sermons against the British.

BRITISH IMPERIALISM

West of the prime meridian a person would get the impression that the British empire was the greatest assemblage of nations ever put together by man. East of the same line one would get the impression that the same empire was the most oppressive tyranny ever attempted, worse even than that of the Assyrian empire of ancient times, the state that called forth the malediction of God: "When the Lord has finished all his work on Mount Zion and on Jerusalem he will punish the arrogant boasting of the king of Assyria and his haughty pride. For he says, 'By the strength of my hand I have done it' " (Isa. 10:12-13).

Britain's empire was usually pictured as a monster of some kind, a giant spider or octopus, or a beast resembling the creatures of the apocalyptic books of Daniel and Revelation. Tolzien gave this description:

England is like Goliath. His head and heart are the London island, half as large as all of Germany. His belly lies in faraway India and he gorges himself on this part. Like a crude monster he straddles the world and stamps his feet down on Africa and Australia. The claws of his hands are fixed like anchors in the Atlantic and Pacific Oceans.[6]

Scarcely a dark chapter of British history was left unmentioned as the German preachers called the roll of Albion's perfidy: the oppression of the American colonists, the taking of slaves from Africa, the subjugation of India, the seizure of South American trade during the Napoleonic period, the Opium Wars against China, the crushing of the Boers in South Africa, the massacre of natives in the Sudan under Kitchener, and so on. But now the crowning blow comes when Germanic, Protestant England goes to war with a racial and religious brother—Germany. If Britain were fighting alone it might be different but she organizes the rest of Europe against Germany and then brings in all of her imperial minions to spill the blood of brothers. She is a "robber motherland" who treats her children like stepchildren. She sacrifices her offspring to the Moloch of money in order to control the business and trade of the world.

Preachers charged that Britain considered herself the chosen people of the world in these modern times. She looked upon herself as the *Mustervolk*, the model nation for all the others to emulate. Her arrogance and self-righteousness caused her to violate the rights of smaller nations, to weaken their unique cultures and reduce them to sickly imitations of her own shallow, commercial culture. Britain thought that God had installed her as the international schoolmaster to the nations, the norm for all future development. But she was wrong, for God never intended the nations to be smelted into a cultural uniformity, therefore, when the Germans fight the British empire they are fighting for the rights of small nations and unique cultures.

This fight is really a continuation of the struggle against Napoleon during the great War of Liberation (1806-15). Napoleon I tried to create a "one world" culture with French military power and Britain is trying to do the same, but Germany will defeat the latter attempt just as she defeated the former. God always destroys these movements to create a monolithic world culture. Troeltsch summed up this sentiment well: "In this sense, we believe that we are the ones really fighting for the progress of mankind—we, who give freedom to all and never violate anyone."[7]

Ferdinand J. Schmidt enlisted Luther in this struggle for national freedom. Luther had destroyed for all time the absolutism of the church but now England was attempting to establish an absolutism of the land and sea. "Therefore, this war is just as good as a Luther war previously fought against papal absolutism. The hero of the faith from Worms has risen from the dead and gives his blessing as he hovers over his nation's war for freedom."[8]

Reinhold Seeberg, world-famous scholar in the history of dogma, interpreted the war as Germany's arrival in the world as an independent nation, able to stand on her own without slavish emulation of Britain or any other nation. "From now on," he asserted, "we need to strengthen our national self-consciousness. We don't want to be arrogant, but neither do we want to be too humble; not suspicious but also not credulous; not obnoxious but also not fawning; neither rejecting people nor running after them."[9]

Many German clerics mentioned the British mistreatment of German missionaries and their families in Africa during the war as a special illustration of British insolence. The British imprisoned missionaries, separated them from their families, destroyed their homes and mission outposts, robbed them of their possessions, tore them from their families, and prevented them for years from writing to their relatives or their congregations. They took away the land and the facilities that Germans had accumulated for 200 years in the mission field. They placed the poor natives at sea so far as instruction was concerned. All of this was blatantly contradictory to Article Six of the Congo Acts, which granted liberty of conscience to all Christians regardless of nationality. Yet Britain posed as the champion of international morality.[10]

BRITISH HYPOCRISY

One can know a person or a nation for a long time, observed Pastor Witte of Berlin, before one really comes to know the true personality and character of that person or nation. It takes a decisive moment, a crisis, to tell what is pretense and what is reality. When the chips were down and England had to decide where she stood she finally showed her greatest fault: hypocrisy, sanctimonious Phariseeism.[11] This pretense came out in several ways.

First, there was Belgium. German churchmen found it laughable that Britain would tell the world she was going to war just for poor little Belgium. That was merely the reason she gave to her conscience and to the world press so that her naked aggression would be cloaked under a facade of humanitarianism. This putative "protector of small nations" had suppressed India, Persia, Egypt, Armenia, Tripoli, the Boers, and numerous other small peoples. To now pose as the protector of Belgium, Poland, and Serbia was the quintessence of mendacity. Germany was now occupying these small nations out of military necessity, but Britain had rolled over many such nations in her imperial history.[12]

Then there was Britain's strange diplomatic alliance in the war. If Palmerston or Salisbury or Pitt could have seen the allied menagerie they would not have been able to believe it. We say that "politics makes strange bedfellows" but this group seemed to defy all reason: Germanic, Protestant Britain in alliance with Slavic, Orthodox Russia, the land of superstition and the whip, and with Gallic, Roman Catholic France, the land of Enlightenment and the Revolution. It was a bizarre mélange of hypocrisy, atheism, and superstition, of Puritans, freethinkers, and Cossacks. What had created this strange alliance? Jealousy of Germany, envy of German growth and German power.[13]

Britain was a monarchy. Her people loved and venerated their sovereign and showed deep devotion to the principle of monarchism. Yet Britain threw in her lot with Serbia, the nation that had committed regicide. How could a morally healthy people do such a thing?[14]

Ernst Troeltsch traced British hypocrisy back to the time of Cromwell and Puritanism, noting that it was a distinct tendency of English and American mentality to moralize everything political. This tendency he traced back to the deep influence of Calvin on Anglo-Saxon civilization. The English Christian feels divinely appointed to bring the kingdom of God to earth, not at the end of time, but now, in history, and thus he feels morally obligated to give the world the values he considers most important: freedom, order, and personal liberty. For this purpose, God expects Britain to maintain a great navy at all times. Militarism is wrong for the Germans, of course, but navalism is permitted the British—another example of Albion's double standard.[15]

Britain was flayed in hundreds of sermons for the lies she was telling around the world. Pastors referred variously to the "international lie press," the "lie bureau," the "lie factory" or the "lie machine." Tolzien modified an old saying to read, "Talking is silver, silence is gold, and lying is Britannia."[16] He maintained that "this war was instigated with falsehood. Who can dispute it? England is the nation of falsehood. Richard III could only be an Englishman and all England is now like a Richard III. . . . England is the Mephistopheles of the entire tragedy."[17]

"Has the world become a madhouse," asked Troeltsch, "or a monster of evil and meanness?"[18] "What a flood of lies, treason, and atrocity are now going out from England over the entire world," exclaimed König, adding that Germany had an obligation to the truth and to herself not to sheathe the sword until a judgment against England had been rendered: "Down with England! That alone is Europe's future and Europe's peace!"[19] Rump contrasted British lying with German truthfulness, buttressing it with an ancient proverb: "One man, one word." He asserted: "We cannot lie like England!"[20] Harnack warned: "They do not want to believe the truth, well, then, now they will have to believe our weapons!"[21] Dr. Friedrich Delitzsch warned the British with Ps. 5:7—the Lord destroys those who speak lies.[22]

Paul Le Seur, garrison pastor in Brussels, detected a hypocritical strain in the moral judgment of Englishmen. He related that he once asked an Englishman about the profligate private life of King Edward VII. The man replied that Edward's private life did not concern him; if the king fulfilled his public duty, that was enough. This showed, like a flash of lightning, said Le Seur, the great gulf between German and English ethics. "Comrades," he concluded, "thank God the German Michael is too naive to judge with such a double standard. We Germans would say that a king who leads a wicked private life has spurned his royal duty."[23]

BRITISH BETRAYALS

German pastors expressed the depth of their strong feelings against Britain when they compared her with Judas Iscariot, the man who betrayed the innocent Son of God to his enemies (John 13:30). Many also compared Germany to Joseph, the innocent son of Jacob who was unjustly sold into slavery by his jealous brothers (Gen. 37). Britain was depicted as a treacherous colleague, who violated the rules of sacred fellowship by selling out his brother. They say that "blood is thicker than water" but the British had proved that money was stronger than blood.

The list of betrayals was long.

First, Britain betrayed Christianity, especially Protestant Christianity, when she attacked Germany. In September, 1914, a number of prominent German theologians sent out a document from Berlin called "Address of the German Theologians to the Evangelical Christians Abroad," in which it was stated that a possible rent in "Teutonic Protestantism" would ensue from the war, a war caused by "those who have long secretly and cunningly been spinning a web of conspiracy against Germany." The same document quoted Tsar Nicholas II of Russia as saying that the war was a struggle against "Teutonism and Protestantism."[24] (British clerics denied that the tsar ever said this.)

Second, Britain betrayed the white race when she brought in all kinds of colored soldiers from her colonies to throw against the Germans in the trenches of the western front. Germany, on the contrary, fought only with her native troops. She had no colonies to draw from, no cannon fodder to exploit. Not only were the enemy troops colored, they were nearly always pagans and heathens, Hindus or animists. Albion compounded these sins by asking the pagan Hindus of India to pray to their plethora of gods for victory over Germany. How could a people dedicated to the true Gospel and to historic monotheism do such a thing? The British were turning the clock back to the times when the Hebrews launched their historic assault on polytheism and idolatry.[25]

German preachers were especially convinced that Britain had betrayed European culture or western civilization by attacking Germany in concert with Asiatic Russia. Running through all these sermons is the central idea that *Russia is not really a part of Europe.* Russia is too far East, too different, out of the orbit of western culture, "a land of assassins and pogroms," said Dr. J. Haller of Tübingen.[26] D. O. Baumgarten called Russia "the strongest refuge of all bondage, all punishment for ideas, all intolerance, all reaction."[27] Titius, quoting General Hindenburg, argued that the Russian soldiers did not have true discipline, based on inner character, but merely "stupid, dull obedience." They were very different from German soldiers whose discipline was based on the spirit and on morality, which created a feeling of individual responsibility to the fatherland.[28]

Tolzien insisted that the Russians committed the fallacy of thinking that mass, the legendary steamroller, could conquer *Geist.* He said that Russia did not have enough life and spirit in the individual soldier to make its mass effective, as did the Germans. The Russian masses had no "inner culture," but only external force, the kind used to drive cattle. Ministers of the gospel are sometimes uncertain about the will of God but Tolzien was dogmatic about the will of God in this matter of Russia and Europe:

Can it be the will of God that Russian barbarism, Mongolian heathenism, and English criminality will destroy beautiful Europe? . . . It cannot be the will of God that the heathen peoples of Asia should get a foothold in Europe, the ancient, holy, mother soil of the Christian religion! It cannot be the will of God that this our German *Volk*— the most efficient and most thorough, the most loyal and most honorable of all nations—should be crushed. No, that cannot be the will of God![29]

Harnack felt keenly the future threat of Russia to European civilization. In a speech to a group of Americans he told his listeners that the common German-American culture rested on respect for the individual personality, an entity unknown to Russian history. In Russia, you have the "culture of the herd," the "culture of the heap," ruled patriarchically, massed, and held together like a pile of sand by a strange Byzantine-Mongolian-Muscovite framework. Great Britain was trying to break the dam that protected western Europe from the desert sands of the Asiatic *Unkultur* (nonculture) of Russia. Germans, therefore, must take up the cry of the kaiser: "People of Europe, protect your most holy possessions!" Ironically, noted Harnack, we are fighting for Great Britain, though she is ignorant of this great truth. If Germany should fall, he concluded, Britain would bear a major responsibility for the demise of western civilization: "The day that Great Britain broke the dam will never be forgotten in world history."[30]

BRITISH ENVY

There was a time when the term "German" referred to a being so pure and harmless that one would think him too good for this world. Historically the Germans were the nation of toy makers, musicians, philosophers, and poets, not the nation of Prussian soldiers and rigorous businessmen. In the eighteenth century the quip was current that the French had the empire of the land, the British the empire of the sea, and the Germans the empire of the air.

All that changed after 1871. When Bismarck unified Germany under Prussia he put an end to all these "soft" impressions of Germany. The Reich forged ahead and became the leading nation of Europe in several categories: industry, banking, trading, manufacturing, mining, scholarship, and science. In fact, one could argue that Germany grew too fast. She did not give the other nations of Europe a chance to adjust their estimate of her to her new-found leadership in so many categories. She reminded folks of a teenager who has grown large and strong in body but is still considered immature in emotions and judgment.

Like most Germans, the Protestant clergy was firmly convinced that the Great War had one primary motive—*envy*. The great powers, especially Britain, were simply jealous of the new Reich and its obvious strength in so many fields. The German Michael had knocked John Bull off his throne; Great Britain was no longer the "workshop of the world." Otto Zurhellen declared, "Not our sin, but our efficiency, is the cause of this war."[31] The

British wanted Germany to remain a nation of poets and musicians and philosophers so they organized the world against the new Reich.

This jealousy was similar to the sin of Abel, the first murderer in world history (Gen. 4). It was the same sin that caused Joseph's brothers to sell him into slavery and that drove the Jews to perjure themselves to kill Christ. Envy distorts reality and causes one to see things in a perverted way. This helps explain the unnatural alliance of England with France, Russia, and Japan. It is unnatural because it corresponds to no logical diplomatic principle; its only unifying motif is *Germany must be stopped*! Why must Germany be stopped? Walter Lehmann answered, "Because Germany is too large and powerful, too strong, too flourishing, too pure and moral, too healthy and blameless, too efficient and striving, too deep and rich, too inward and spiritually fruitful."[32]

Clergymen preached hope to their parishioners when they pointed out the injustice of Germany's situation. Although Joseph's brothers sold him into slavery, Joseph later, by hard work and patience, rose to be the ruler of all Egypt. Although the Jews killed Jesus out of envy, Jesus later rose from the dead and God judged the Jews in A.D. 70 by sending the Romans to destroy Jerusalem. Like Paul, the German nation could boast, "I have worked harder than any of them" (1 Cor. 15:10). Work is always what makes the difference, with both God and man. Work will win out in the long run. The best *Realpolitik*, said Harnack, is for the three great Germanic states—England, America, and Germany—to remain sisters who carry on "honorable competition." "If one is more industrious than the other, then the latter must double her industry; if one is more inventive than the other, then the latter must increase her initiative; if one is morally stronger . . . then the latter must exert her moral powers."[33]

The worst thing to do would be to organize the world against the most efficient *Volk* in Europe, just because that *Volk* was overtaking one in production. Surely a universe structured by moral principles would prevent such an injustice.

ALBION, THE PEDDLER

In 1915, Werner Sombart, distinguished German economist and authority on modern capitalism, wrote a withering indictment of England called *Händler und Helden*, which translates roughly as "shopkeepers and heroes" or possibly, "peddlers and heroes." Sombart argued that the British were a nation of sordid, petty shopkeepers while Germany was a nation of deep, spiritual heroes. The Englishman is incredibly narrow, he claimed, totally incapable of rising above the superficial reality of the cash nexus that his commercial civilization worships devoutly. A glance at English philosophers from Bacon to Spencer will show in a minute how superficially empirical is the English mentality. The trader is guilty of the reductive fallacy on a grand scale; he reduces everything to a series of monetary transactions—life, art, religion, science, war. The entire British empire is a great trading enterprise and its wars are merely wars of pecuniary calculation. But the Germans will never be conquered by this damning taint of commercialism and their special *Geist* will stamp it from the earth.[34]

The Protestant clergy took up this theme of England as the land of the *Krämergeist*, the petty, shopkeeper's mentality (from *Kram*, "junk"). They echoed the view of the kaiser, that this war was one of worldviews, the German versus the Anglo-Saxon, which was another way of saying that money was struggling with honor, freedom, and morality! These two worldviews, said Bruno Doehring, must fight to the death; no diplomatic settlement can end such a conflict. If the British should win "then gold, power, and brutality" will become the ruling principles of the world, and the globe would become a "loathsome department store" in which men would be only machines and the powerful would rule the weak.[35] Ott assured his parishioners that, "Spirit is struggling with matter, idealism with petty shopkeeper's mentality, the nobleman with the predator."[36]

But what exactly is this petty, ignoble spirit? It comes out in a number of small ways. For example, the Englishman shows his innate selfish individualism by capitalizing the personal pronoun "I" even when it occurs in the middle of the sentence. The German, on the contrary, always spells *ich* with small letters unless it occurs at the beginning of the sentence. The Englishman demonstrates his incredibly narrow mentality by using the slogan, "My country, right or wrong!" Yet he also illustrates his personal cupidity with the slogan, "My fatherland is wherever it goes well with me."

The Germans say, "We will fight to the last drop of blood," but the English say, "We will fight to the last penny." All through his history the Englishman has supplied the pennies but he always finds someone else to do his actual fighting for him, like the French or the Russians or the colonials. He is essentially a craven coward, not a brave knight, and the crowning proof of his cowardice is the naval blockade. He does not have the courage to fight like a man so he uses starvation. He wars against women and children. In a letter to Archbishop Davidson, Adolf Deissmann called the blockade "the most brutal and inhuman way of annihilating innocent people."

One thing must be admitted. The blockade does not look as brutal as it is. It has a certain appearance of "*Eleganz*" that avoids blood, bomb, and "brand." It works in the world as a gentleman criminal, quiet and unobtrusive, and decks its visiting card with the doctorate of international law. In contrast with the dramatic scene on sea and land, it cannot be worked into the atrocity film; its victims do not fly into the air or into the deep mutilated by explosions, but are extinguished unheeded and noiseless in some miserable garret in a crowded town. They do not even die of "Blockade." That illness is not on the register. Modestly the Blockade yields the *pas* to her murders, decline, tuberculosis, pneumonia.[37]

The British war technique was scored even by Troeltsch, who avoided most of the crude formulations of the German clergy. "No war," he declared, "has been so economic in its technique as this English starvation and financial war."[38] König spoke for many when he formulated the fall of Britain into a German war aim:

We cannot change English jealousy or the cold policy of England which fills their entire political character, but our determined will must be to shatter this jealousy and the means of power connected with this political egoism. . . . It will not do any good to humble France; it will help nothing to smash Russia. The evil spirit of Europe is that cold, English power politics, which is bereft of any noble feelings.[39]

Some pastors compared England to the temple where Christ cleaned out the shopkeepers and moneychangers (John 2:13-22). Just as Christ had once demanded the purging of the temple from those who bought and sold, said Horn, "so now he speaks to the Christian nation of Germany: 'Clean up the temple of mankind from those who desecrate it!' " Germany had been entrusted with this task and just as God had once given power to Christ and his apostles to work miracles, so also in the crisis of the Great War God would grant Germany supernatural strength to rid the world of English gold.[40]

Thus British crass commercial mentality stood in sharp contrast to the ideals of *Geist* and heroism held forth by Germany. The German clergy would have applauded lustily the following tribute from William James:

In heroism, we feel, life's supreme mystery is hidden. We tolerate no one who has no capacity whatever for it in any direction. . . . No matter what a man's frailties otherwise may be, if he be willing to risk death, and still more if he suffer it heroically, in the service he has chosen, the fact consecrates him forever. Inferior to ourselves in this or that way, if yet we cling to life, and he is able to "fling it away like a flower," . . . we account him in the deepest way our born superior.[41]

ROOTS OF BRITISH MENTALITY

Not many German clerics engaged in a deep analysis of the historical roots of Britain's defective mindset, but those who did divined a crucial difference between the British and the German *moral* philosophies, a difference that had momentous implications in many directions. It could be reduced to a struggle between Kant and Bentham, between duty and utilitarianism.

To understand British behavior, argued many, one must grasp the direction of her axiology for several centuries, which has been in the direction of what we call *utilitarianism*. If you want to go far enough back, you could start the apostolic line with Pelagius (360-420), who misunderstood the doctrine of salvation by grace and thought rather too much of free will. Certainly the empirical school goes back as far as Roger Bacon and William of Occam, and then comes through Hobbes, Locke, Berkeley, Hume, Bentham, and Mill. Out of the school of empirical epistemology comes the ethical norm called the "principle of utility." This asserts that good and evil are merely matters of pain and pleasure. All men seek to maximize pleasure and minimize pain. Pleasure is good and pain is evil, so whatever leads to pleasure is good and whatever leads to pain is evil. All moral behavior, therefore, is grounded merely in human usage and physical consequences. Such thinking will lead eventually to the maxim, "The greatest happiness for the greatest number." Utilitarianism finally degenerates into a cow's morality, where simple fleshly contentment is the *summum bonum*. It seems ludicrous on its face because most people will be caught at some point in their lives doing things that cause pain, for example, a mother running into a burning house to save her child.

Now utilitarianism is easy to refute if you define it simplistically, which is what the German preachers did. They had fun contrasting this patently selfish view with the (alleged) German view illustrated so beautifully by history's greatest moralist, Immanuel Kant.[42] Kant insisted that only confusion could result from the premise that morality must terminate in pleasant consequences, in "personal happiness." One must do his duty, regardless of the consequences; he must do what is right, though the heavens fall. If one seeks happiness directly he will end up neglecting many solid values in this life. One does his duty, he pursues the good as apprehended by reason, and then, perhaps, he may find happiness, he may be "surprised by joy." But he will certainly find no true happiness if he pursues it directly. When utilitarianism becomes writ large in the behavior of an entire nation, said Titius, the result is especially frightening: "The goal turns out to be: if we can secure greater happiness and greater profit for England, then let us pursue a reckless, brutal business morality (*Geschäftsmoral*), even if it be at the cost of faith and loyalty."[43]

Perhaps no German thinker in the war labored more sincerely to uncover and elucidate the errors of Britain and the special qualities of German thought than Ernst Troeltsch. He frankly admitted that the key to German thought was the Romantic movement of the early nineteenth century, the time when Germany turned away from many western ways of thought. He felt that the Germans had a special perspective on "freedom" that was different from the West. German freedom was not the individual secular liberty of France, Britain, and America, but the "free self-inclusion" of the person into the subordination of the state. Germans looked upon the total state organism alone as sovereign, he noted, and individuals as only members of it. This concept one could not understand if, like the British, he lived in a culture shot through and through with empiricism, materialism, and nominalism. The nation, however, that studied Plato and produced Hegel could easily comprehend it. Germans want parliaments and elections at times, but these things are not the essence of true freedom. Rather, "German freedom will never be purely political. It will always remain tied up with the idealistic notion of duty and the romantic idea of individuality."

Troeltsch admitted that the German brand of freedom could easily degenerate into obsequiousness, but, he noted, the English brand can deteriorate into crass egoism and the French version into anticlerical philistinism. In ideal form, German freedom implied "an organized national unity, based on a dutiful yet at the same time critical devotion of the individual to the group, completed and justified through the independence and individuality of free intellectual education." The state, in sum, controls the body but not the mind. The dialectical notion of "critical yet dutiful devotion" of the individual to the state marked the primary difference between Germany and the West. In the West, the individual always held a final veto.

With this formulation, Troeltsch had a base from which to launch an attack against the British for their imperialistic aggression. England was trying to "atomize" the nations of the world so she could subject them to her uniform institutions. Germans—Allied propaganda to the contrary notwithstanding—believed in the individuality of all national institutions and therefore in "the world principle of the freedom of different national spirits without English control over the moral-political world order." Germany should build a great *Mitteleuropa* that would stand under the German spirit to break the monopoly of the big powers. Such a federation would be a free association of many nations with the uniqueness of each *Volk* carefully preserved, just like the federation Fichte suggested in 1810 as a response to Napoleonic caesarism. This bloc of powers would be led by Germany but not dominated by Germany. Germany was thus the only power that could save the world from "Anglicization and Russification."[44]

Throughout his entire system of thought, Troeltsch was consistently faithful to the romantic principle of "irreducible and individual vital forms."[45] The important thing to remember, however, is that the *forms* he exalted were not the individual persons, as in England, but the *Volk* or the state, or some social unit. It makes a great deal of sense to talk to a German about the freedom of a social unit, but it makes little sense to an Englishman.

CONCLUSION

"One plus God is a majority," runs an old proverb. Germans had to console themselves with such sayings when they looked at the odds against them in the Great War. Though perfidious Albion had organized the world to fight against them, they would win because their cause was just. Most pastors considered the war as a great culmination of German history; they dramatized this idea by listing the great heroes of German history, the poets, artists, philosophers, musicians, generals, statesmen, and religious thinkers. One could compile a *Who's Who in German History* from the patriotic sermons delivered in the war. Rittelmeyer urged his listeners: "Just look around—who is really fighting?" Not just contemporary Germans, he responded, but "a Kant is fighting, one with his teaching about the holy law of morality. Also a Fichte is fighting with him, with his wonderful disclosure of the nobility of the German nationality. A Hegel is fighting with them, with his great, wide-reaching thoughts about the state."[46]

Johann Kessler, pastor of the Lukaskirche in Dresden, asserted, "We believe in a world calling for our nation. A nation that God has equipped with such gifts of the spirit and such depths of mind, that he called to be a bearer of the gospel in the days of the Reformation, that he chose in the War of Liberation to be a harbinger of the new era, a nation to which God has given a Luther and Lessing, a Goethe and Schiller, a Kant and a Bismarck—this nation cannot be cast aside!" The conclusion was obvious: "God has great things in store for such a nation. Such a nation could defy a world of enemies and still triumph."[47]

NOTES

1. *Kriegspredigten* (Wurster), 56.

2. *Vom Feld fürs Feld*, 92.

3. For a very complete source of internal developments in Germany during the war one should see the reports and proceedings of the Fourth Subcommittee of the National Assembly and the Reichstag, edited by Albrecht Philipp and released under the title, *Die Ursachen des deutschen Zusammenbruchs im Jahre 1918*, 12 vols. (Berlin, 1928). Extracts from this collection are available in English translation in *The Causes of the German Collapse*, selected by R. H. Lutz (Stanford, 1934).

4. See e.g., Dunkmann, *Katechismus des Feldgrauen*, 26-38; König, *Neue Kriegspredigten*, 44; Tolzien, *Kriegspredigten*, 53.

5. See e.g., Martin Rade, "Hass oder Pflicht?" *CW*, No. 41 (1916), 781ff; G. Freybe, *P*, 48:10 (March, 1915), 150; Rolffs, *Evangelien-Predigten*, 19.

6. *Kriegspredigten*, V, 59-60.

7. "Geist und Kultur," *Deutschland und der Weltkrieg* (Hintze), 90; see also Schubert, *Erziehung unser Volkes*, 15; Planck, *Sieg des Deutschen*, 13; Sardemann, *Das Reich Gottes*, 14-15; Ott, *Religion, Krieg, und Vaterland*, 39; Horn, *1813 und 1914*, 2; Reetz, *An meine Soldaten*, 105; Hintze, *Die englischen Weltherrschaftspläne*, 8, 29; König, *Kriegspredigten*, 21; Tolzien, *Kriegspredigten*, III, 133; Hoover, *Gospel of Nationalism*, ch. 3.

8. *P*, 47:44 (October 28, 1914), 932.

9. *Geschichte, Krieg, und Seele*, 276; also Wurster, *MP*, XI, 304.

10. See Karl Axenfeld, *Germany's Battle for the Freedom of the Christian Missions* (Berlin-Steglitz, 1919), 8, 20; Dr. Wolfart, *Kriegspredigten* (Wurster), 297; Wurster, *MP*, XI, 234.

11. *EF*, XIV, 370-71.

12. Paul Wurster, *Das english Christenvolk und wir* (Tübingen, 1915), 13-16; Pott, *Vom Feld fürs Feld*, 93.

13. Cordes, *Kriegsbrot*, 87; Pott, *Vom Feld fürs Feld*, 19; Haller, *Warum wir kämpfen*, 12; Herzig, *Kriegspredigten* (Wurster), 113.

14. Althaus-Göttingen, *Kommt last uns anbeten!*, 51; *Kriegsvorträge in der Heimat*, I, 93.

15. "Der Kulturkrieg," *Deutsche Reden in schwerer Zeit*, III, 227.

16. *Die Tragik in des Kaisers Leben*, 12.

17. *Kriegspredigten*, I, 52.

18. *Deutsche Reden in schwerer Zeit*, III, 217.

19. *Neue Kriegspredigten*, 5.

20. *Kriegspredigten*, II, 180; *Berliner Kriegs-Betstunden*, 92.

21. *Aus der Friedens- und Kriegsarbeit*, 314.

22. *Deutsche Reden in schwerer Zeit*, 82. See also Hilbert, *Weltkrieg und Weltregierung*, 13; Deissmann, *Inneres Aufgebot*, 79; Löber, *Christentum und Krieg*, 9; Lehmann, *Von deutschen Gott*, 27; Wurster, *Kriegspredigten*, 370; Guthke, *MP*, XI, 196.

23. *Frohbotschaft*, 46-47; for a similar estimate of King Edward see Sardemann, *Das Reich Gottes*, 15.

24. Some prominent signatories were Harnack, Deissmann, Dryander, Eucken, Lahusen, Le Seur, Meinhof, Richter, Spiecker, and Wundt. The document is printed in Besier, *Die protestantischen Kirchen Europas im Ersten Weltkrieg*, 40-44. See also Wurster, *Kriegspredigten*, 121; Gennrich, *Ein feste Burg* (Doehring), II, 92; König, *Kriegspredigten*, 37.

25. Rump, *Berliner Kriegs-Betstunden*, 52; Ohly, *Ein feste Burg* (Doehring), II, 64-65; Lehmann, *Vom deutschen Gott*, 112-14; Häring, *Kriegspredigten* (Wurster), 146. Troeltsch denounced this race argument, pointing out that the Central Powers had just as many races in their coalition as the Allies (*Deutsche Glaube*, 21).

26. Haller, *Warum wir kämpfen*, 25.

27. *EF*, XVII, 159.

28. *Unser Krieg*, 43-44.

29. *Kriegspredigten*, V, 30, 35; I, 73. See also König, *Neue Kriegspredigten*, 13; Pott, *Vom Feld fürs Feld*, 53, 58; *Kriegsvorträge in der Heimat*, I, 91; Axenfeld, *Unter Gottes gewaltiger Hand*, 13; Roethe, *Vom Tode fürs Vaterland*, 27; Vorwerk, *Was sagt der Weltkrieg*, 18; Zurhellen, *Kriegspredigten*, 22; Ihmels, *Evangelium in schwerer Zeit*, 109.

30. *Aus der Friedens- und Kriegsarbeit*, 287, 295.

31. *Kriegspredigten*, 15.

32. *Vom deutschen Gott*, 23, 44; see also Bürckstümmer, *Ein feste Burg*, 90; Evers, *1870 und 1914*, 5, 26; Dunkmann-Greifswald, *Krieg und Weltanschauung*, 5; Naumann, *Stark in Gott*, 43; Risch, *Mit Gott*, 21; König, *Kriegspredigten*, 62-63; Kessler, *Durch Gott zum Sieg*, 20; Lahusen, *Christbaum und Schwert*, 26-27; Dryander, *Evangelische Reden*, II, 6, 7; Nielsen, *EF*, XIV, 292; Titius, *Unser Krieg*, 10; Tolzien, *Kriegspredigten*, I, 5.

33. *Aus der Friedens- und Kriegsarbeit*, 281; see also Buchholz, *Glaube ist Kraft!*, 91-92; Kirmss, *Ein feste Burg* (Doehring), I, 219.

34. See Hammer, *Kriegstheologie*, 124, 144, 367; Pressel, *Kriegspredigt*, 150; and Lasswell, *Propaganda Technique*, 68.

35. *Ihr habt nicht gewollt*, 140, 144.

36. *Religion, Krieg, und Vaterland*, 80.

37. Bell, *Randall Davidson*, 942. See also Rhode, *Kriegspredigten*, 24; Althaus-Göttingen, *Kommt lasst uns anbeten!*, 55; Doehring, *Ihr habt nicht gewollt*, 147; Dieterich, *Gott mit uns*, 56; Wurster, *Kriegspredigten*, 153; Haecker, *Von Krieg und Kreuz*, 28.

38. *Deutscher Geist*, 38.

39. *Neue Kriegspredigten*, 4.

40. *Gott—unser Zuflucht*, 3; see also Hasse, *Der grosse Krieg*, 48-49; Reetz, *An meine Soldaten*, 126; Tolzien, *Kriegspredigten*, III, 74; Le Seur, *Frohbotschaft*, 48; Haller, *Warum wir kämpfen*, 17; Vorwerk, *Was sagt der Weltkrieg*, 16; Spanuth, *Weltkrieg im Unterricht*, 31; Planck, *Sieg des Deutschen*, 2, 5; Kirn, *Acht Dorf-Kriegspredigten*, 22; Schneller, *Drei Kriegspredigten*, 13; Blume, *Der deutsche Militarismus*, 14; Herzog, *Kriegspredigten* (Wurster), 112.

41. *Varieties of Religious Experience*, 356.

42. See Kant's *Grundlegung zur Metaphysik der Sitten* (Riga, 1785).

43. *Unser Krieg*, 41. See also Hasse, *Grosse Krieg*, 48; Planck, *Sieg des Deutschen*, 13; Rittelmeyer, *Deutschlands religiöser Weltberuf*, 16-19; König, *Kriegspredigten*, 9, 21; Suderow, *Aus ernsten Tagen*, 27-28.

44. "Die Ideen von 1914," *Deutscher Geist*, 32, 48-49, 52-55, 63, 78-79, 94-95, 103. See also "Geist und Kultur," *Deutschland und der Weltkrieg*, edited by Otto Hintze, Friedrich Meinecke, Hermann Oncken (Leipzig & Berlin, 1915), 65, 90.

45. H. R. Mackintosh, *Types of Modern Theology* (London, 1937), 121. The most learned study of German ideas of freedom is Leonard Krieger, *The German Idea of Freedom* (Boston, 1957).

46. *Christ und Krieg*, 157.

47. *Unser Glaube ist Sieg*, 83.

5

Responses

The sins of Germany and Britain seemed obvious—to the other side. The religious patriots of both nations were generally acquainted with the principal charges made against their fatherland. Probably the British knew a bit more than the Germans since they lived in an open (perhaps we should say "more open") society. Since the German newspapers were more controlled than those of Britain we are not surprised to find that the German people did not know all of the charges made against the nation and its military leadership. The Germans had been told for so long by their government that they were surrounded by an iron ring of enemies they just naturally assumed when hostilities began that the Entente had attacked first. They had been hearing of a "defensive war" for so long that they assumed their government's policy was merely one of defense—self-defense. Hence German war sermons often show a surprising lack of knowledge about the real state of affairs on the fronts. But this is true also of the British sermons, though to a much lesser degree. In both cases, we should not judge the clergy too harshly because we now have the facts that they did not have and could not have had at the time.

BRITISH RESPONSES

Most of the British responses to German attacks dealt with four broad issues: the British empire, the charge of betraying the white race, the charge of betraying western civilization, and the charge of hypocrisy concerning Belgium and the beginning of the war.

The British churchmen gave a spirited defense of the British empire against the German attackers in the Great War. The Germans compared Britain to a retired burglar, who, now that he had his plunder, preached law and order to the rest of the world and called in the police when someone else tried to imitate his former crimes. When Britain, who wrote the textbook on imperialism, became satiated with colonies she suddenly discovered international morality and the error of imperialism; she called peace conferences and chattered about disarmament.

New Testament theologian William Sanday saw the weakness in this charge very soon: it was too neat. It was a propaganda version based on a few abstract categories, all of them bad. The British empire was "something more than a bundle of vices. The description . . . bears its own refutation on the face of it. It is not only a libel upon British nature, but upon human nature in general. Men are not made that way."[1] To compare the British empire to a burglar was a patent misuse of analogy, implying that British imperial policy had had a single directing will and a single coherent plan for over three centuries—which was absurd.

The Germans had obviously become victims of their own myth—the "myth of the British empire." To set the record straight the British went to some lengths to show that their empire was almost an accident. In the process they did too good a job and distorted the facts in the other direction. They said the empire grew slowly, haphazardly, pragmatically, changing by response to specific needs and precise historical circumstances. It was a curious mixture of force, vision, fraud, realism, and idealism. There was much less actual, premeditated violence in its history than its enemies supposed. This defense reminded one of the old saw about the Romans, that they conquered the world in self-defense.

Basil Mathews accused the Germans of blindness to realities "freely revealed to babes." The word *empire*, he said, sent the typically professorial Germans like Treitschke scurrying to their textbooks, where they discovered Assyria, Babylon, Rome, and Spain as examples of empires and judged the British empire by that abstract idea. "But the British Empire eludes that definition," he declared; it is rather "a colossal experiment in international government with a minimum of compulsion and a maximum of freedom."[2] In our empire, said Oman, "the whole national idea disappears in an amazing agglomeration of races, tongues, and religions."[3] "The British Empire," claimed Drummond, "is not only the most significant experiment in civilization of which we have any record; in spite of the worst faults which its critics can lay to its charge, it is also by far the noblest."[4] Woods concurred: "We may venture to say that here we have the best attempt at a union of nations which has so far been made."[5]

Since the British empire grew by no single human plan, it must have been the work of divine providence. This conclusion seemed forced on many Britons in 1914 when they observed the unusual response of the empire to defend the English motherland. Since the motherland was fighting for a moral and spiritual principle, the empire must be based, not on greed as the Germans charged, but on some higher principle. Look at the evolution of the empire over three centuries, said many; at the time of Henry VIII England had only Calais for her overseas holdings. Who would have predicted that by 1914 she would be greater than Rome, controlling about one-fourth of the globe, boasting that "the sun never sets on the British Empire?"[6]

Preachers found a fitting verse in the Old Testament. "For what great nation is there that has a god so near to it as the Lord our God is to us?" (Deut. 4:7,8). Like the Germans, the British were not ashamed to claim that they were a chosen people. "Who are we?" asked John Hancock in his book, *God's Dealings with the British Empire.* "We are God's chosen people, His inheritance, the salt of the earth, His loved ones, His glory, the people He delights in, His sons and His daughters. What more can we wish for? I know nothing more."[7] "Let us not fall into the old mistake," warned Dawson, "of counting Jewish history as sacred and English history as secular. . . . You cannot shut up God in a section of time or a corner of the globe. You cannot have him speak for a few generations and be dumb for all succeeding ages."[8] Winnington-Ingram borrowed a figure from Isaiah 49:2 and designated Britain as a "polished arrow" in the quiver of the Almighty, a nation prepared for years by divine discipline to perform a special task.

What was this task? Most churchmen identified it with the idea of freedom. F. T. Woods, Rural Dean and Vicar of Bradford, typified this belief:

God has done much with many lands. Many countries are marked upon His map— Palestine for religion, and Greece for culture, and Rome for law. What if He has marked out Britain for liberty? Britain to win new freedom for the nations? Britain to show them how to use it by her own example? Britain to breed a race of men who have learned their freedom from the Prince of Freedom?[9]

Richard Roberts explained Britain's world mission in a work entitled *Are We Worth Fighting For?*

Great Britain is charged with the obligations of a great tradition. Within its own borders and its empire it has achieved liberty; and with liberty, domestic peace. It is its splendid mission to pass on this gift to the world. The ideal that is implicit in its history is that of "a world set free." It makes no boast of a culture which it would impose upon the world for its good; it is simply vested with a gift in trust for the world. . . . It is the vocation of Britain to proclaim and practise the faith that in the supremacy of moral ideas lies the promise of the liberty and the peace of the world.[10]

Many clerics stressed Britain's ethical mission. T. W. Crafer, vicar of All Saints Church, Cambridge, quoted Zechariah 2:8 in such a way that God declared of Britain, "He that touches you touches the apple of my eye." He continued:

We believe that we are a nation wondrously favoured by God, and we like to think of ourselves as a chosen people, whose name stands in the world for righteousness and peace, for honest dealing with other nations, and respect and protection for small states and weaker peoples. . . . We cannot doubt that so powerful an Empire, in which we are striving after the ideal that right should be preferred to might, must be a precious instrument for good in the hands of God.[11]

Several preachers mentioned the American Revolution as a salutary event in British imperial development. It introduced a new policy of toleration the empire badly needed. Joseph Newton, Minister of the London City Temple, blamed the revolt of the colonies on "a German King [George III of Hanover] and a stupid prime minister." When the United States joined the Allies in 1917, he argued, it disclosed the true nature of the British empire as "an empire of common culture, a common political idea, and common spiritual inheritance."[12]

But, one could say, all this is mere theory until some proof from experience is given. As Jesus said, "By their fruits you shall know them." Was there any real proof of this alleged imperial unity? Was the empire truly an organic entity? The Germans charged that the British empire was a fraud, based on greed and tyranny, destined to fall like a house of cards. They predicted that when war came India would rise in revolt, Ireland would go into civil war, the Boers would hasten to avenge their recent defeat, Canada would remain neutral, and America would opt for German culture. General Bernhardi predicted that England's self-governing colonies would be a negligible military factor in a war.

The Germans were wrong. They were wrong so many times in that fateful year 1914 that their country came to be called "the classic home of political miscalculation." But they were never more wrong than when they predicted the collapse of the British empire. Far from collapsing, the empire responded with a unity and strength that startled everyone, even the mother country. This response struck Drummond as a divine revelation, the voice of God: "All over the world, these millions of men are banded together, not for purposes of aggression or because their material possessions are in danger, but first and last to defend the riches of the soul."[13] "No need to ask now whether we are an Empire," exclaimed Dawson; "The blood of our sons across the seas has mingled with our own, and the blended flood calls heaven to witness that we are one."[14] Mathews exulted that the "hammer of Thor in the hands of the Teuton has welded the Empire's noble metal into a single sword of tempered steel."[15]

Archbishop Davidson was deeply impressed by the same event:

An Empire, a Commonwealth, vast beyond the dreams of any seer of other days—an Empire, a Commonwealth, with roots planted deep in every region of the round world—felt itself suddenly athrob with one impulse, one eager, prayerful purpose, one unshakable resolve: to prevent a great wrong, to stand for what is just and true.[16]

The preachers called the roll of commonwealth nations to dramatize the world-wide imperial response. Soldiers streamed to the front from Australia and New Zealand. Even Tibet sent 1,000 soldiers to the trenches. Louis Botha, the Boer from South Africa, helped England, the nation that had beaten and conquered the Boers just fifteen years before. "Would they have done so," asked Smith, "had they not realized in the Empire something essential to their life, something which is worth battling for against all the bribes and menaces of Germany?"[17]

Canada could have remained neutral but she too came to the aid of the stricken mother. Davidson quoted an eminent Canadian: "We came to your side, not merely or mainly for love of the old mother, but because we felt the old mother was right."[18] Mathews saw a grim, poetic justice in the fact that it was Canadian troops at Ypres, November, 1914, that broke the last German efforts to reach the coast of Calais and menace England.[19]

There was something especially sweet about the entry of India. Pagan India, Hindu-Moslem India—why should she want to help the state that kept her in colonial subjugation? Dawson dramatized the situation in these words:

Let India speak, our greatest, richest possession. She has spoken, she is speaking, and what are her words? "Let England live, let England rule, let no one smite her power. She has our trust, she has our swords, she has our lives, and he who would crush her to the earth must first of all crush us." That is a splendid witness to the righteousness of England's rule, a voice issuing from the present, but bearing in it the testimony of the past.[20]

Winnington-Ingram thought Japan was a special case. Although not a part of the empire, she came in on the Allied side soon after the beginning of the war. He claimed that once the war started the Japanese seemed more favorably disposed to give a hearing to the Christian religion than before. Unlike many, they did not think the war had refuted Christianity. When Japan observed England entering the war to defend Belgium, she "saw a great nation act up to the principles of the religion it professed." She saw in Britain the spirit of Christ, who had sympathy for the poor. "The good old British race never did a more Christlike thing," he concluded, "than when, on August 4, 1914, it went to war."[21]

Thus were the Germans refuted. The British empire had proved itself to be an organic community, the greatest union of nations in history. "French-Canadian Catholics, Irish Protestants, Canadian Anglicans and Dissenters, Moslems and Hindoos, Pagans and Christians, dwell happily and contentedly under the Pax Britannica."[22] God had summoned this great fellowship to stop Germany. He had asked, "Are you able to drink the cup?" and the empire had responded, "We are able!"

The British clergy reacted sharply to the charge that Britain was betraying the cause of the white man by bringing nonwhites from India and other regions to fight the Germans. On first reading, admitted Edwyn Bevan, this argument sounded as if it came from a deep loyalty to Christianity, but further reflection revealed that it came simply from racial prejudice, "the pride of the white colour, which is the very antithesis of real Christianity."[23] This spirit that treats whole races of men as unclean, said Moberly, "is the very opposite of the spirit of Christian brotherhood."[24] Bishop Gore put the issue in clear terms: "We recognize a humanity wider than the white races. . . . We acknowledge that God has given no right to the white races to treat those of other colour as 'lesser breeds' who can be exploited for the white man's purposes."[25]

The Oxford scholars who wrote *To the Christian Scholars of Europe and America* addressed this racism charge in detail. They accused the Germans of inconsistency, since the German empire had an alliance with Moslem Turkey, a non-European, non-Christian state, and a state, furthermore, that had historically frustrated the legitimate aspirations of the Christian Balkan peoples. The fact that Britain received help from her Indian and African colonies constituted, not a fault, but the "crowning token of the true inner cohesion of the British Empire." The address concluded with the ringing declaration that "if we stand, as we claim to do, on behalf of right against might, of respect for the law of nations and for plighted word, and for the defense of the weak, then we can only rejoice if these Christian principles find an echo in the breast of non-Christian peoples."[26]

Many clergymen, while attacking German racism, admitted that Britain's imperial history had contained much of the same evil. While deploring this, they usually concluded from the empire's response of 1914 that, on the whole, Britain's treatment of her subject peoples had been essentially humane.

The British reacted just as strongly against the charge that their country had betrayed western civilization by warring against Germany. Germans depicted their *Kaiserreich* as a great dam, holding back the Russian steamroller, protecting the West like a shining knight against the hordes of Asia. They described Russian civilization as a nonculture, based on a strange religion and a Byzantine-Mongolian superstructure.

British critics responded to this scenario with something like "Humbug!" As with most German propaganda it was just too neat. British clerics pointed out that, contrary to German claims, Russia was not the quintessence of despotism; in recent decades Russia had made more progress toward freedom and self-government than Germany. Furthermore, Russia treated her Poles better than the Germans did theirs. Germany's treatment of the people in Belgium and northern France made Prussianism a far greater threat to any kind of civilization than the alleged "Asiatic barbarism."

It was a *non sequitur* to suppose that Britons were trying to pit Slavs against Teutons just because they went to war with the Russians as allies. Nor did friendship with Russia mean that Britain supported Russian foreign policy in the Balkans, or anywhere else for that matter. As Sanday explained, "We should resist any state that showed Napoleonic ambitions. . . . Only at the last moment and under the severe pressure of honourable obligations, did we allow our friendship to involve us in war with the enemy of our friends."[27]

Last, there was that ugly charge of hypocrisy, revealed in the sudden sympathy for poor little Belgium. The British took the accusation and hurled it back into the Germans' faces and asserted that, on the contrary, August 4, 1914, may have been the finest hour in all British history, the hour when Britain *instinctively*—for there was little time for prolonged reflection—made the right moral decision, a decision that would be remembered through the centuries for its heroism. It was comparable to Luther's resolution at Worms: "Here I stand, I cannot do otherwise, God help me!" Several recalled the famous lines of James Russel Lowell:

> Once to every man and nation
> Comes the moment to decide,
> In the strife of truth with falsehood,
> For the good or evil side,
> Some great cause, God's new Messiah,
> Offering each the bloom or blight,
> And the choice goes by forever
> 'Twixt that darkness and that light.

There are a few times in human history when a moral issue becomes so sharply focused and so clearly understood by millions of people that one could say an entire nation decided to do something. Britons felt that the beginning of World War I was just such an occasion. Everyone felt the strange, mystical unity surrounding the collective purpose in August, 1914. What was it that united the British people? "The consciousness of a nation which has kept its word," answered L. P. Jacks. "No refinements of social mechanism can unite a nation which has broken its faith. A promise betrayed means a people divided."[28]

"I never was so proud of my own nation," confessed Sanday, "as I was in the first week of the war."[29] "The eyes of Britain were wider open at the beginning of the War," declared Dawson, "than they had been for a hundred years."[30] Once we saw Belgium crushed, said Carnegie, we knew that war with Germany was the "only decision worthy of our traditions."[31] Jones recalled that the crisis brought to mind the proverb, "We can send no proxies to meet duty or death."[32] The lines of Tennyson cropped up in many sermons: "His strength is as the strength of ten, / Because his heart is pure."

F. H. Dudden, rector of Holy Trinity, London, gave eloquent expression to the common feeling in England:

Yes, we are on the winning side. The great currents of life are with us; the great forces of the world are for us; we are venturing on a certainty. . . . Let us bow before that power—the Divine Power that makes for righteousness. Let us make a firm alliance with it, and find our salvation in its energy. For right is might and integrity is stronger than iron, and moral force must conquer.[33]

What if Britain had remained passive in August, 1914? Potter answered: "We could never again have held up our heads among civilized honourable nations."[34] Several sermons quoted Lord Asquith who said that "sooner than be a silent witness, which means in effect a willing accomplice, to this tragic triumph of force over law, and of brutality over freedom, I would see this country of ours blotted out of the pages of history."[35]

Gilbert Murray did not believe in the biblical God but he did believe in transcendent values and found moral encouragement in Greek history. He pointed to the Battle of Thermopylae, where Leonidas and his brave 300 Spartans went on a suicide mission to save Greece from the Persians. "In some cases," said Murray, "it is better to fight and be broken than to yield peacefully; . . . sometimes the mere act of resisting to the death is in itself a victory." The Spartans knew they were going to die but "they would not consent to their country's dishonour." Murray argued cogently that honor and dishonor are real things; he declined to define them, but insisted that "they admit of no bargaining."[36]

The Bible contained an excellent example of what God thinks of a nation that will not fight for the right. In Judges 5:23 God cursed a small region of Palestine called Meroz for not helping Deborah and Barak fight the Canaanites: "Curse Meroz, says the angel of the Lord, curse bitterly its inhabitants, because they came not to the help of the Lord against the mighty." Winnington-Ingram used this passage in a notable sermon and said that if Britain had given the wrong answer in 1914, "not all the glories commemorated in this Guildhall, not Waterloo, not Agincourt, not any of our great victories, could have saved us from the reproach, the eternal disgrace, of having failed in our word." Britain would have become the "Meroz of Nations." But the British lion, followed by all his cubs, placed his paw on that Belgian treaty and said, "My word is my bond; I stand by my friends. God defend the right."[37]

Thus by a curious twist the Great War was not the refutation of Christianity but rather a vindication of the moral claims of Jesus Christ. It was the passionate protest of civilized men against the abandonment of Christian ideals and the attempt to substitute force for them. When brave Christian men die fighting for the right, said Henson, you can hear over the battlefields the ancient words of the Emperor Julian, "Thou has conquered, O Galilean!"[38]

GERMAN RESPONSES

German clergymen lived in a less open society than Britain, but it was not hermetically sealed against things coming from the West. Most clerics knew that the Allies were attacking their fatherland in the neutral nations and they defended Germany over key issues like Belgium, militarism, the kaiser, and some of the unique features of German culture.

Protestant pastors jumped quickly to the defense of the imperial government in the matter of Belgian neutrality. Several of them criticized Chancellor

Bethmann for apologizing in the Reichstag, August 4, with this admission: "Our invasion of Belgium is contrary to international law but the wrong—I speak openly—that we are committing we will make good as soon as our military goal has been reached." Admiral von Tirpitz considered this the greatest blunder ever committed by a German statesman and many of the clergy agreed with him.

Harnack put the shoe on the other British foot and asked what Britain would have done if France had decided to advance through Belgium on the way to attack Germany? Or better, what would Britain have done if (say) the Prince of Wales had been murdered by someone from a small enemy state that had always helped the Irish revolt against the British? Would Britain not have sent an ultimatum to that country? And would that ultimatum not have been just as stern as the one Austria-Hungary sent to Serbia? Harnack reminded the British that their government had found it convenient to break promises now and then, like not pulling out of Egypt after they had promised it over a dozen times.[39]

But this is just arguing *ad hominem*, proving your opponent inconsistent. The Germans went further than this, invoking an ancient maxim, "Necessity knows no law" (*Not kennt kein Gebot*). They defended the violation of Belgian neutrality as a military and therefore national necessity. Harnack compared the event to an incident in the life of King David, who once took the holy, consecrated bread from the table of God and gave it to his soldiers to eat, bread that only the appointed priests were allowed to eat. His act was justified because he and his men were engaged in a vital mission and were desperately in need of food (1 Sam. 21:6). This must have been a good argument, because Jesus Christ used the same passage to defend his disciples for plucking grain on the Sabbath day (Mark 2:25). Just as Jesus said, "The Sabbath was made for man, not man for the Sabbath," so also Harnack was arguing that, "Treaties are made for nations, not nations for treaties." He concluded: "There is a right of necessity that breaks iron, not to mention a treaty."[40]

Pastor Karl Reimers argued in a similar vein, using the analogy that Germany in 1914 was like a man outnumbered by three robbers. He can escape only if he darts through a small garden with a "No Trespassing" sign on it. He has the right to commit this peccadillo against a small neighbor to avoid harm from three larger predatory neighbors.[41]

Dr. W. Dibelius explained Germany's dilemma this way: "We were in the position of a man who, being attacked from two sides, has to carry on a furious fight for life, and cannot concern himself overmuch as to whether one or two flowers are trodden down in his neighbor's garden."[42]

Dr. Arthur Titius, professor of systematic theology at Göttingen, defended Germany in a volume entitled *Our War: Ethical Observations*. He recalled how Britain had contemplated the violation of Belgian neutrality in 1870 just in case the Franco-Prussian War required British intervention. "There can be no higher principle of politics," he averred, "than the welfare of one's own nation, when it must be, even in opposition to that of every other nation." It would have been wrong, therefore, for the leaders of Germany— given Germany's geographical location—to have planned any other course of action than the violation of Belgium. Titius reminded his readers that even the great English historian Thomas Macaulay justified Frederick the Great's sudden attack on Saxony in 1756, an act that started the Seven Years War.[43]

Ernst Dryander, a high church official, stated the crucial principle that justified Germany in these terms: "Unlike the individual, the state cannot and may not proceed according to the principle, 'Better to suffer injustice than to commit injustice.' If it did, it would relinquish its right. The state has the duty to protect the interests of everyone belonging to its association and entrusted to its protection."[44]

We notice that all these churchmen assumed that Germany was being attacked, not doing the attacking, as the historical record indicates.

As noted earlier, the British attacked the Germans over Belgium by connecting the violation of neutrality with the pernicious theory of the amoral state. They insisted that the violation of Belgium followed logically from the operation of *Realpolitik*. The German clergy contradicted this assertion vehemently. "Germany has never used its power," said Philippi, "to endanger the independence of others."[45] Dryander assured the world that Germans took their stand not on moral relativism but on a belief in the righteousness of the God who rules history, the God who tells us that *Recht muss doch Recht bleiben*!—"the right must surely remain the right!"[46] Hilbert said, "The belief in the victory of the good in this world is the only firm basis for our moral striving."[47] Tolzien took an oath on German innocence: "We raise our pure hands to God and swear that never was there a better and more peaceful nation than we in relations with our neighbors."[48] Lehmann discovered German probity in the *Volksgeist*: "We Germans believe we understand Christ better than all other people on earth, because we feel God in the soul and we turn our moral conscience into a principle of action."[49]

Otto Hättenschwiller contrasted the morality of the Reich with that of the French, who, when the war started, boasted, "The Germans fear God and nothing else in the world [a famous remark from Bismarck]. We French fear even less—we do not even fear the God of the Germans!" Someone high in the French government remarked that "science has put out the lights in heaven." Hättenschwiller reassured his readers that the eternal lights of God were still burning and that Germans still followed those lights.[50]

But what of the awful trinity—Bernhardi, Nietzsche, and Treitschke? They must have been a creation of the British; at least this is the impression one gets from the paucity of references in the German clerical literature. Blume asked how many people had read Nietzsche much less how many had become his followers?[51] Wurster ridiculed the notion that these three thinkers dominated the intellectual life of Germany.[52] Dr. August Stock, pastor in Berlin-Lichterfelde, reported that the best-selling books in Munich at the outbreak of war were the New Testament, Goethe's *Faust*, and Nietzsche's *Zarathustra*; but he proceeded to attack Nietzsche for speaking ill of Christ.[53]

It would appear that the British furor over the awful trinity was much ado about little. Perhaps Germany's military clique agreed with Bernhardi, perhaps a few thinkers agreed with Nietzsche, perhaps a lot of people tended to agree with the general tone of Treitschke . . . perhaps, but one finds very little of these three in the Protestant clergy's war sermons.

The clergy's defense of militarism was one of the most interesting aspects of German clerical nationalism. Preachers complained that foreigners could not possibly understand German militarism because it was a peculiarity of the *Volksgeist*, a unique product of German heredity, history, and divine providence. The English, protested Deissmann, cannot even get the words right when discussing the topic. They translated *allgemeine Wehrpflicht* as "compulsory service" (which would be properly *Zwangdienst*) instead of "general military duty." By this linguistic trick they distorted the voluntary aspect of German military service and perpetuated the myth that Germans had to be rounded up by the police and driven like cattle to the front.[54]

Dryander assumed a defiant mood when meeting attacks on militarism; he quoted Saint Paul: "With me, it is a very small thing that I should be judged by you or by any human court" (1 Cor. 4:3).[55] Baumgarten pointed out that "For us Germans 'militarism' is certainly no problem but a bitter necessity; it is not even amenable to discussion, but a simple given."[56] Blume noted the hypocrisy of the British in attacking militarism in 1914 but praising the Prussian spirit a century before when everyone was fighting Napoleon and the French. "Yes," he admitted, "we are a military state and will remain one, if we must, to keep our nation from becoming booty to a neighbor."[57] König said that German militarism had been a blessing from God, a great schoolmaster through whom God was making the German *Volk* into a glorious instrument to free Europe of three devils: the French thirst for glory, the Muscovite thirst for power, and the English spirit of petty commercialism, gluttony, and envy.[58]

Many clergymen insisted that there was a genuine connection between militarism and the moral health of Germany. Military training develops discipline, obedience, frugality, loyalty, self-control, love, and comradeship. These are all moral virtues that any nation would desire to have in its citizens. Perhaps the key virtue instilled by militarism is the sense of duty. As one pastor explained it: "The German nation has surpassed every nation in the world in extolling the command of duty in its national education, in its professional work, in its civic spirit, and in its great poets and philosophers. . . . Our children become great in the consciousness that each person has his duty to fulfill!"[59] Pastor Koehler gave a similar eulogy:

To do a thing of your own free will, compelled by your own free conscience—that is German. The German is before all else a man of duty and loyalty. His is upright and modest, brave and devout. His blessing and his reward come from the iron sense of duty that leads and informs all of his actions. Doing something for the sake of duty is a pleasure to him. His sense of duty makes him proud, but he still remains humble and modest. Humility and trust are lodged in his soul. That is German piety.[60]

Extolling the frugal soldier gave Zurhellen another opportunity to bash the British and the sin of materialism. He cited an old German proverb, "Freedom and black bread go together." The free man is the one "who recognizes nothing higher than the good of his soul . . . but the materialistic spirit is slavery." Only the idealist, therefore, is free. The British had connected materialism and militarism in their critique of German culture, but the truth was too subtle for them to grasp: militarism actually cultivates idealism![61]

Baumgarten resented the allegation that militarism was opposed to the free, scientific spirit. On the contrary, he asserted, the two emphases have grown up together in Germany. In fact, German thoroughness and efficiency can be traced to the beneficent effects of military training in German history. Military training was thus a primary cause of German industrial power.[62]

Adolf Stoecker (1835-1909), one of the strongest religious patriots in the Second Reich, affirmed that "we Prussians make no distinctions between king and fatherland. Where the king is, there is the fatherland also, and where the fatherland is, there is the king."[63] One could shift this remark to conditions of the Great War and most Protestant clergymen would say the same about Kaiser William II. Allied propaganda claimed that all the German vices were incarnated in the person of the kaiser but German churchmen found this idea outrageous.

William II predicted that when the war was over and the truth was known, he would become known as the "peace emperor" (*Friedenskaiser*). Many clerics echoed the same prediction. Tolzien reminded people of how the kaiser held back the German army for a day in August, 1914, waiting for a certain message from Great Britain. He thus nobly forfeited a clear advantage Germany had at the outset of hostilities. He already had his niche in history as "the waiting emperor."[64]

The Allies had compared William II to Julian the Apostate but the truth was that he was the only ruler among the great powers who could truly be called a Christian. He, like Christ, could say, "They hated me without a cause." He bowed the knee to God, but not to Britain! "Never," said Tolzien, "did a more noble man sit upon a throne, never one more worthy, never a prince with a more religious heart, with a more serious conscience."[65] "The real secret of this man," said Ihmels, "is the deep seriousness with which he believes in a divine mission. . . . Today we feel that nothing better could happen to our nation than to learn from the Kaiser to believe in its calling, or better, to believe in the God who calls it."[66]

The year 1915 was the 500-year celebration of the coming of the Hohenzollern dynasty to north Germany, and naturally, there were numerous sermons on the providential care of the ruling family. God had chosen and directed Germany and the Hohenzollerns just as surely as he had chosen Abraham and guided the destinies of Israel. William II was eulogized as the most fortunate of the dynasty for being Kaiser at this culmination of German history. The general thrust of such sermons went like this:

In the year 1415, when the Hohenzollerns started ruling in Berlin, no one would have dreamed that the dynasty would someday dominate most of central Europe. The German cause had just five years before received a mortal blow from the Poles in the Battle of Tannenberg (1410). God nevertheless called the Hohenzollerns from south to north Germany, just as he once summoned Abraham from Ur to Canaan—without telling him the purpose of his migration (Gen. 12:1-3). It took a lot of faith for the chosen family to pick up everything and move into the Mark Brandenburg, a land so sandy and infertile it was called "the sand box of the Holy Roman Empire."

Under God's guidance, this special family produced a line of remarkable rulers, twenty princes in all, including nine kings and three emperors, all of whom displayed the godly, Prussian-German virtues of frugality, gravity, responsibility, and devotion to duty. The family produced Frederick the Great, who wrote a treatise called *Anti-Machiavelli*, extolling the notion that the prince is the "first servant" of the state, a ruler who must look not to himself but to the welfare of his people. The family produced serious, religious men like the Great Elector, whose last words were, "Come Lord Jesus, I am ready."

The Hohenzollerns adopted the Protestant faith and spread it over all northern Germany. They defeated Napoleon I and Napoleon III, thus checking the spread of rotten, French culture. As God had obviously planned, they united all Germans into the great Reich of 1871. Now, in the fullness of time, in 1914, Germany has grown to be the leading nation of Europe militarily, economically, culturally, and intellectually—poised to take its place as the leading nation of Europe, perhaps the world. Truly, the mills of the gods grind slowly but they grind exceedingly fine.[67]

Defending the kaiser and extolling the Hohenzollern dynasty gave some pastors an excellent chance to expatiate on the virtues of monarchism and the evils of republicanism. Albert Lorenz testified that the war had opened his eyes on this topic: "I believe that the war has shown us what a republic is—example France. What a sham monarchy is—example England and Italy. What a capricious autocracy is—example Russia. We give thanks to God in heaven that he has given us the strong and righteous government of the Hohenzollerns."[68]

When Woodrow Wilson declared war on imperial Germany, April 6, 1917, he said that the United States was fighting for the privilege of every man to lead the life of his choice. When Pastor Hartwick read these words he exclaimed, "I laughed out loud at this contradiction in the speech of a man who wants to force a democratic republic on the Germans. But then," he continued,

then I hit myself on the head, no I strike my breast! Have we Germans not complained about our government before the world and posed as enslaved vassals and led Wilson and his group to believe that they would be doing a good work if they would liberate us from our government? Father, forgive us, because we did not know what we were doing![69]

In general, German pastors felt that German culture, as God had developed it through history, was all of one piece. Hohenzollerns, kaisers, Protestantism, monarchy, militarism—it was all meant to hang together, to be a unique mosaic of features defining the peculiar German nation with its unique *Volksgeist*. To remove the kaiser or the principle of monarchy from the gestalt would be as shameful as removing the Torah from Judaism. What God had joined by historical development man should not put asunder.

Many pastors quoted the familiar words of Schiller in expressing the importance of the Great War: "Every nation has its day in history, but the day of the Germans will be the harvest of the entire world." British clergymen held the conviction that Germany was in a period of temporary insanity, but the truth was that Germany was reaching her harvest, the culmination of her history. She was facing the greatest struggle of her national life, a struggle that would install her as the leading nation of Europe. Perhaps the most ecstatic expression of this belief came from Franz Rhode of Karlsruhe, whose kingdom of God was almost identical with the geopolitical abstraction *Mitteleuropa*:

Now it must come, a great dual empire [Germany and Austria-Hungary] that will be washed by the blue tide of the Adriatic and the North Sea, a central kingdom, indivisible, German forever, a bulwark of peace, crouched in peaceful stubbornness like a lion against the tide of the national chaos in the east [Russia] and the restless neighbor in the west [France] and the envious sea-ruling shopkeeper on his isle of security [England]. Now it must come, in this war, whose advent our great men have always expected—the empire that the most noble among the people have been anticipating for a long time. It must come, the completion of German history. The old Red Beard [Frederick Barbarossa] climbs again out of the Kyffhäuser and beholds the flight of the ravens around the German hearth and his eyes are gleaming because his people in the north and in the south have drawn the sword in a fellowship of arms for the Holy German Empire of the German nation.[70]

One notable condition that heightened the sense of historical destiny in the Great War was the cluster of four major celebrations that coincided with the conflict: (1) 1913, the centennial of the War of Liberation; (2) 1915, the 500-year celebration of the arrival of the Hohenzollerns; (3) 1915, the centennial of Bismarck's birth; and (4) 1917, the 400-year celebration of the

Reformation. With so many anniversaries of so many wonderful events falling so close together it was easy to flow with the feeling that the war was a culmination of German history. The period 1914-18 seemed to be a giant ganglion of historical threads.

The conviction was almost universal that God had been developing Germany for a long time, tempering her like fine steel to be used on this momentous occasion. "The path of our history," said Showalter, "is strewn with monuments of the love of God."[71] Over and over one hears the refrain, "Look at our history. God has something special in store for this nation." God had now arranged it so that Germany's greatest trial was also to be her greatest hour.[72]

A few pastors got carried away and sounded close to *Realpolitik* in describing Germany's world mission. Zurhellen said Germany needed *Raum* (space) instead of *Ruhm* (fame) to fulfill her calling in history.[73] Titius argued that it was quite natural for a healthy nation to strive to spread out.[74] Witte protested that "our sixty-seven million need more space than we have in our narrow, original home."[75] Pott bordered on the ridiculous when he uttered the faulty dilemma: "After the war we will either be the uncontested first nation of Europe or we will be nothing at all."[76] Shades of *Weltmacht oder Niedergang*! Leonhardt even used Nietzsche's "Will to Power" as a sermon title in which he claimed:

Every normal and healthy nation carries in itself the will to power, grounded in the consciousness of a moral superiority over other nations. Any nation that thinks otherwise demonstrates thereby that it is degenerate and in the process of dissolution because it is in doubt about its right of existence. It is therefore completely wrong to characterize the aspirations of a nation without further ado as megalomania or arrogance.[77]

But these were the exceptions, not the rule. Most clergymen talked in vague, general terms about Germany's spiritual and cultural mission in world history. This mission, however, was not usually depicted as an imperialistic one in which foreign peoples would be conquered or Germanized—certainly not liquidated.[78]

CONCLUSION

Both sides, German and British, defended the fatherland against its detractors. Both committed a common fallacy called special pleading, which is selecting the material that favors your theory and suppressing the material that refutes it. The British eulogized the bright episodes of imperial history and ignored the dark chapters, while the Germans praised the good results of militarism and ignored the negative results. To get an impartial history of anything involved in these accusations one would certainly not use war sermons as his source.

NOTES

1. *Meaning of the War*, 69.

2. *Three Years War*, 38. See especially H. E. Egerton, *Is the British Empire the Result of Wholesale Robbery?* (London, 1915).

3. *War and Its Issues*, 108.

4. *Soul of a Nation*, 22.

5. F. T. Woods, *War Watchwords from Bradford Parish Church* (Leeds, 1914), 62.

6. Plowden-Wardlaw, *Test of War*, 14; Wace, *War and the Gospel*, 114, 121-23; Orchard, *The Real War* (London, 1914), 14; Sanday, *Meaning of the War*, 73-75; Robinson, *Holy Ground: Sermons Preached in Time of War* (London, 1914), 22, 61.

7. (Cambridge, 1916), 3.

8. *Christ and the Sword*, 74.

9. *War Watchwords*, 93.

10. *Are We Worth Fighting For?*, 14-15. See also Robinson, *Holy Ground*, 20; Smith, *War, Nation, and Church*, 32; Gough, *God's Strong People*, 107.

11. *A Prophet's Vision and the War*, 37.

12. *The Sword of the Spirit: Britain and America in the Great War* (London, 1918), 21. See also Robinson, *Holy Ground*, 20; Mathews, *Three Years War*, 46; Plowden-Wardlaw, *Test of War*, 33.

13. *Soul of a Nation*, 20-21.

14. *Christ and the Sword*, 74.

15. *Three Years War*, 39.

16. *Testing of a Nation*, 211. See also E. W. M. Grigg, *Why the Dominions Came In* (London, n.d.), 8; Winnington-Ingram, *Day of God*, 8.

17. *War, Nation, and Church*, 34; also Sinker, *The War*, 79; Plowden-Wardlaw, *Test of War*, 35.

18. *Testing of a Nation*, 189.

19. *Three Years War*, 38.

20. *Christ and the Sword*, 76. See also Worsey, *Under the War Cloud*, 59.

21. *Potter and Clay*, 227-29.

22. Plowden-Wardlaw, *Test of War*, 34. See also Potter, *Judgment of War*, 32; Orchard, *The Real War*, 14; Mursell, *Bruising of Belgium*, 17; B. W. Randolph, *Sermons for the Times*, I, 10; Renshaw, *Christ and the War*, 10.

23. *Brothers All: The War and the Race Question* (London, 1914), 14.

24. *Christian Conduct in War Time*, 15.

25. *Patriotism in the Bible*, 18. See also Holland, *So as by Fire*, 70-72. Smith cited Troeltsch, writing in the *Neue Rundschau* (February, 1915), to the effect that Germany admitted a fellowship of European states—thus denying Bernhardi's and Treitschke's doctrine of *Realpolitik*; but what Germany found wrong was Britain's denial of this fellowship by bringing in nonwhites (*War, Nation, and Church*, 11-12).

26. *To the Christian Scholars*, 6, 12. Thompson pointed out in his *Prussia's Devilish Creed* (p. 11) that Kaiser William II in November, 1898, told a crowd in Damascus, Syria, that the 300 million Moslems scattered over the globe could be assured "that the German Empire will be their friend at all times." Fisher describes in some detail the policy Germany pursued for several years of destabilizing the British Empire by appealing to the separatist ambitions of various nationalities (*Germany's Aims in the First World War*, 120ff.).

27. *Meaning of the War*, 104; also Winnington-Ingram, *Potter and Clay*, 231; *To the Christian Scholars*, 1, 9-11; Valentine Chirol, *Germany and the Fear of Russia* (London, 1914), 3, 19.

28. "Mechanism and the War," 37.

29. *Meaning of the War*, 50.

30. *Christ and the Sword*, 127.

31. *Sermons on Subjects*, 12.

32. *Ethical and Religious Problems* (Carpenter), 41.

33. *Problem of Human Suffering*, 60-61; also Davidson, *Testing of a Nation*, 130; A. C. Buckell, *The Greatest War: Six Addresses* (London, 1915), 27; Paterson-Smyth, *God and the War*, 38.

34. *Discipline of War*, 22.

35. See his Guildhall speech, September 4, 1914; also Foakes-Jackson, *Sermons for the Times*, IV, 13; Muir, *War and Christian Duty*, 212.

36. *How Can War Ever Be Right?* (London, 1914), 6-7. The examples of Marathon and Thermopylae were also used in Dudden, *Problem of Human Suffering*, 55; and Black, *Around the Guns*, 62.

37. *Church in Time of War*, 24; also Henson, *War-Time Sermons*, 49; Denison, *Spiritual Lessons of the War*, 16.

38. Henson, *War-Time Sermons*, 252.

39. *Aus der Friedens- und Kriegsarbeit*, 294-95; 299ff.

40. Ibid., 296. Harnack held to what would today be called "situation ethics." He wrote: "There is a private ethic and a social ethic and a political ethic. There is an ethic in peacetime and another in the situation of necessary defense, and so forth. One cannot simply pass from one field to another; in face, one would be unethical if he did." See Zahn-Harnack, *Harnack*, 359.

41. *Krieg und der Christ* (Hamburg, 1914), 21.

42. *Was Will England?* (1914), 5, cited in William Archer, *501 Gems of German Thought* (London, 1917), 120.

43. *Unser Krieg*, 13-14.

44. *Evangelische Reden*, II, 38; also König, *Neue Kriegspredigten*, 14; Schönhuth, *Kriegspredigten* (Wurster), 137; Tolzien, *Tragik in des Kaisers Leben*, 15; D. H. Kerler, *Deutschlands Verletzung der Belgischen Neutralität, Eine sittliche Notwendigkeit* (Ulm, 1915).

45. *An der Front*, 8.

46. *Evangelische Reden*, V, 32.

47. *Krieg und Kreuz*, 13.

48. *Kriegspredigten*, II, 7.

49. *Vom deutschen Gott*, 14.

50. *Kriegsbeispiele*, 81.

51. *Der deutsche Militarismus*, 14.

52. *Das englische Christenvolk*, 20-21.

53. *Gott nimmt von uns alles Weh! Drei Festpredigten zu Weinacht und Neujahr im Kriegsjahr 1914/15* (Berlin-Lichterfelde, 1915), 28; see also Baumgarten, *EF*, XVI, 192.

54. *Schwertsegen*, 18-20.

55. *Evangelische Reden*, III, 18.

56. *Deutsche Reden in schwerer Zeit*, 128.

57. *Der deutsche Militarismus*, 17.

58. *Neue Kriegspredigten*, 14.

59. *Kriegsvorträge in der Heimat*, I, 90.

60. *Kriegspredigt*, 39, cited in Hammer, *Kriegstheologie*, 138.

61. *Kriegspredigten*, 74-75.

62. "Deutscher Militarismus," *EF*, XIV, 389-91. For additional sermons on militarism see Schwarz, *Kriegspredigten* (Wurster), 313; Troeltsch, *Deutsche Glaube*, 9-11; Planck, *Sieg des Deutschen*, 69; Schubert, *Erziehung unser Volkes*, 12; Dunkmann, *Katechismus des Feldgrauen*, 16-17; Klein, *Du bist mein Hammer*, 17-18; König, *Kriegspredigten*, 26; Tolzien, *Kriegspredigten*, III, 8; Titius, *Unser Krieg*, 54-56; Nowak, *Stark und getrost*, 37.

63. Hammer, *Kriegstheologie*, 40.

64. *Tragik in des Kaisers Leben*, 7; also Häring, *Kriegspredigten* (Wurster), 150; Hättenschwiller, *Kriegsbeispiele*, 82; Kirmss, *Das Reich muss uns doch bleiben*, 41.

65. *Kriegsausgang*, 66.

66. *Evangelium in schwerer Zeit*, 33; also Buchholz, *Glaube ist Kraft!*, 50-57; Showalter, *Krieg in Predigten*, 16; Rendtorff, *Aus dem dritten Kriegsjahr*, 50-54; Kirmss, *Kriegspredigten*, 38; Dunkmann, *Katechismus des Feldgrauen*, 11; Faulhaber, *Schwert des Geistes*, 262-64; Römer, *Des Christen Weg*, 265; Wurster, *Das englische Christenvolk*, 22; Cordes, *Kriegsbrot*, 104.

67. See e.g., Rump, *Kriegspredigten*, II, 213-22; Dryander, *Evangelische Reden*, 34-35; Kirmss, *Das Reich muss uns doch bleiben*, 4-8, 41; Blume, *Der deutsche Militarismus*, 15; Kramer, *Kriegs- und Friedens-Predigten*, 73; Reetz, *An meine Soldaten*, 154; Lahusen, *Christbaum und Schwert*, 25; Pott, *Vom Feld fürs Feld*, 12; Ihmels, *Darum auch wir*, 85-87; Suderow, *Aus ernsten Tagen*, 22; Lorenz, *Warum blüht der Hohenzollern Krone?*, 5-7; Horn, *Begeisterung*, 2.

68. *Warum blüht der Hohenzollern Krone?*, 10.

69. *P*, XV (April, 1917), 237; also Zurhellen, *Kriegspredigten*, 91.

70. *Kriegspredigten*, 19.

71. *Krieg in Predigten*, 26.

72. For representative sermons on this general theme see Ihmels, *Darum auch wir*, 24; Hasse, *Grosse Krieg*, 82; Deissmann, *Deutsche Schwertsegen*, 60; Dietrich, *Gott mit uns*, 58; Kessler, *Unser Glaube*, 67; Keller, *Ist Gott neutral?*, 7; Le Seur, *Vom werdenden Deutschland*, 8; Kirmss, *Kriegspredigten*, 19; Klein, *Du bist mein Hammer*, 39; Rittelmeyer, *Deutschlands religiöse Weltberuf*, 3; Meyer, *Kriegspredigten* (Wurster), 31; Nowak, *Stark und getrost*, 34; Meyer, *Vom ehrlichen Krieg*, 88; König, *Kriegspredigten*, 12-13; Lehmann, *Vom deutschen Gott*, 63-64; Tolzien, *Kriegspredigten*, IV, 16-18; Suderow, *Aus ernsten Tagen*, 15-16; Pott, *Vom Feld fürs Feld*, 21; Philippi, *An der Front*, 21-22.

73. *Kriegspredigten*, 29.

74. *Unser Krieg*, 9.

75. *EF*, XIV, 370.

76. *Vom Feld fürs Feld*, 72.

77. *P*, XLVII:41 (October 7, 1914), 880. Dunkmann-Greifswald affirmed that "if it should be necessary that French culture be totally destroyed in order for us to live, then it has to be. That is the hard logic of war!" (*Krieg und Weltanschauung*, 17).

78. See Aner's sharp attack on the Social Darwinism of the Pangerman Society in *Hammer oder Kreuz?*, 31.

6

Varieties of Christian Nationalism

We have seen that the British and German clergy disagreed sharply with one another on such questions as empires, heroism, Russia, France, idealism, militarism, monarchism, western civilization, freedom, and equality. It comes as somewhat of a surprise, therefore, when we discover that they were in close agreement on one subject—nationalism. Nearly all clerics on both sides of the North Sea agreed that the nation, or *Volk*, was one of God's primary creations, a community of great value like the family and the church. Both sides used the same biblical passages and the same philosophical arguments to defend nationalism. Both felt that God had brought the nations into being for a special purpose and that the Christian had a moral obligation to discover that purpose and to dedicate his individual life to its fulfillment.

APOLOGY FOR NATIONALISM

Dean William R. Inge once described a nation as "a society united by a delusion about its ancestry and by a common hatred of its neighbors." This definition is a bit cynical but not entirely wrong, because there is, unfortunately, a great deal of delusion and emotion mixed into modern nationalism. Nationalism is a sense of identity held by any group that prides itself on being a nation. A nation, loosely speaking, is an earthbound in-group that thinks it constitutes a unique cultural entity, a special fraction of the human race. Nations usually have some common features such as language, culture, territory, and history.[1]

The safest definition one could give of a nation is "a subdivision of the human race." Our churchmen would hasten to add one qualification: a nation is a *divinely ordained subdivision of the human race*. Some students of nationalism make the mistake of saying we must either believe that God designed the nations or that they developed, somewhat accidentally, from race, climate, and environment.² This is a faulty dilemma; it overlooks the fact that God can use secondary causes like race, soil, climate, and history to mold a special people to use in his plan for history. He kept Israel in Egyptian bondage for centuries and in the wilderness for decades before he let them enter Canaan. British preachers were fond of Shakespeare's line, "There is a divinity that shapes our ends, rough hew them as he may."

Man is a social being. Individualism, especially atomistic individualism, is a great error because man does not live alone in this world. Man has a will to love, a drive to personal relationships; he must always be reaching forth beyond himself. This drive, however, always stops short of total humanity, a concept that most nationalists consider a mischievous abstraction. Just as Aristotle warned us to beware of "watery friendships," the clergymen of Britain and Germany warned us against nebulous concepts like internationalism, cosmopolitanism, and "good Europeanism." Barry noted that "a union of developed nation-states with all their rich, concrete varieties would be a far more fruitful issue than a sad denationalized uniformity."³ To be a good fruit, reasoned Harnack, you must be a good specific fruit, like a good pear or a good apple. "A culture without a national character is bland, watery, and insipid."⁴ Dibelius agreed: "Everything great, everything powerful, everything truly holy and noble is native, growing up from the ground of a sound nationality."⁵

God shows his wisdom in the creation of separate nations. The gathering of people into ethnic subdivisions enables the individual to accomplish what would otherwise be impossible. It places within our reach, said Dawson, "a mutual service, a culture, a security, a power of enrichment and expansion, never to be arrived at singly and apart."⁶ Sociologists always point out that man would remain a brute animal without society and the Christian patriot takes this insight and runs with it—straight to the conclusion that nationality is necessary to be truly human. "We are brought into the world as members of families, tribes, or nations," said Gore, "and only in such memberships do we come to know either ourselves or God. In particular only in and through the family and nation can we reach forward to the idea of humanity."⁷

If a nation is a divine creation, it follows logically that the collective mind or soul of a related ethnic group could be called a *Volksgeist*, a national spirit or soul. This spirit is something divine and essentially moral. "National spirit is a sacred thing," declared Mursell, "it is something God meant to be; and he meant it for something."⁸ Any race that has become aware of its soul, said Holland, would rather die a hundred deaths than submit to a conquest of it. "When once an Englishman has become conscious of his type, of his inheritance, of his racial quality, he will know why he could never endure to live unless he were free to be himself."⁹ In a passage extolling the national spirit, Dunkmann-Greifswald got carried away and illustrated the dangers of praising the fatherland too highly: "This fatherland is our highest commitment, our highest earthly good. We have nothing higher in the world, therefore the fatherland is our absolute."[10]

Otto Zurhellen reached back into German history and used a romantic argument for nationalism; he argued that each *Volk* is meant to illustrate or reflect the variegated splendor of God's nature and of man as God's image.[11] This idea had been given popular expression by Johann Gottfried Herder (1744-1804), sometimes called the father of German nationalism. Each nation represented, as it were, a plant of unique growth in the great garden of God's creation, where each pursued its course "according to its instincts and character."[12] The same idea was championed during the War of Liberation by the greatest of all German patriotic preachers, Friedrich Schleiermacher (1768-1834). "Each *Volk*," he claimed, "was designed to illustrate a special aspect of the image of God, in its own peculiar setting and by its own specially determined position in the world."[13]

Perhaps the best statement of this Christian nationalism came from the pen of theologian Paul Althaus (1888-1966):

The belief that God has created me includes also my *Volk*. Whatever I am and have, God has given me out of the wellspring of my *Volk*: the inheritance of blood, the corporeality, the soul, the spirit. God has determined my life from its outermost to its innermost elements through my *Volk*, through its blood, through its spiritual style, which above all endows and stamps me in the language, and through its history. My *Volk* is my outer and my inner destiny. This womb of my being is God's means, his *Ordnung*, by which to create me and endow me. . . . The special style of a *Volk* is his creation, and as such it is for us holy.[14]

But does the scripture allow this patriotism? Christians are told to honor, respect, and obey the government (Rom. 13:1-7; 1 Pet. 2:12-17), but the New Testament never mentions *love* of a government. Could it be that patriotism is never mentioned in the New Testament because it is an unjustified contraction of the Christian's love, which should be universal?

Different preachers handled this objection in different ways. Some Anglican divines pointed out that it was based on a defective Puritan hermeneutic, the assumption that omission equals condemnation. Some German pastors noted that patriotism is not mentioned in the New Testament because there were no fatherlands in the Roman empire of Jesus' time; everything was merged into a single political unity.

Most churchmen on both sides, however, denied that patriotism is not mentioned in the Bible. They argued that scripture does teach love of country, by example if not by precept. To begin with, the prophets of the Old Testament were the finest examples of patriotism; their love of Yahweh and Israel was identical. Especially impressive was the picture of Jeremiah, the prophet who loved Judah so much that his sorrow over her sins earned him the epithet "the weeping prophet."[15]

Even in the New Testament one could find sterling examples of religious patriotism. The preachers' favorite example, of course, was Jesus Christ himself, who loved his nation deeply, as can be seen from several passages. One can detect an undertone of patriotism in his statement to Nathaniel, an early apostle: "Behold, an Israelite indeed, in whom is no guile!" (John 1:47). He told the Samaritan woman at Jacob's well that salvation was of the Jews, not the Samaritans (John 4:22). To the Phoenician woman who begged him to heal her daughter, Jesus replied rather curtly, "It is not right to take the children's bread and throw it to the dogs," the Jewish term for gentiles (Mark 7:27). According to Matthew's account of this conversation, Jesus explained his mission to the woman by saying, "I was sent only to the lost sheep of the house of Israel" (Matt. 15:24). Then there was the time Christ sent his apostles out to preach and commanded them not to go among the Gentiles or Samaritans (Matt. 10:5). But most impressive was the weeping over his capital city, Jerusalem (Matt. 23:27). Nothing demonstrated the sincere patriotism of Jesus better than this agony suffered at the rejection of his own people. If he had been a bland "citizen of the world" he could have easily shrugged it off. There seemed to be no doubt about it: the Son of God was a nationalist.

The apostle Paul provided another genuine case of religious patriotism from the scripture. Although God sent him away from his homeland to preach to the gentiles, Paul could say to the Romans, "I could wish that I myself were accursed and cut off from Christ for the sake of my brethren, my kinsmen by race" (Rom. 9:3). To the Philippians he boasted that he was "circumcised on the eighth day, of the people of Israel, of the tribe of Benjamin, a Hebrew born of Hebrews" (Phil. 3:5). He told Timothy that if a Christian did not provide for his own family and his own people "he has disowned the faith and is worse than an unbeliever" (1 Tim. 5:8). From this verse, Dieterich drew the inference, "Whoever does not love his fatherland has denied the faith."[16]

The Bible teaches both the principle of universalism and the principle of nationality. Once a person recognizes that both principles are valid, he will be able to speak without blushing of a "German Christian" or a "British Christian." God created both the Gospel and the *Volk* and he would not have made them antagonistic. Like Hegel's dialectical process, the thesis of universalism cannot exist in isolation; it must live in tension with the antithesis of nationality. Mankind is inadequately conceived without this polarity. Or, to vary the metaphor, Christian universalism and Christian nationalism are like faith and reason in the system of Thomas Aquinas—two harmonious spheres that never really contradict each other.

THE DANGERS OF NATIONALISM

But this is a bit too neat, is it not? Surely someone spoke up and pointed to the obvious dangers inherent in nationalism? Yes, they did, on both sides, but it is important to note that the warning voices were stronger in Britain than in Germany.[17] The British ministers were so alarmed at the sins of Germany in the Great War that they warned repeatedly of the sin of chauvinism, or overdeveloped nationalism. Archbishop Davidson said, "we are seeing . . . how perilously easy it is for the noble plant of loyal patriotism, if it be wrongly nurtured, to degenerate into a coarse and baneful tree."[18] "Nationalism can never be used as a principle," said Holland, "unless it sanctions all nations alike. This is the extraordinary blunder of the German claim that their Ideal of Culture is so specially precious that it must cancel all other ideals."[19] Mursell attacked the slogan *Deutschland über alles* as meaning "Germany before everything: before honour, before decency, before pity, before chivalry, before all morality." It is good, he concluded, to fight for your country and to die for it *but not to worship it*.[20]

Percy Dearmer, in a perceptive study called *Patriotism*, analyzed the paradoxical nature of nationalism. He admitted that the nation was an abstraction and yet, he confessed, "we love it, and our love for it is wonderful; quite ordinary people are glad to die in agony for it, and base people are transformed, and careless people become heroic, and selfish people offer great, joyful sacrifices to the unseen."[21] This makes nationalism a religion, he admitted, "but at least we may assert that subjectively patriotism is a form of religion; of this communal charity it may be said that love is of God, and he that loveth is born of God."[22] Patriotism, that is, is at least a step up on regular selfishness. But Dearmer goes on to argue that "the best Englishman is also a good European—nay, he is a humanitarian; the best churchman is a Catholic—one who loves the whole of Christendom as well as his own group. We have to be patriotic and loyal like Christ, and like Him also to be universal."[23]

Other British clerics pointed out that traditional British patriotism often harbored an unchristian element. Henson called attention to a deeply rooted tendency in human nature to monopolize the divine favor and spoke critically of John Milton for his reference to "God's Englishmen."[24] Lenwood admitted that "we idealize our own country and our own people, while in relation to a hostile nation we practice that kind of realism which . . . involved the selection and emphasis of all the ugly and sordid facts."[25] "Have we not," asked Burroughs, "in effect created a British God, in our own image and after our likeness?"[26] Clutton-Brock said that while the Germans preach racism now the Anglo-Saxons were just recently doing the same by comparing themselves with the "decadent Latins."[27] Plowden-Wardlaw exclaimed, "Thank God, England has outgrown that vice of contempt for alien civilizations!"[28]

Some British churchmen made an emphatic distinction between common or heathen patriotism and Christian or biblical patriotism. Common patriotism is always narrow and selfish and makes an idol of the nation and tries to annex God to the nation, while biblical patriotism is deeper and broader.

Biblical patriotism is seen in the prophet Jeremiah, who spoke the word of God against his compatriots and was accused of opposing the national welfare and weakening the hands of the men of war (Jer. 38:4). Biblical patriotism is seen in Jesus Christ who tearfully informed his apostles of the coming ruin of the Jewish temple and the holy city, Jerusalem (Matt. 24). This is the patriotism that says God's will must be done regardless, even if it means the loss of my nation for the sake of God's kingdom. Charles Gore, Bishop of Oxford, affirmed, "This vivid sense of the moral independence of God, and the searching severity of His moral requirement upon the people of His choice, is the keynote of the higher patriotism of the Bible."[29] Dearmer's words are a classic summary: "A Christian cannot turn to the State for his ethics, or take diplomats for his spiritual directors; the only patriotism which we can respect is that which bows before the God of truth and righteousness."[30]

Canon Holland of Oxford used Revelation 21:26 very effectively to express the beauty of God's creation of the nations. In this passage John says that in the next world the nations will bring their glory into the New Jerusalem, each making the unique contribution God had designed for it. Holland declared:

The Nations of the earth bring in their glory; and walk in the light of the Lamb. Each has its own worth, its own contribution, its own allotted place. Not one is specialized and privileged; but also, not one is unnecessary, or uncounted. Christ interprets Nationalities to themselves. He gives to each its separate meaning, by exhibiting its relationship to the rest in the unity of His Body. Does Christianity then abolish Nationality? Nay! It establishes it. A nation can never know its full and true value, until it has brought itself under the scales of CHRIST and entered into the combination which He consummates. For it is as an organ and medium of international Fellowship that CHRIST established and sanctified Nationality. He has Himself brought about and revealed the absolute equality of Peoples. . . . All claims to superiority or supremacy are cancelled.[31]

A. H. Gray explained God's plans for the nations in these words:

Whenever any nation, by the exercise of its peculiar genius, has attained to some measure of success in the art of enriching or ennobling our civilization, then immediately it becomes possessed of something which it must hold in trust for the world. For the ultimate glory of His Kingdom Christ needs all the glories and honours which all the nations can bring into it, and when it is built each nation will then have its life enriched by contributions from all the other nations.[32]

Paterson-Smyth explained to his readers that one could believe in the divine calling of Britain and still retain proper humility:

In the mysterious calling and election of God, Britain is the elect nation of the world to-day. We say it in all wonder and humility. For it is not we, but God who has done it. We know not why. Just as we don't know why one man is born in a princely home and another, no worse than he, is born in a slum—we don't know why a little island in the Atlantic mists, which might well be but a fishing station or one of the little appendages of some foreign despot, should be the proudest empire of the world—or why it should bask in the light of Christianity for fifteen centuries while poor Africa and India are in darkness of heathendom. We know not. That is the mystery of God's election. The Potter has power over the lump of clay to make one vessel to honour and another to dishonour.[33]

Wace's warning to his fellow Britons was salutary: "If God has given us wealth, and strength, and prosperity, and imperial power, we may be sure it is in order that we may be His instruments for the spread of the kingdom, for bringing the knowledge of Christ and of Christ's salvation to the ends of the earth. . . . Do not let us suppose that there is any other object whatever in God's dispensations."[34]

This biblical and Christian patriotism could therefore never degenerate into chauvinism or national idolatry. Nations are judged in time; individuals in eternity. Nations are merely tools in the hands of God, tools to be used in history for his purpose. Their function is instrumental. They arise in history and they pass away in history. One could hardly make a god out of such an ephemeral entity. Yet, it is precisely this insight that seemed to be largely missing in the German clergy.

THE ANATOMY OF "GERMAN PIETY"

The British had a point when they claimed that the Germans possessed a certain radicalism in their intellectual life. When the Germans latch onto an idea they cling to it with fervor and try to carry it to its logical conclusion. They usually reduce it to absurdity. The British and the Americans, on the other hand, seem blessed with a certain brake of common sense that keeps them from going over the edge in their beliefs. A Briton might say, "Well, of course, I'm a patriot, but let's not get ridiculous about it!" In the Great War one can see that patient, methodical, orderly German mind pressing the doctrine of nationalism to its logical conclusion.

For example, if a nation is a unique divine creation, it follows logically that each *Volk* wil have not only a *Volkstum*, a national essence, but also a *Volksgeist*, a national spirit or soul. This national mind will be as unique as the nation itself and thus we are driven to the conclusion that each nation will have a special perspective on nearly all questions. This style of nationalism will eventually lead to a volkish epistemology, to an ethnic relativism in all knowledge, all disciplines. Truth will cease to be absolute and will become a matter of perspective, with the national perspective being the most crucial. Even "eternal" truths, like those of mathematics and science, will become colored by the volkish viewpoint. Universal reason or the general mind will become, like the human race, mischievous abstractions.

But if the notion of humanity is an abstraction, then the notion of universal law is also an abstraction. There is no common conscience, no general norm for good and evil, no Tao. One is driven to agree with Nietzsche that there are no moral facts, only a moral interpretation of the facts. Morality becomes merely a volkish prejudice, an ethnic perspective. When you reach this point, it becomes much easier for you to commit genocide with a clear conscience. It would appear, then, that a radical volkish nationalism could easily produce a relativism in ethics that would, in time, prepare a nation for an event as terrible as the Holocaust.

In the Great War certain thinkers began to press this relativism as a necessary implication of Christian nationalism. In a passage praising nationality, Walter Lehmann went so far as to say that we cannot have an objective picture of Jesus Christ, since each of the four gospels—Matthew, Mark, Luke, and John—was written from a special ethnic perspective and, on top of that, each German viewed this fourfold picture from his own unique ethnic perspective. Thus, concluded Lehmann, "an absolutely valid picture of Christ is absolutely impossible."[35] Each nation will have its own unique perspective on Jesus and hence it makes a great deal of sense to speak of *deutsche Frömmigkeit*—German piety or German religion.

Dr. Hans von Schubert, a high church official and professor of theology at the University of Heidelberg, wrote a book in 1916 called *The Education of our Nation to a World Nation*. He affirmed the existence of a "German Christianity" in Europe, a unique version of the Gospel that would become just as legitimate as Greek Christianity or Roman Christianity. Christianity, he argued, is not a cold, simple, mathematical formula that passes from generation to generation without alteration but a living thing that takes on the traits of the people who believe in it and practice it. We speak of the "Hellenizing" of Christianity in the East and the "Romanizing" of Christianity in the West; we now are compelled by the history of Europe since Luther to speak of a "Germanizing" of Christianity in the north.[36]

It was characteristic in the war to hear Protestant clergymen affirm that God had been preparing Germany since the Reformation for her role in world history. Bruno Doehring was typical of those pastors who emphasized Luther and the German Bible as the indispensable key to German history and nationality:

I must confess: I cannot imagine our German nation without its Bible! What I mean is this: we would have passed out of existence long ago if God had not given us the gift of the Bible through the German, Martin Luther! What the south European Renaissance with its humanism was not able to do was accomplished by the faith of a German and his Bible! . . . Luther and his Bible made our German nation possible; they molded the German form of nobility and nurtured the powers with which we have defied half the world . . . in this universal conflagration.[37]

Friedrich Rittelmeyer, pastor in Nuremberg and Berlin, got more specific than most German clerics on the matter of God's role for Germany. He specified three traits that God would use in history. First was *Verständnisfähigkeit*, empathy or the ability to understand; this virtue would make the Germans the special *Volk* to bring Christianity to the non-Christian nations, a virtue that would neutralize the "culture shock" usually suffered by western missionaries. Second was *Ehrlichkeit*, honesty or sincerity. This virtue equipped the Germans to carry on and finish the battle between religion and natural science that had raged for the last two centuries. Third was *Innerlichkeit*, inwardness or spirituality. This virtue meant that the Germans would be the nation to win the struggle with superficiality, shallowness, and materialism, the great errors of the modern world. God will use Germany, he concluded, to be the conscience of the world.[38]

Paul Le Seur, garrison pastor in Brussels, discovered some different virtues that God had employed in German history. "Why," he asked, "has Germany brought forth so many deep thinkers?" "Because the will to truth urged and compelled her to keep searching through all the debris of human errors, searching in the depths of her own being." "Why does the fountain of music gush forth in Germany purer than anywhere else?" "Because the sincerity of German feeling is born from the truth and therefore cannot rest until it releases itself in authentic beauty." He concluded, "It was because the will to truth in the German *Volk* is unconquerable that Germany became the *Volk* of the Reformation."[39]

The German preachers showed their deep belief in German Christian nationalism by the way they used—and abused—the Bible. They appropriated statements from the scripture that spoke of Israel and the church and applied them—often with no explanation—directly to Germany. Deissmann applied, "You are the salt of the earth" (Matt. 5:13) directly to the fatherland.[40] Bode did the same with "You shall have no other gods before me" (Ex. 20:3) and followed it with the statement: "The German God is speaking the same word to us today!"[41] Schwarz told his parishioners that their nation was "holy ground" just as certainly as the land on which Moses stood and beheld the burning bush (Ex. 3:5).[42] Rosmer quoted God's promise to Abraham—"I will make of you a great nation" (Gen. 12:2)—and assured patriots that the nation had found God in the experience of war fellowship.[43] Tolzien and Nowak compared the conquered states of Belgium, Poland, and Serbia to the Philistines who were finally subdued by the Israelites in the Holy Land.[44] Several pastors borrowed the biblical idea of the chosen people and called Germany "the Israel of the New Covenant." Kessler bordered on insolence when he asserted: "We are the tools with which God will construct his kingdom today. We are the soldiers with which he will win his victory. Just as it is certain that we can do nothing without God, it is also certain that God will do nothing without us."[45] As noted earlier, many pastors interpreted August, 1914, as a clear visitation of the Holy Spirit, a sort of patriotic Pentecost.[46] Hasse even used the wording of Christ's Great Commission to encourage his compatriots: "Go into all the world, teach all nations, baptize them with [German] spirit—for their salvation!"[47]

A few pastors were bold enough to state it outright—*Christentum* and *Deutschtum* belong together; Christianity and Germanness are the same. Martin Rade boasted that after the war there would be no more talk about separation of church and state: "In this war, church people and ordinary citizens have become the same, more so than for a century. Immediately one is reminded of the saying, 'What God has joined together no man should put asunder.' "[48] Reinhold Dieterich, city pastor at Ulm Cathedral, introduced his volume of war sermons with the expressed hope that the war would bring about "the Christianizing of Germanness and the Germanizing of Christianity."[49] Dieterich and Kessler both adapted Revelation 2:10 while equating Christianity and Germanness: "German *Volk*, hold what you have, let no one take away your crown!"[50] Rittelmeyer quoted with pride a statement from a Christian soldier at the front:

This liberation [the war experience] came over me like a miracle performed by God. My earthly and heavenly homes are no longer divided by a great gulf. The depth of this experience united both worlds into one kingdom. I am now the subject of one king, the child of one home, of one faith, of one love, full of one hope. Now I have my home, one fatherland. . . . Because from now on to be a German and to be a Christian are one and the same for me.[51]

Did the Germans, then, believe that they were the only true Christians on earth? No, but they spoke as if they were the best Christian nation, the spiritual model for the world. As Naumann alleged, "The German national soul is saturated with the spirit of God. We fight for this soul on behalf of the world, because we know that it is a work of God and contains God's blessings for the entire world."[52] Tolzien claimed that Germany was a nation with a special relationship to God, a bond with God.[53] Dieterich insisted that no other nation of recent history had taken the greatest question of mankind—what do you think of eternal things?—and made it into a central problem of national life.[54] Chaplain D. G. Goens asserted that "the evangelical Germany is the center for the evangelical church of the entire world" and "if we lose the leadership of the world then the entire evangelical church will suffer."[55] Rittelmeyer mused, "When one gets an inkling of the splendor of German spiritual gifts, he will feel a deep pleasure in being a German and will believe it must be a joy for God to see himself mirrored in the German soul." He said in another sermon: "If I could have had the choice of time and place in which to be born,

I would have chosen no other nation but Germany. . . . Indeed every individual among us has been personally entrusted with a German soul. We take a grand and hopeful look into the future. . . . The day of the Germans is still yet to come in the history of the world. So, let us sing from the deepest, fullest, most inward part of our being the song of the Germans that will echo down through the centuries.[56]

"Sing the song of the Germans!" When Israel was delivered from Egyptian bondage the Hebrews sang "the Song of Moses and the Lamb" (Ex.

15). When God visited Germany in 1914 the Germans sang "the song of the Germans." But which was it—*Ein feste Burg ist unser Gott* or *deutschland über alles*? Or was it both?

PATRIOTISM AND IMMANENCE

All this enthusiasm for the *earthly* fatherland is something new in German religious history; it cannot be found in this degree of intensity before the War of Liberation and the era of Napoleon. We have already noted how the Romantic movement contributed to the new German conception of nationality that developed in the nineteenth century. We now need to mention the contribution made by Liberal Protestantism to this intense nationalism.

The transcendent God of traditional Christian theology slowly changed in the nineteenth century to the immanent God of liberal theology. Immanence theology is very close to pantheism or theistic monism. In pantheism God loses his identity and personality; he becomes indistinguishable from Being per se. Mysticism in its broadest sense is pantheistic; it posits the mutual immanence of the human and the divine, the sacred and the secular, earth and heaven, the kingdom of God and the culture of man. This mystical pantheism was given a great boost by the theology of Schleiermacher, especially in his *magnum opus, The Christian Faith* (1821). Schleiermacher emphasized that feeling, the feeling of "immediate self-consciousness" or the feeling of "absolute dependence" (*Abhängigkeitsgefühl*) was the psychological locus of true Christian piety. Religious doctrines, instead of being a priori standards of belief, were "accounts of the Christian religious affections set forth in speech."

All religious emotions to whatever type and level of religion they belong, have this in common with all other modifications of the affective self-consciousness, that as soon as they have reached a certain stage and a certain definiteness, they manifest themselves outwardly by mimicry in the most direct and spontaneous way, by means of facial features and movements of voice and gesture, which we regard as their expression.[57]

Those who followed Schleiermacher's direction—and they were many— insisted that the task of dogmatics was one of introspection, not of listening to God. The job of the systematic theologian was to provide an orderly view of the doctrines received in a specific church at a specific time. Doctrine was a statement describing one's subjective feelings, not a proposition revealing the objective content of religion. Dogma was a historical study; its work was to deal with what Christians actually believe, not what they ought to believe. Orthodox theologians would claim that dogma was a propositional revelation of God to man, but Schleiermacher held that all Christian doctrines had their "ultimate ground so exclusively in the emotions of the religious self-consciousness, that where these do not exist the doctrines cannot arise."[58] E. A. Burtt summarized this approach: "Human experiences of whatever has religious significance to people became the touchstone of theology."[59]

The rise of immanence theology was significant for Christian theology and especially for Christian nationalism. This "empirical theology" put religious experience in the place of God; the conscious individual and his personal experiences became the decisive court of appeal by which one tested the validity of any religious idea. Now this move toward spiritual monism made the process of adapting religion to nationalism easier for the pastor and the patriotic theologian. In pantheism the cleft between sacred and secular is bridged; every secular pursuit becomes *ipso facto* a service to God, including love of country. Patriotism becomes a valid religious experience, regardless of the contraction of universal love. Culture is merely a continuous demonstration of God's will for mankind. The spirit that drives soldiers to defend the fatherland (or ravage Belgium?) is the same spirit that works in all historical processes, the same divine spirit that permeates all Being, that *is* all Being. There is a danger here and Gwilyn Griffith states it with precision:

If religion and piety are fundamentally a state of feeling, and if this feeling is itself the raw material of dogma, how shall the Church which indoctrinates its people in this belief safeguard them against the errors of "strong delusions" which may arise at any time of widespread emotional eruption and mass hysteria? Under the powerful influence of some dominant personality, or of national propaganda, millions of religiously minded people may be swept up into frenzied enthusiasm and feel—really feel—themselves religiously exalted. . . . What is to be the answer of the Church which has taught them insistently that religion *is* feeling, that revelation *is* intuition, and that experience *is* the basis of doctrine?[60]

Empirical theology pulls God from the sky and absorbs him into history. Another powerful intellectual movement that produced a similar result was the philosophy of Hegel. Hegel's system was an idealistic pantheism, a logical-spiritual monism. The One or the All (Being or God) is unitary but nevertheless evolving through eternity, developing through a process called the Dialectic. By this process, reality constantly changes and progresses by a conflict of opposite principles: thesis, antithesis, and synthesis. The Absolute is not transcendent but rises to consciousness of itself in man; God has reality only in the thought of those who believe in him; God knows himself only in the knowledge man has of him. The eternal movement of the Triad produces a continually greater consciousness in God.

If Hegel is correct, then not even the Absolute/God is a finished or irreducible fact; everything is forever becoming. The world is required to make God no less than God is required to make the world. God does not make history, but history develops God. This means that the historical Christ is no longer unique because that would imply that an event two millennia ago was more developed than the present. The story of man is the history of God's growth and maturation, the self-evolution of the Absolute Reason. This idea will destroy any notion of the Second Coming of Christ and the consummation of all history. There is no consummation, just eternal becoming, everlasting growth, incessant evolution. We can be certain, say Hegelians, that the latest is the greatest, the newest is the truest. One can see, therefore, how a cleric that followed Hegel could see God continually revealing himself in the great events of German national history: 1517, 1813, 1871, and 1914. August Showalter, military pastor for the province of Antwerp, claimed that "whoever has not experienced God in the history of his nation will not experience him in the church or the creed."[61]

The obvious danger with this view, as Troeltsch saw, is that it usually results in a deification of the actual particular state, "and this deification not only excluded the possibility of any revolutionary impulse . . . it ultimately resulted in a mystical elevation of every State, even the State which was actually as imperfect as it could be, to the position of a sort of deity."[62] Baron von Hügel noted that German pantheism "did not shrink from finding the State to be essentially founded upon force alone," thus achieving that fatal combination of pantheism and Machiavellianism.[63] If Hegelian pantheism is true, then the British churchmen were wrong to criticize German *Realpolitik* because "whatever is, is right."

A third movement reinforcing the immanential perspective was the theological system of Albrecht Ritschl (1822-89), a theologian so influential that one of his disciples, Adolf von Harnack, referred to him as the latest of the church fathers. Although he was opposed to mysticism, the net result of Ritschl's system was to reinforce immanentalism and absorb the kingdom of God into history. Ritschl rejected knowledge of God through metaphysics and asserted that only history could unfold the true nature of the deity. Similarly to Kant, he insisted that the kingdom of God was equivalent to the moral unification of the human race, brought about through action prompted by universal love of neighbor. All this invites the error of "Cultural Protestantism" and comes close to the naïve belief that *Weltgeschichte ist Weltgericht*—"the history of the world is the judgment of the world." It all ends in a religious historicism where ethical values are the first interest of faith. Gone is the biblical view that the world is at all times under the judgment of a righteous, transcendent God, that it never attains to perfection until the consummation of all things.[64]

This Ritschlian mentality came out clearly in the Franco-Prussian War in this utterance of Pastor Schwarz: "How could we separate our faith from our most holy duties as citizens, our Christianity from our love of fatherland? Both are one, inseparably one. The fatherland, our nation to which we belong . . . is our holiest inheritance and entitlement. . . . Only in it and with it can we be what we are and fulfill our human and Christian duties."[65]

The immanental formula was subtle in most German clergymen during the Great War, but it came out sharply in some preachers, like Walter Lehmann.

"God," he said, "is nothing but our moral activity, our honest and righteous behavior, the deepest, final reason for our fighting." He cited Meister Eckhart and Johann Fichte to the effect that "God is what the god-inspired people do." "God is inner-worldly, his existence immanent—that is the first article of faith in the German religion!" He denounced the traditional idea of Christ as a sin-offering, as "abominable" and "thoroughly ungerman." In the place of "Christ-for-us" the German will put "Christ-in-us." Heroism is the great link between *Christentum* and *Deutschtum*: "Germanness and Christianity agree at bottom in heroism: nothing is greater than laying down your life for your brothers. Both are fulfilled in the death of the hero."[66] Evidently, the doctrine of the Atonement must be jettisoned when the unique German perspective constructs its theology!

A more dangerous expression of the immanental formula was heard in the voice of Reinhold Seeberg, the most outspoken academic-theological champion of German annexations in the war. Seeberg's rationale for annexation was a vague, irrational volkish voluntarism, which asserted that the will of the nation, like the will of the individual, is the only thing that matters in the discussion. The basic *Lebensinstinkt* ("life instinct") reaches much deeper into the nature of things than mere reason, whose power is puny compared to such elemental forces. The primal fact of all politics is the will of the *Volk* to life. Reason, understanding, argument—these are mere tools of the will, which needs no justification at all—it just *is*. The Categorical Imperative for Seeberg is: "Do whatever serves the realization of the life will of your *Volk*!"[67]

Günther Brakelmann has performed a masterful analysis of Seeberg's religious nationalism and its inherent dangers. He stresses how perilous it is to make prerational realities like the will the basis of politics instead of reason. Seeberg's emphasis on the *Volk* life will would make diplomacy very difficult. His ethnocentrism was so strong that Brakelmann called it "mystical autism," which is a form of abnormal subjectivity that turns the person to fantasy rather than reality.[68] One could make a good case for the thesis that the immanental formula promotes ethnocentric autism.

Thinkers like Lehmann and Seeberg would not say, "My country, right or wrong!" They would say, "My country, right, always right!" If the volkish life will is all that matters, then a *Volk* can never be wrong. Only reason could deliver a judgment that asserts, "My *Volk* is wrong!"

CONCLUSION

We began this chapter by emphasizing the agreements between the British and the Germans on the subject of nationalism. We must end it by summarizing the differences. As the topic developed we began to notice certain subtle differences that corresponded to the dissimilar intellectual backgrounds of the two nations.

British Christian nationalism was shaped by the unique background of ideas like empiricism, realism, and individualism, while German Christian nationalism was shaped by Lutheranism, romanticism, idealism, and immanentalism. The result is that British nationalism is broader and more tolerant than German nationalism. British preachers showed more critical distance from their patriotism; they showed a greater awareness of the dangers of nationalism. German clerics annexed God to the fatherland with more alacrity than the British. For example, interpreting August, 1914, by the Pentecostal motif was almost the rule in Germany but the exception in Britain. The British seemed to have missed the Holy Spirit in the enthusiasm of the time. The immanental formula was much stronger in Germany than in Britain.

On balance, therefore, the British brand of nationalism seems less a contraction of Christian love than the German brand. One must be careful in making such a generalization, however, because a lot of British preachers were just as ethnocentric as some of the Germans, and not all German clergymen went as far as Lehmann and Seeberg. But, in the main, the British clergy did a better job of pushing nationalism without pushing it too far. They kept a tighter rein, as it were, on the animal.

Individualism has always been weaker in Germany than in England because England is an island and Germany has always been surrounded by enemies. Germany's geopolitical position has produced a protracted crisis of national security that finally gave us the nation of Prussia and Prussian militarism, which eventually grew into the German empire and German militarism. In such a climate the individual must constantly be told to forget self and defend the community and the Christian preacher is one of the main people that has to tell him. It is asking a lot of Christian preachers to be so aloof, objective, and critical in such a severe national crisis as that of August, 1914, especially if the government controls all the channels of information and can exaggerate the severity of the crisis.

One can understand the Germans' problem but one cannot defend them. German Christian nationalism became too narrow in the Great War, so narrow that it could scarcely be harmonized with Christian universalism any longer. A few people interpreted Germany's defeat in 1918 as God's rebuke for the fatherland's narrow nationalism in the war.

NOTES

1. For good studies of nationalism see Louis L. Snyder, *The Meaning of Nationalism* (New Brunswick, NJ, 1954); Boyd Shafer, *Nationalism: Myth and Reality* (New York, 1955); Carlton J. H. Hayes, *Nationalism: A Religion* (New York, 1960); Salo Baron, *Modern Nationalism and Religion* (New York, 1947); W. B. Pillsbury, *The Psychology of Nationality and Internationalism* (New York, 1955); Max Lenz, "Nationalität und Religion," *Preussische Jahrbücher*, CXXVII, 403.

2. David Potter, for example, implies this in his *People of Plenty: Economic Abundance and the American Character* (Chicago, 1954), 21.

3. *Religion and the War*, 71.

4. *Aus der Friedens- und Kriegsarbeit*, 318.

5. *Gott und die deutsche Zuversicht: Drei Reden in dunkler Zeit* (Berlin, 1918),

6. See also Holland, *So as by Fire*, 3; Barry, *Religion and the War*, 72; Temple, *Our Need for a Catholic Church*, 12.

6. *Christ and the Sword*, 149.

7. *Patriotism in the Bible*, 3.

8. *Bruising of Belgium*, 56.

9. *So as by Fire*, 19.

10. *Krieg und Weltanschauung*, 9.

11. *Kriegspredigten*, 29.

12. This is taken from Herder's *Ideen zur Philosophie der Menscheit*, as translated in Patrick Gardiner, *Theories of History* (Glencoe, IL, 1953), 35-49.

13. *Predigten* (Part II of *Sämmtliche Werke*, Berlin, 1834-36), I, 228.

14. This translation is by Robert Ericksen in his article, "The Political Theology of Paul Althaus: Nazi Supporter," *German Studies Review*, IX:3 (October, 1986), 558. The original is from Althaus, *Völker vor und nach Christus* (Leipzig, 1937), 3-5. For additional sermons see König, *Kriegspredigten*, 51; Kramer, *Kriegs- und Friedens-Predigten*, 211; Geyer, *Stimme des Christus*, 62-63; Bürckstümmer, *Ein feste Burg*, 26; Buder, *Gottes Heerdienst*, 33-36; Pauli, *EF*, XVI, 99-100; Meyer, *Kriegspredigten* (Wurster), 281; Emil Pfennigsdorf, *Wie predigen wir heute Evangelium?* (Leipzig, 1917), 40; Le Seur, *Frohbotschaft in Feindesland*, 45; Schowalter, *Krieg in Predigten*, 29-30; Titius, *Unser Krieg*, 10; Lehmann, *Vom deutschen Gott*, 35-37; Ihmels, *Aufwärts die Herzen*, 204; Schubert, *Erziehung unser Volkes*, 8-10; Zurhellen, *Kriegspredigten*, 24-26; Otto, *Religion, Krieg, und Vaterland*, 52; Woods, *Christianity and War*, 116-117; Gough, *God's Strong People*, viii; Denison, *Spiritual Lessons of the War*, 51; Dunkmann, *Katechismus des Feldgrauen*, 27.

15. See C. Lieber, "Vaterlandsliebe," *EF*, XV, 403; Dibelius, *Ein feste Burg* (Doehring), II, 73; Rhode, *Kriegspredigten*, 9; Köhler, *Predigten aus der Kriegszeit*, 3.

16. Dieterich, *Gott mit uns*, 20; see also Dryander, *Evangelische Reden*, V, 14; Ihmels, *Darum auch wir*, 84; Ott, *Religion, Krieg, und Vaterland*, 11-15; Rhode, *Kriegspredigten*, 63; Naumann, *Stark in Gott*, 4; Ingram, *Church in Time of War*, 12; Gore, *Patriotism in the Bible*, 4-6.

17. For some German warnings see Blumhardt, *Gottes Reich kommt!*, 379; Pfennigsdorf, *Wie predigen wir heute Evangelium?*, 39; Troeltsch, *Deutsche Glaube und Deutsche Sitte*, 25; Dryander, *Evangelische Reden*, V, 14; Ott, *Religion, Krieg, und Vaterland*, 29; Steltz, *Krieg und Christentum*, 8-9.

18. *Testing of a Nation*, 68.

19. *So as by Fire*, 30.

20. *Bruising of Belgium*, 186-87.

21. *Patriotism*, 4.

22. Ibid., 5.

23. Ibid., 9.

24. *War-Time Sermons*, 130.

25. *Pharisaism and War*, 14.

26. *Fight for the Future*, 37.

27. *Cure for War*, 9.

28. *Test of War*, 91.

29. *Patriotism in the Bible*, 8. See also Gore, *War and the Church*, 4; *The League of Nations: The Opportunity of the Church* (London, 1919), 25; Barry, *Religion and the War*, 77; Woods, *War Watchwords*, 88; Hügel, *The German Soul*, 211; Ramsey Muir, *The National Principle and the War* (London, 1914), 31; Henson, *War-Time Sermons*, 282; Stanley Miller, *Which Gospel Do You Accept?* (Liverpool, 1914), 33.

30. *Patriotism*, 7.

31. *So as by Fire*, 17.

32. *Only Alternative to War*, 15.

33. *God and the War*, 12.

34. *War and the Gospel*, 167. See also Temple, *Church and Nation* (London, 1915), 44; *Our Need for a Catholic Church*, 16; Gough, *God's Strong People*, 42; Crafer, *Prophetic Vision*, 37.

35. *Deutsche Frömmigkeit*, 5-6; also Titius, *Unser Krieg*, 23-24.

36. *Erziehung unseres Volkes*, 21, 27; also König, *Kriegspredigten*, 8.

37. *Gott und wir Deutsche*, 181; for more sermons stressing Luther's role see Dryander, *Evangelische Reden*, XII, 30; XI, 40. Dryander spoke of Luther "germanizing" the Bible.

38. *Christ und Krieg*, 166, 170.

39. *Frohbotschaft in Feindesland*, 47.

40. *Deutsche Schwertsegen*, 60.

41. *P*, XLVII:38 (September 16, 1914), 837.

42. *Kriegspredigten* (Wurster), 314.

43. *P*, XLVII:42 (October 14, 1914), 894.

44. Tolzien, *Kriegspredigten*, IV, 16; Nowak, *Stark und getrost*, 34.

45. *Unser Glaube*, 111; see also Ihmels, *Darum auch wir*, 85; Horn, *Heilige Zorn*, 3; Broecker, *Der Erlöser Israels*, 12.

46. See ch. 1, sec. D. See also Tolzien, *Kriegspredigten*, V, 69; Kirmss, *Eine gute Wehr*, 32; Kramer, *Kriegs- und Friedens-Predigten*, 215; *Gottes Frage an unser deutschen Volk*, 2.

47. *Der grosse Krieg*, 82.

48. Cited in Hammer, *Kriegstheologie*, 171. Kramer quoted the same verse from Christ in *Kriegs- und Friedens-Predigten*, 69.

49. *Gott mit uns*, iv.

50. Ibid., 58; Kessler, *Furchtlos und Treu, Erste Sammlung von Predigten und Ansprachen in den Kriegstagen 1914* (Dresden, 1914), 35.

51. *Zukunft des deutschen Geistes*, 4.

52. *Stark in Gott*, 18.

53. *Kriegspredigten*, I, 115-16.

54. *Gott mit uns*, 9.

55. Cited in Mehnert, *Evangelische Kirche und Politik*, 34.

56. *Zukunft des deutschen Geistes*, 17; *Deutschlands religiöser Weltberuf*, 24-25.

57. *The Christian Faith Systematically Presented According to the Fundamental Propositions of the Evangelical Church*, ed. H. R. Mackintosh and J. S. Stewart (Edinburgh, 1928), 76. For an analysis of this mature theology see Mackintosh, *Types of Modern Theology*, 66-100. See also Schleiermacher, *On Religion: Speeches to Its Cultural Despisers*, trans. John Oman (New York, 1955) and *Soliloquies*, trans. H. L. Friess (Chicago, 1926). The pioneering work that explored the connection between

liberal theology and nationalism was K. S. Pinson, *Pietism as a Factor in the Rise of German Nationalism* (New York, 1934).

58. *The Christian Faith*, 78.

59. *Types of Religious Philosophy*, 288; see also J. H. Randall, *Religion and the Modern World* (New York, 1929), 42ff; Karl Barth, *Die protestantische Theologie im 19. Jahrhundert: ihre Vorgeschichte und ihre Geschichte* (Zollikon and Zurich, 1947), 598-605.

60. *Interpreters of Man: A Review of Secular and Religious Thought from Hegel to Barth* (London, 1943), 24.

61. *Krieg in Predigten*, Introduction. For Hegel's religious thought see I. Iljin, *Die Philosophie Hegels als kontemplative Gotteslehre* (Bern, 1946), and J. M. E. McTaggart, *Studies in Hegelian Cosmology* (Cambridge, 1901).

62. "Ideas of Natural Law," 213. Friedrich Meinecke commented that "the chief deficiency of the German historical thought was the euphemistic idealization of power politics through the doctrine that it corresponded to a higher morality." See *Die Ideen der Staatsräson in der neureren Geschichte* (Munich and Berlin, 1924), 533.

63. *The German Soul*, 133.

64. See the treatments of this in Borg, *Old Prussian Church*, 32-33; Pressel, *Kriegspredigt*, 51; and Hammer, *Kriegstheologie*, 90-94. For treatments of Ritschl see Otto Ritschl, *Albrecht Ritschls Leben*, 2 vols. (Freiburg and Leipzig, 1892-96); G. Ecke, *Die theologische Schule Albrecht Ritschls* (Berlin, 1897-1904); J. Wendland, *Albrecht Ritschl und seine Schüler* (Berlin, 1899).

65. Cited in Piechowski, *Kriegspredigt von 1870-71*, 75. For another example see Ott, *Religion, Krieg, und Vaterland*, 63.

66. *Vom deutschen Gott*, 95, 106; *Deutsche Frömmigkeit*, 10, 12.

67. See Seeberg, *Geschichte, Krieg, und Seele*, 283.

68. *Protestantische Kriegstheologie*, 95.

7

The Just War

The clergy of Britain and Germany agreed in many ways on the question of Christian nationalism. They were in even closer agreement on the matter of the just war. Hundreds of sermons on both sides of the North Sea were devoted to proving that a Christian may go to war and kill to protect his family, home, and country. The arguments, both biblical and philosophical, were similar on both sides and one may cautiously suggest that the Protestant clergy of the Great War carried the defense of the just war theory to its ultimate heights. If the theory has any validity at all it was surely established in the war sermons of 1914-18. This chapter is a summary of those sermons.[1]

The just war theory is centuries old and it came into existence as a child of the tension between practical patriotism and Christian teaching, a tension between this world and the next. War demands the taking of life, yet killing another human being seems to contradict the ethical ideals of the Bible, especially of the New Testament. In the Decalogue, Yahweh said to the Jews: "Thou shalt not kill" (Ex. 20:13), a prohibition repeated by Jesus Christ in the New Testament (Matt. 5:21). In the Sermon on the Mount Christ went beyond this mere external act of murder and condemned even the thought that prompted it: "Everyone who is angry with his brother will be liable to judgment" (Matt. 5:22).

Christ is called "the prince of peace" and was born amid exaltations of "peace on earth good will to men." He commanded his followers to resist no evil, turn the other cheek, go the second mile, give up the cloak, and love and pray for enemies (Matt. 5:39, 44). At his own arrest he rebuked Peter for using a sword to protect him: "All who take the sword will perish by the sword" (Matt. 26:52). Saint Paul seems to put the crown on the pacifist position in the epistle to the Romans: "Bless those who persecute you . . . repay no one evil for evil . . . if possible as far as it depends on you, live peaceably with all" (Rom. 12:14, 17, 18). The pacifist argues, therefore, that the

Christian must renounce war if he takes these passages seriously. War by its very nature requires the Christian to kill and to motivate him to kill it creates a hostile spirit diametrically opposed to Christian love. War and love are two masters that no man can serve at the same time.[2]

CHRIST AND WAR

If the Christian patriot wants to go to war he must explain the Sermon on the Mount, especially statements such as "love your enemies" and "resist not evil." The most startling means of rendering the sermon irrelevant was the special approach of Albert Schweitzer, set forth in his epoch-making study, *The Quest for the Historical Jesus* (1910). This "eschatological interpretation" maintained that Jesus taught only an "interim ethic," a set of guidelines for the interval between his day and the imminent inauguration of God's kingdom on earth. Since Jesus was wrong about the coming of the kingdom, the impractical injunctions of the sermon are no longer binding on Christians. Commands like "turn the other cheek" would obviously never work in a normal situation.[3] This position required a liberal view of Christ that many clerics were loathe to accept.

The overwhelming majority of Lutheran and Anglican preachers, however, held to the traditional authority of the sermon but tried to deflect its troublesome precepts. They developed a careful hermeneutic on the sermon, which amounted to saying that Jesus never intended us to take certain remarks literally or to absolutize them into immutable regulations. Thomas stated the general tone of this approach when he accused the pacifist of *legalism*:

We want some firm, precise, infallible phrase that will fit every problem of practice, without any exception. *There is no such formula to be found.* Let us thank God there is none, for if there were, we should be back once more in Judaism and Pharisaism. . . . There is no letter of law that can bind the free limbs of the human personality.[4]

Pacifists make the typical legalistic mistake of camping on one verse like "resist not evil" and ignoring the rest of the revelation, the total context of scripture. Much mischief usually results from harping on isolated passages in the scripture. Jesus never meant us to understand him in a wooden, literal sense, making an isolated statement contradict other statements. For example, if you press "resist not evil" to an absolute degree you make it contradict "resist the devil and he will flee from you" (James 4:7). Holland argued that "resist not evil" is a proverb, not a command, with all the natural limitations of a proverb, which means that it can be flatly contradicted by another proverb.[5] Muir noted that the paradoxes of the sermon are designed to startle the mind and awaken thought and conscience, "to stimulate even more than to reveal."[6] Thomas insisted that in interpreting the sermon we must avoid the "literalism that destroys" by making nonsense of Christ's splendid parabolic imagery. We must abandon our western prose and pedestrian literalism and remember that Jesus was an Oriental who loved the strong glowing colors and the violent contrasts and shocks of Eastern speech. Jesus said, "Hate your father and mother" but no one in his right mind takes this literally; instead we translate it, "All or nothing." Jesus said cut off your hand if it offends you, but no one takes this literally; instead we translate it, "Control your body." But the way Jesus said it was concrete, immediate, and gripping.[7]

In sum, we would never wish to change the way Jesus said it, but then, on the other hand, we would never wish to misunderstand what he said!

Several churchmen maintained that we must understand Christ's teachings through his actions; his life must be a commentary upon his doctrines. Now, as a matter of fact, Jesus did not give in to evil, as the pacifists might lead us to believe. He said call no one a fool (Matt. 5:22), yet he called the Scribes and Pharisees "blind fools" (Matt. 23:17). He said do not be angry with your brother (Matt. 5:22), yet he himself became angry with his disciples (Mark 10:14), and for good reason.

Furthermore, had not Jesus declared that he came not to bring peace but a sword (Matt. 10:34)? Did he not instruct his disciples on one occasion to purchase a sword (Luke 22:36)? Did he not enjoin his disciples to render to Caesar what rightfully belongs to Caesar (Luke 20:25)? Did he not predict that the history of man would be full of wars to the very end of time (Matt. 24:6, 7)?[8]

But there is more. If the pacifist will just read carefully he will find Jesus behaving in a belligerent, aggressive way at times. *Christ made war.* He believed in conflict; he practiced what the Germans called *heilige Zorn*—holy anger (close to the English expression, "righteous indignation"). He sternly denounced the Scribes, Pharisees, Sadducees, and Herodians of his day for their hypocrisy and false beliefs. At his trial, when struck by the officer of the High Priest, he did not turn the other cheek but rather rebuked the man for his sinful act (John 18:22). He cast out demons all over Palestine, which is certainly a case of "resisting evil."

The most popular thing Jesus ever did for these nonpacifists was to chase the money-changers out of the Temple (Matt. 21:12-14). To describe his actions the disciples had to use Psalm 69:9—"Zeal for thy house will consume me" (John 2:17). Using a whip with consuming zeal is clearly inconsistent with the pacifist Jesus. The same gentle hands that healed the sick and raised the dead doubled up a cord and lashed the bodies of evil, greedy man out of God's house. Mursell pressed the point effectively:

It was with a scourge he drove the traders from the temple and cleared the holy place of their sordid traffic; it is with a scourge also that we must drive aggression and savagery from the plains of Europe, since they will not be disturbed or dislodged in any other way, and make it a place where honest men can live in safety, prosperity, and peace.[9]

On both sides there was a concerted effort to rescue the image of Jesus Christ from the "meek-and-gentle" stereotype fostered by so much historical Christian art. Gray complained that artists and hymn writers have done us a disservice by picturing Christ so meek and mild that vigorous men would not want to be led by him.[10] Muir presented the ideal of Christ as a well-rounded moral person in whom anger and pity were perfectly blended. "There are sins," he noted, "for which every good man should show not pity but determined hostility."[11] Drummond said of the influence of Christ: "It created St. Francis, but it also created General Gordon. The lowly brother of the poor and the chivalrous soldier are two of its distinct types of character. It may be hard to find a formula which will include them both; but there is ample room in the world of spiritual reality to which they eventually belong."[12] Ballard defended the manhood of Jesus with a rhetorical question:

Does anyone suppose for a moment that if the crowd had set upon Mary, His mother, as the German brutes have done upon the poor women of Belgium and Poland, Jesus Himself, or John, to whom He committed her, would have stood by and done nothing to rescue or protect her, but would have allowed them to murder her without resistance?[13]

Otto Baumgarten insisted that it was precisely the austerity of Christ, not his mildness, that gave his message its appeal through the ages. Baumgarten's summary of Christ's attitude was good: "He never commanded us to practice love at the expense of truth, forgiveness at the cost of righteousness, or to seek peace at the price of honorable conviction about our own rights."[14]

In general, the preachers of Germany and Britain argued that love of enemies and nonretaliation were ethical principles that one should evaluate critically before applying. Not even Christ applied them uncritically. One would err if one absolutized these principles in a way that would contradict other duties, such as love of family, nation, truth, Christ, or God.

THE BIBLE AND WAR

If love of enemies is not an absolute principle, argued the clergy, it does not surprise the student of the New Testament or of the Christian creeds to find that nowhere is the soldier told to give up his occupation to please God. The Anglican Articles of Religion, Article 37, state that "It is lawful for Christian men, at the command of the magistrate, to bear weapons and to serve in the wars." Similar statements can be found in the Lutheran Augsburg Confession (1550), the Presbyterian Westminster Confession of Faith (1647), and the Congregationalist Savoy Declaration of Faith and Order (1658). The historical Christian community has nearly always considered the soldier's life as a necessary calling in society.

The Bible, too, is free of any antimilitarism. Christ was pleased with the statement of the Roman centurion from Capernaum: "I am a man under authority . . . I say to one 'Go!' and he goes'' (Matt. 8:4-13). Jesus noted his strong faith, something strange if his vocation was inherently sinful. John the Baptist did not require discharge from the army for the Roman soldiers who asked him how they could improve their lives; he simply instructed them to ''rob no one by violence or by false accusation, and be content with your wages'' (Luke 3:14). Peter did not make Cornelius, the first Gentile convert, quit his military post (Acts 10). At the foot of the Cross only a Roman soldier recognized the true greatness of Christ and said, ''Surely this man was a son of God'' (Matt. 27:54). If the military life is so immoral you would think that Paul would have taught this to the officers on board his ship to Rome (Acts 27-28).[15]

Pacifists have always had a low view of soldiers. In their misguided zeal they sometimes call soldiers murderers; they assert that war is just a license for mass homicide. They overlook the patent fact that war is just like a police action; soldiers use judicial force on criminal nations just as policemen use judicial force on criminal individuals. The cases are exactly parallel, even though we may have great difficulty determining the meaning of ''criminal nation.'' If a soldier starts engaging in private warfare, then he has become a private criminal; if he relapses into freebooting he is shot—by his own general, ideally. A soldier is the official representative of a fellowship; the sword he wields is the sword of community justice, not a private sword. He is resisting evil, not because he has been struck on the cheek but because someone else has.[16]

We recall the question at the beginning of the war: ''Why hasn't Christianity abolished war?'' The answer was another question: ''Why hasn't Christianity abolished police and law courts?'' Christianity never promised to abolish all evil in human society; evil will be around until the consummation. That means that soldiers and armies will be around as long as police, law, and courts. And in the meantime, as Streeter said, ''Lynch law is better than no law.''[17] Woodford noted that it would be ludicrous to suppose that robbery would come to an end by disbanding the police. It would be just as ludicrous to think that war would cease by disbanding armies.[18] This is why, said Oman, that the Bible says ''blessed are the *peacemakers*,'' not the *peaceable*. This is also why no biblical prophet ever preached disarmament, even while he was preaching the folly of trusting in arms.[19] There is no absolute biblical prohibition on weapons, urged Harnack: ''The weapon that I grasp to protect brother, wife, child, and fatherland, so that they will not starve physically or spiritually, so that coming generations may live and that my *Volk* will not lose its mission in the world—this weapon is sacred!''[20]

Dawson drew the conclusion that most clergymen in both nations knew must be drawn: *the Sermon on the Mount simply does not apply to war between nations. Jesus never intended the precepts of his sermon to regulate the judicial control of evil before the consummation.* Several British clerics quoted Edmund Burke: ''War is the sole means of justice amongst nations.''

Dawson said, "Because you can bless Jones or Robinson when he curses you, and offer him the second cheek on his smiting the first, does not make it either feasible or desirable for your country to . . . forgive the injuries inflicted by Germany."[21] Holland said that the British people could not say to Belgium, "We are very sorry; but we have been reading again the Sermon on the Mount; and we cannot therefore keep our word. We must advise you to take it lying down."[22]

British and German preachers did an outstanding job in the Great War of praising the soldier. Far from being innately sinful, the life of the soldier was actually one of the most exemplary lives one could choose, an occupation illustrating moral courage, devotion, and self-denial. The Bible justly praises the heroes of God who "through faith conquered kingdoms, enforced justice . . . escaped the edge of the sword, won strength out of weakness, became mighty in war, put foreign armies to flight" (Heb. 11:33-34). The soldier of faith deserves praise because, like Paul, he must learn to be content in whatever state he finds himself (Phil. 4:11). Like Christ, he must face times when he cannot find a place to lay his head (Luke 9:58). He must train his body to obey his will and spirit. He must master the sins of hedonism, materialism, greed, and covetousness. He must learn that there is something higher than "things," something spiritual, ideal, and eternal. William James observed that "lives based on having are less free than lives based either on doing or on being, and in the interest of action people subject to spiritual excitement throw away possessions as so many clogs."[23]

This semiascetic ideal of life has some obvious affinities to biblical values— "naked came I into this world" . . . "sell all you have and give to the poor" . . . "take no thought of the morrow." The nature of war makes it easy for the soldier to understand the essence of Christianity: heroism, love, sacrifice, devotion to duty. As Patten said, soldiers understand the Cross because they have borne a cross themselves.[24] They know instinctively what Jesus meant when he said, "Greater love hath no man than the man who would lay down his life for his friends" (John 15:13). Donald Hankey left us a priceless description of a group of unruly British soldiers who proved in death to be exemplary:

. . . they, who had formerly been our despair, were now our glory. Their spirits effervesced. Their wit sparkled. Hunger and thirst could not depress them. Rain could not damp them. Cold could not chill them. Every hardship became a joke. They did not endure hardship, they derided it. And somehow it seemed at the moment as if derision was all that hardship existed for! Never was such a triumph of spirit over matter. As for death, it was, in a way, the greatest joke of all. In a way, for if it was another fellow that was hit it was an occasion for tenderness and grief. But if one of them was hit, O Death, where is thy sting? O Grave, where is thy victory? Portentous, solemn Death, you looked like a fool when you tackled one of them! Life? They did not value life! They had never been able to make much of a fist of it. But if they lived amiss they died gloriously, with a smile for the pain and the dread of it.

What else had they been born for? It was their chance. With a gay heart they gave their greatest gift, and with a smile to think that after all they had anything to give which was of value. One by one Death challenged them. One by one they smiled in his grim visage, and refused to be dismayed. They had been lost, but they had found the path that led them home; and when at last they laid their lives at the feet of the Good Shepherd, what could they do but smile?[25]

The soldier was compared to the monk or the saint. It does not surprise us, therefore, to find many preachers on both sides taking a leaf from Mohammed and suggesting that the good patriotic soldier will automatically go to heaven, or something close to that. For example, no less a churchman than Archbishop Davidson made this comment on the simple devotion of the soldier who dies in battle:

It is the function of Christianity, of us would-be followers of Christ, to raise this unacknowledging trustfulness and self-giving out of dumb sub-consciousness and to give it speech and to crown it with the glory of the fully human self-devotion. We have to declare that it is God who they find in the offering of themselves, His love in which they can lose themselves, His purpose to which they can cleave, His will to be done—and that to give him joy is the supreme end of man.[26]

More candid was the Primate of Belgium, who said in a famous pastoral letter:

If I am asked what I think of the eternal salvation of a brave man who has conscientiously given his life in defense of his country's honour, and in vindication of violated justice, I shall not hesitate to reply that without any doubt whatever Christ crowns his military valour, and that death, accepted in this Christian spirit, assures the safety of that man's soul.[27]

This is a dangerous idea but it is amazing how many clergymen on both sides said this and how few warned against it.[28] Harnack said that soldiers can claim the promise of scripture: "We know that we have passed out of death into life, because we love the brethren" (1 John 3:14).[29] "Whoever dies in battle dies in the Lord," claimed Windisch, "because he has subordinated his bodily good to the good of the *Volk* and has offered his life for his own."[30] Speaking of soldierly sacrifice, Meyer said, "Truly, here is holy ground. Here is the gate of heaven. Sacrifice is the key that breaks it open."[31]

To switch to the British, Kelman said of fallen soldiers: "They have trodden the *Via dolorosa*, and have found high company there, for there they have met with that great Brother who trod it first alone."[32] Plowden-Wardlaw claimed that God even accepted the sacrifice of a German life: "God accepts all sacrifice rightly offered, even for a bad cause (when the badness of it is not known), and will reward it in some spiritual sense."[33] "We may confidently be assured," said Wace, "that those who meet their death on the battlefields of this war in the spirit of Christ and in simple devotion to duty, will be received by Him in the sense of those gracious words, Well done, good and faithful servant.''[34] Winnington-Ingram assured parents that ''if it so happens that some dear boy, the darling of your home, passes, with unsullied honour and to uphold the nation's name, into the presence of the Unseen, you will find him there waiting for you when your time comes, one of God's own children, kept most safely, in His care.''[35] Dawson scolded the legalists by saying that he would ''rather a thousand times die with these noble fellows and share their chance than be the theological inspector who goes poking round to find out what were the credentials they carried with them into the other world.''[36] One cleric, writing as ''the Temporary Chaplain,'' declared:

Many of our lads who have fallen in this struggle have been, like the Holy Innocents, unconscious martyrs. They have died for a faith but dimly understood. But while they answered the call of their country, and offered themselves in that service they were also serving Christ. For everything that makes up a Christian life, all kindness and love of men, is at issue in this war.[37]

Potter argued for the reinstatement of the old Roman Catholic doctrine of the Intermediate State. He suggested that the soldiers who gave their all for the nation might pass into that blessed place and Christ might reveal his mercies to them there.[38] Should we call this a ''patriotic purgatory?''

THE EVILS OF PACIFISM

If Christ and the Bible are not against war, it follows that pacifism is wrong. But it is more than wrong—it is dangerous, vicious, criminal, immoral, irrational, and unchristian. It must be exposed and refuted, especially in the Great War, when the nation must mobilize all possible power to defeat the enemy. If nationalism is a surrogate religion, then pacifism becomes the sin against the Holy Ghost. The nationalistic cleric has a moral obligation to wage a relentless war against pacifism and nonresistance.

One could say, first of all, that nonresistance is actually illegal, at least in Britain. Britain had a law that stipulated that ''any person who is present when a felony is committed not only may, *but is bound* without warrant to arrest the offender.'' If a felon escaped through your negligence you were liable to fine or prison.[39] Thus a nonresisting pacifist would become a *particeps criminis*, a participant in the crime. Capt. E. J. Solano captures one's emotions with this striking hypothetical situation:

Suppose for instance, that our country was invaded by the Germans, and that a number of them came to the pacifist's home and, led by their officers, proceeded, as they have frequently done in Belgium, to strip naked and rape in his presence his mother, his wife, his sister, and his daughter—or indeed any Englishwoman—one man following another in succession; after which they proceeded to slice off the breasts of these women, hack off their limbs, disembowel them by ripping them open, or to kill them in other ways, concluding their entertainment in his presence by mutilating and hanging little children, or by pinning them to his door with bayonets run through their bodies.

This tense passage ends with the question: *"What would the pacifist do?"*[40] If true to his principles, he would "resist not evil" or "turn the other cheek." Such cowardice would cause intense revulsion in most sane people, argued the clergy. As a matter of fact, when actual war breaks out and citizens are faced with a real decision on this matter, many putative pacifists become activists; they move instinctively to protect their loved ones. This leads to the widespread charge that pacifists are hypocrites, as Samuel Johnson once said about the Quakers.

Pacifists never really carry out the complete doctrine of nonresistance. The same Jesus who said "resist not evil" said also "lend, expecting nothing in return" (Luke 6:35). Quakers abstain from war but they do not lend money to people unconditionally, as the literal sense of Jesus' words would require. Nor do they leave their houses unlocked, which would be required by a literal obedience to "resist not evil." The pacifist wants peace and order but is unwilling to pay the price for them; he wants health but he stops the surgeon from cutting. Quakers pay taxes and thus their money pays for the use of force; they fight by deputy but say they cannot fight in person. They reap the benefits of those who die but are unwilling to die themselves.

Paul Bull pointed to the contradiction in a clergyman who gets a thousand pounds in salary yet espouses pacifism. His salary comes by force since the government must use rent-collectors, police, magistrates, judges, soldiers, and sailors to gather taxes to pay his salary. He concluded, "I do not think any words of condemnation are strong enough for those priests and teachers who have misled you into the refusal of your Nation's call by preaching a literal obedience which they themselves do not practice."[41]

Clergymen in both countries attacked the notion of "peace at any price," insisting that righteousness and justice were just as important as peace. "Is not such a war better than a foul peace?" asked Rhode.[42] "Without war," claimed Doehring, "man would become dissolute and be lost in materialism."[43] Blumhardt insisted that "man falls into a lot of foolishness when he never has to endure any tribulation."[44] Titius admonished his flock:

Not every peace has moral value. A peace that serves only to increase material culture and sensual enjoyment, that weakens the spiritual life and leads nations into practical materialism would be thoroughly bad. A peace that lamed all our progressive powers and tried to perpetuate a condition of injustice would be a foul, dishonorable peace.[45]

Several British sermons used the line, "We could not love fair peace so much, / Loved we not honour more." To prattle about peace while evil runs rampant calls to mind the wise warning of Francis Bacon: "In this theatre of human life it is only for God and the angels to be spectators." Man must get involved; he must reduce evil when it is in his power to do so. Pacifists are people who sing psalms to the fire rather than using the fire department, said Ballard.[46] "There is a worse sight than that of a nation at war," said Paterson-Smyth, "it is the sight of a nation at peace because she is too selfish to risk her blood."[47] Thomas affirmed that nonresistance is "not an act of piety or forebearance, it is really infidelity to the Human Race, apostacy from Christ, and high treason against God." One actually arms evil people with the Quaker interpretation of the Sermon on the Mount.[48] G. K. Chesterton said that the Great War was "the most sincere war of human history."[49] Jacks agreed, claiming that "those who are deaf to the call of duty now may be rightly judged incapable of hearing it under any circumstances whatsoever."[50] Pacifists usually hold to a theory of moral equivalence, where all belligerents are equally reprehensible. Against such people, Dawson stated the British position in an extreme form:

What are the Germans at present but obstructions to moral progress, a hotbed of flies, bearers of the worst ethical and spiritual maladies? Are they not rats carrying typhoid from the drains, and has not a Christian State the right to call upon us all to aid in their extermination.[51]

The pacifist may reply that we are to curb evil but we must use "spiritual force" and "moral persuasion" to accomplish it. Paul said we must live at peace with everyone as much as possible. But, replies the activist, it is not possible to live at peace with some evil people. Look at the Bible and you will see the folly of the pacifist position, said Thomas. When God wants to bring about some "behavior modification" he often uses physical force: he sends plagues on the Egyptians, he rains fire and brimstone on Sodom, he has Elijah slaughter 400 prophets of Baal, he has Jesus clean out the Temple with a whip, he strikes Ananias and Sapphira dead for lying to him.[52] Obviously the Almighty has not read Tolstoy.

Part of the preacher's task in refuting pacifism is to defend enthusiasm, zeal, ardor, passion, indignation, maybe even anger . . . maybe even hate. The pacifist argues that anger distorts rational thought but the activist replies that anger drives the whole person, reason and emotion, to accomplish great things. A man with reason and no passion is like an automobile without fuel. As Naumann said, only the man who is capable of a certain "God-anger" can accomplish anything important: "Everything truly great originates in a holy inspiration; in this inspiration God unlocks the soul and lets his spirit flow in."[53] Pott argued cogently that to love God is necessarily to hate evil; Jesus proved this when he said that you cannot serve two masters at the same time for you will love one and *hate* the other (Matt. 6:24).[54] Wilhelm Meyer confessed he was glad to hear poems and hymns about hate in the Great War; anger and hatred have more than once brought something great to Germany—they stopped the Romans in the Teutoburger Forest in 9 B.C. and chased the French over the Rhine in 1813. Meyer declared:

Yet, I must hate them, hate them with my whole soul, those who would destroy the German way of life root and branch, those who have betrayed us to the yellow race and the black race. . . . I must hate them for God's sake, who created the German way of life and wants to maintain it. . . . We hate the powers who want to blot out the German way of life, because God established the special traits of Germany and because our holy duty is to keep them pure.[55]

British clerics were just as anxious to recommend holy anger. Gough thundered, "There is no such thing as neutrality in this day of the Lord! . . . There are times—and this is one of them—when to be without passion is to betray a moral deficiency."[56] Drummond quoted Lloyd George: "Doubting hand never yet struck a firm blow."[57] Thomas spoke of a "guiltless wrath" that a moral person must show to evil people and "to fail to shew toward such a darkened conscience this kind of indignation would be to rob love itself of its due function."[58] Carnegie argued that a nation should be able to show resentment and if it could not it "may prove false to its world responsibility, and by doing so may lose its right to a place in the upward movement of the human race." He reminded his people that it was anger that swept Britain into war in August, 1914:

The overwhelming majority of English-speaking folk agree that had we felt and acted otherwise we should have been untrue to ourselves and to the part in the world's drama which we are called to play: that we should have declared ourselves decadent and degenerate, a people no longer to be accounted for in that great march of events through which God is working out His purpose for mankind.[59]

Not all preachers realized that in defending passion they were placing themselves in agreement with Friedrich Nietzsche, whose philosophy they were supposed to despise. One who did see this was F. R. Barry of Oxford, who conceded that Nietzsche was closer to the truth than Tolstoy. "If you *merely* endure aggression, letting the other cheek be smitten, without actively striking at the wrong, you leave the total ethical value of the Universe unchanged."[60]

THE GERMAN PERSPECTIVE ON WAR

Once again it is necessary to point to a significant difference among the Germans on this matter of war. Both sides believed in the just war and argued against pacifism but there was something extra with the Germans, a certain intensity about the topic that probably is explained by Germany's geopolitical position and her historical militarism. Ever since the War of Liberation, or perhaps even earlier, the Germans have had no difficulty at all in fitting war into God's world order. God has used war for thousands of years to accomplish his will. German pastors were fond of the passages that say God controls war in the world (e.g., Ps. 46:9). They could never forget how a deft use of war by Bismarck cut the Gordian knot of Central Europe and unified Germany after centuries of division and weakness. In three great fatherland wars from 1813 to 1914 German Protestant pastors had advocated the idea that war was a valuable, divinely ordained arbiter between nations. In the heat of the Franco-Prussian War Karl Köhler explained to his parishioners:

When two great nations are at war it is a test between them to see which of them possesses the greater inner capacity, the greater intelligence and spiritual resources, the greater moral earnestness, the stronger will and the more manly determination, the greater *esprit de corps*, the stronger ability to sacrifice one's self, the stronger conviction of one's value and of the greatness of the calling that one must fulfill in the world.[61]

A Latin proverb says, *In vino veritas*, "in wine there is truth." One could also say, *In bello veritas*, "in war there is truth." Among the nations, war is the great final examination among the powers; it separates the wheat from the chaff. The question of national superiority—military, economic, cultural, moral, and spiritual—can sometimes be settled only by war. Men may prattle about "competition short of war" or "the moral equivalent of war" but in the final analysis some issues can be settled only by Mars.

As we have seen, most German pastors in 1914 believed that war had suddenly disclosed the true colors of England, perfidious Albion, whose rottenness had been artfully concealed during peacetime. By attacking Germany so treacherously and by spreading lies around the world, the British had let their true moral depravity come out into the open, a depravity that few could have suspected prior to 1914. Germany had grown so powerful since unification that the nations of Europe were unwilling to admit that a significant alteration of the balance of power had occurred. Hence, a war seemed necessary to establish the change.

There was something extra special about World War I to the Germans. Running through the sermons of the Great War is a unique vibration, a special feeling that this was going to be the greatest war of all history. Many pastors agreed with Paul de Lagarde that Germany was not completely unified in 1871 and that it was going to take another war, a very special war, to complete her inner unification. Maybe this was why Schiller's remark was a favorite: "Every nation has its day in history, but the day of the Germans will be the harvest of the entire world." The remarkable Reichstag session of August 4, 1914, finally unified the German people spiritually. Koehler's analysis was typical: "What a wonderful master war is! What man could not do with all his deliberation and industry war has accomplished in a stroke of magic—the inner unification of Germany. While war was declared on us from the outside, God bestowed peace on us from the inside. . . . The Lord caused this and it is a miracle in our eyes!"[62]

Tolzien told his parishioners that the kaiser drew the sword "to protect something sacred." The sacred things that were in danger were "land and people, wife and child, *Volk* and fatherland." When these things are in danger, "the cherub must appear"—referring to the angel with the flaming sword placed at the entrance to the Garden of Eden (Gen. 3:24). "Therefore, we have a pure conscience, in contrast to our enemies, who used the sword as a weapon of aggression, as a tool of robbery."[63]

In a book with the suggestive title, *German Faith and German Morals*, Ernst Troeltsch explained carefully why Germany was fighting:

We fight not only for what we are, but also for what we will and must become. . . . Our faith is not just that we can and must defend our state and homeland but that our national essence [*Volkstum*] contains an inexhaustible richness and value that are inexpressibly important for mankind, a value that the Lord and God of history has entrusted to our protection and development. The German faith is a faith in the inner moral and spiritual content of Germanness [*Deutschtum*], the faith of the Germans in themselves, in their future, in their world mission. . . . This is a belief in the divine world ruler and world reason that has allowed us to become a great world nation, that will not forsake us or deny us because our spirit comes from its spirit.[64]

Note the Hegelian and immanental undertones in this passage. The Lord and God of history is also the world ruler and world reason whose spirit has given the Germans their spirit and their unique national essence.

For the Germans the only war worthy of the adjective "holy" would be a *Völkerkrieg*, a struggle between the nations, a contest between national spirits, national moralities, and national cultures—not a cabinet war or a diplomats' war or a war of mere territorial expansion. Small wonder that the Germans found the Old Testament a favorite source of texts for war sermons; there God is clearly the national God who worries about his *Volk* and leads them into battle and fights for them. He is the Lord of Sabaoth, the "Lord of Hosts," that is, hosts of armies. He has no qualms about you fighting for your nation, for as Ernst Arndt once said, "The God who allowed iron to grow did not want any slaves!" Without shame the Germans could speak of *Kriegsfrömmigkeit*—war piety or war religion.[65]

CONCLUSION

Even as we approach the end of the twentieth century we are still amazed at the war enthusiasm of August, 1914. More important than the question of what caused this boldness is the question, what *sustained* it once the Schlieffen plan bogged down and trench warfare developed? Part of the explanation lies in the work of the spiritual leaders of Britain and Germany, the pastors and theologians who preached a "gospel of nationalism" that stiffened the resistance of the soldiers in the field and the citizens on the home front. Once the war stalemated in the trenches the role of the preacher became crucial. As G. K. Chesterton well put it:

Whatever starts wars, the thing that sustains wars is something in the soul; that is something akin to religion. It is what men feel about life and death. A man near to death is dealing directly with an absolute; it is nonsense to say he is concerned only with relative and remote complications that death will in any case end. If he is sustained by certain loyalties they must be loyalties as simple as death.[66]

Nationalism gives a man a loyalty as simple as death. For the last two centuries millions of patriots have given their lives for the nation, which, in truth, makes nationalism a surrogate religion, as we have argued in this study. As Lewis Mumford said, "If a religion consists of the beliefs and hopes for which men, when challenged, will sacrifice their lives and fortunes in the assurance of participating in a greater life, then nationalism was the vital religion of the nineteenth century."[67]

And, we should add, of the twentieth century also . . . so far.

NOTES

1. For three good general studies of the Christian views on war see Roland H. Bainton, *Christian Attitudes toward War and Peace: A Historical Survey and Critical Re-evaluation* (New York, 1960); Paul Ramsey, *War and the Christian Conscience* (Durham, NC, 1961); Michael Walzer, *Just and Unjust Wars: A Moral Argument with Historical Illustrations* (New York, 1977). All three works operate in the shadow of the A-bomb, of course, and end with a discussion of the threat of nuclear devastation. Walzer's study was deeply affected by the American Vietnam experience.

2. For good studies of the pacifist position see Keith Robbins, *The Abolition of War: The "Peace Movement" in Britain, 1914-1919* (Cardiff: University of Wales Press, 1976); John Rae, *Conscience and Politics: The British Government and the Conscientious Objector to Military Service, 1916-1919* (London, 1970); Jo Vellacott, *Bertrand Russell and the Pacifists in the First World War* (New York, 1980).

3. See Bailey, "British Protestant Theologians," 212; Marrin, *Last Crusade*, chs. 4 and 5.

4. *Immorality of Nonresistance*, 20-21.

5. *So as by Fire*, 13.

6. *War and Christian Duty*, 117.

7. *Immorality of Nonresistance*, 56; see also Ballard, *Mistakes of Pacifism*, 19, 26.

8. See e.g., Rolffs, *Evangelien-Predigten aus der Kriegszeit*, 3-5; B. J. Snell, *How are we to love our enemies?* (London, 1915), 2-6; Thomas, *Immorality of Nonresistance*, 10; Eger, *Sechs Predigten*, 16.

9. *Bruising of Belgium*, 262; see also Kirchner, *Kriegszweifel*, 17; *Vorwerk, Was sagt der Weltkrieg*, 41-42; Ott, *Religion, Krieg, und Vaterland*, 23; Meinhof, *Sittlichkeit und Krieg*, 15, 30; Naumann, *Stark in Gott*, 50-52; Pautke, *MP*, XI, 179; Rump, *Kriegspredigten*, II, 12-16; Le Seur, *Frohbotschaft in Feindesland*, 40; Muir, *War and Christian Duty*, 14; Thomas, *Immorality of Nonresistance*, 30.

10. *Only Alternative to War*, 9.

11. *War and Christian Duty*, 127; this is a quotation from an article by James Orr in *Hastings Dictionary of the Bible*.

12. *Soul of a Nation*, 28.

13. *Mistakes of Pacifism*, 27.

14. "Jesus und das Recht des Krieges," *EF*, XIV, 300-301; see also Meyer, *Vom ehrlichen Krieg*, 75-77.

15. See Mozley, *On War*, 10; Holmes, *Colors of the King*, 20; Dryander, *Evangelische Reden*, II, 36; Haecker, *Von Krieg und Kreuz*, 5; Vorwerk, *Was sagt der Weltkrieg*, 61; Cordes, *Kriegsbrot*, 3; Mulert, *Christ und Vaterland*, 191; Ott, *Religion, Krieg, und Vaterland*, 21; Faulhaber, *Schwert des Geistes*, 287.

16. See Holland, *So as by Fire*, 24; Studdert-Kennedy, *Rough Talks*, 71; Wace, *War and the Gospel*, 121; Rolffs, *Evangelien Predigten aus der Kriegszeit*, 8; Tolzien, *Kriegspredigten*, II, 137; Sardemann, *Das Reich Gottes und der Krieg*, 12; Cecil Chesterton, *The Prussian Hath Said in His Heart* (London, 1914), 4; Brauns, *Der gerechte Krieg*, 9; Hasse, *Grosse Krieg*, 12.

17. *This War and the Sermon on the Mount*, 10.

18. *Divine Providence and War*, 14.

19. *War and Its Issues*, 28.

20. *Erforschtes und Erlebtes*, 312.

21. *Christ and the Sword*, 103.

22. *So as by Fire*, 84; see also Dryander, *Evangelische Reden*, II, 38; Ihmels, *Aufwärts die Herzen*, 97; Löber, *Christentum und Krieg?*, 13.

23. *Varieties of Religious Experience*, 313.

24. *Decoration of the Cross*, 136.

25. *The Beloved Captain* (London, 1917), 29-31. Hankey died at the Somme, October 12, 1916. For additional sermons praising the soldierly life see Lyttelton, *What Are We Fighting For?*, 21; Sclater, *Eve of Battle*, 69; John Kelman, *The War and Preaching* (London, 1919), 116; Smith, *War, Nation, and Church*, 19; Dennis Jones, *The Diary of a Padre* (Manchester, n.d.), 89; Oman, *War and Its Issues*, 20; Tolzien, *Kriegspredigten*, II, 94; König, *Kriegspredigten*, 11-12; Kirmss, *Eine gute Wehr*, 31; Dryander, *Evangelische Reden*, II, 23; Hasse, *Grosse Krieg*, 13; Risch, *Mit Gott wollen wir Taten tun!*, 78; Klein, *Du bist mein Hammer*, 48; Vorwerk, *Was sagt der Weltkrieg*, 14; Rade, *Krieg und Christentum*, 20-21.

26. *Testing of a Nation*, 107.

27. Cited in Crafer, *Soldiers of Holy Writ*, 69.

28. For some warnings see Bernard, *In War Time*, 106; Hammer, *Kriegstheologie*, 169.

29. *Aus der Friedens- und Kriegsarbeit*, 310.

30. *Totenfest im Kriegsjahr*, 11.

31. *Vom ehrlichen Krieg*, 32; for more illustrations see Foerster, *Heldentod*, 12-13; Rittelmeyer, *Christ und Krieg*, 31; Rendtorff, *Aus dem dritten Kriegswinter*, 59; Naumann, *Stark in Gott*, 45-47; Kirn, *Acht Dorf Kriegspredigten*, 30; Kirmss, *Das Reich muss uns doch bleiben*, 19-20.

32. *War and Preaching*, 119.

33. *Test of War*, 65.

34. *War and the Gospel*, 78.

35. *Drinking the Cup*, 7.

36. *Christ and the Sword*, 47.

37. *The Padre* (London, n.d.), 126.

38. *Judgment of War*, 47; see also Thomas, *Immorality of Nonresistance*, vii-viii.

39. Thomas, *Immorality of Nonresistance*, vii.

40. *The Pacifist Lie: A Book for Sailors and Soldiers* (London, 1918), 50.

41. *Christianity and War*, 9, 10; see also Coulton, *Pacifist Illusions*, 56; Henson, *War-Time Sermons*, 13; Murray, *Christians War Book*, 19; Ballard, *Mistakes of Pacifism*, 32.

42. *Kriegspredigten*, 4.

43. *Ein feste Burg*, II, 317.

44. *Gottes Reich kommt!*, 364.

45. *Unser Krieg*, 3-4; see also Herzog, *Kriegspredigten* (Wurster), 378-79; Spanuth, *Weltkrieg im Unterricht*, 29; Tolzien, *Kriegspredigten*, I, 7; Meyer, *Vom ehrlichen Krieg*, 54-55; Sardemann, *Das Reich Gottes*, 18; Cordes, *Kriegsbrot*, 100. In his *Philosophy of Right* (§324) Hegel observed that "just as the blowing of the winds preserves the sea from long calm, so also corruption in nations would be the product of prolonged, let alone 'perpetual' peace."

46. *Mistakes of Pacifism*, 35.

47. *God and the War*, 23.

48. *Immorality of Nonresistance*, 28, 40.

49. *The Barbarism of Berlin*, 8.

50. "Mechanism and the War," 47.

51. *Christ and the Sword*, 154.

52. *Immorality of Nonresistance*, xv; for more sermons on this point see Worsey, *Under the War Cloud*, 14; Bernard, *In War Time*, 8; Holland, *So as by Fire*, 20; Temple, *Christianity and War*, 7; McCurdy, *Freedom's Call and Duty*, 17-18.

53. *Stark in Gott*, 56.

54. *Vom Feld fürs Feld*, 91.

55. *Vom ehrlichen Krieg*, 73, 75; for more sermons on anger see Dibelius, *Gottes Ruf*, 17; Zurhellen, *Kriegspredigten*, 32; Löber, *Christentum und Krieg*, 12; Philippi, *An der Front*, 19; Rump, *Berliner Betstunden*, 11.

56. *God's Strong People*, 106-7, 110.

57. *Soul of a Nation*, 94.

58. *Immorality of Nonresistance*, 30.

59. *Sermons on Subjects*, 4, 11.

60. *Religion and the War*, 10.

61. Cited in Piechowski, *Kriegspredigt von 1870/71*, 95; see also Hoover, *Gospel of Nationalism*, 94-96.

62. *Der Weltkrieg im Lichte der deutsch-protestantischen Kriegspredigt* (Tübingen, 1915), 43. Koehler was a social Darwinian as can be seen in *Das religiös-sittliche Bewusstsein im Weltkrieg* (Tübingen, 1917), 26 *et passim*.

63. *Kriegspredigten*, II, 136.

64. *Deutsche Glaube und deutsche Sitte*, 19.

65. The phrase is used by Pauli, "Zur Würdigung unserer Kriegsfrömmigkeit," *EF*, XVI, 96. For more sermons giving the German view on war see Ott, *Religion, Krieg, und Vaterland*, 40; Showalter, *Krieg in Predigten*, 6-8; Meyer, *Vom ehrlichen Krieg*, 64; Rendtorff, *Aus dem dritten Kriegswinter*, 34; Kirchner, *Kriegszweifel*, 8; Conrad, *Festhalten bis ans Ende*, 33; Seeberg, *Geschichte, Krieg, und Seele*, 49; Hennig, *Fromm und Deutsch*, 2; Steltz, *Krieg und Christentum*, 13; Meinhof, *Sittlichkeit und Krieg*, 15; Glage-Hamburg, *Der Krieg und der Christ*, 14; Meyer, *Kriegspredigten* (Wurster), 281; Klein, *Du bist mein Hammer*, 8; Broeckner, *Glauben an Gott*, 10; Le Seur, *Frohbotschaft in Feindesland*, 21; Brauns, *Der gerechte Krieg*, 12; Haecker, *Von Krieg und Kreuz*, 38; Lehmann, *Vom deutschen Gott*, 60.

66. *The Everlasting Man* (Garden City, N.Y.), 140.

67. *The Condition of Man* (New York, 1944), 352.

8

The End of the Great War

No war lasts forever, but it seemed to the participants in World War I that the conflict would never end. None of the powers could deliver a final, decisive blow against the other side. From 1915 on, the struggle became a war of attrition in which the western front acted like a black hole, sucking in and annihilating millions of men and tons of material. When Lenin and his Bolshevik party took over Russia in November, 1917, a glimmer of hope appeared for Germany, because the termination of hostilities on the eastern front would release about two million soldiers to break open the western front.

But the United States entered the war in April, 1917, and this more than offset the loss of Russia—if the Americans could get to the front in time to make a difference. Hoping to end the war before the yanks got there in force, General Ludendorff launched an all-out effort in March, 1918, promising the kaiser he would be in Paris by April 1. The Allies finally achieved a unified command by appointing Marshal Ferdinand Foch as General-in-Chief of all the allied armies in France. The Germans reached the banks of the Marne River May 31, just as they had done in September, 1914, but were turned back by the allied forces.

From then until August the Allies gradually pushed the Germans back to their fortified lines. Germany's allies began to make separate peaces—Bulgaria on September 29, Turkey on October 31, and Austria-Hungary on November 3. Germany now stood alone. Then came the mutiny of the High Seas Fleet at Kiel and General Hindenburg told Kaiser William II that to avoid a catastrophe Germany should seek an immediate armistice with the Allies. An appeal was made to President Wilson, who insisted that the Imperial Government step down and allow a government chosen by the people to end the war. The Kaiser, after much soul-searching, abdicated and fled to neutral Holland while the German socialists under Friedrich Ebert proclaimed a republic on November 9. German delegates entered a railway car in the Compiègne Forest at 5:00 A.M. November 11 and signed the Armistice. The fighting on all fronts formally ended at 11:00 A.M., November 11, 1918.

THE END OF THE WAR IN GERMANY

The founder of the Christian religion said, "Blessed are the peacemakers," but one would never have suspected as much from the behavior of some of the clergy in the Great War. On the German side, for example, many churchmen seemed to go out of their way to keep the war going. In July, 1917, the Reichstag passed a resolution seeking to commit the government to a negotiated peace, a peace without total victory, a peace of reconciliation with no annexations. Since it was supported by most Socialists it was called the "Scheidemann Peace." Many Protestant clerics, however, wanted a peace of annexations, a peace that would follow a complete German victory, a peace that would produce an enlarged German Reich having the hegemony of Europe. They called it a "Hindenburg Peace." General Ludendorff insisted right down to the summer of 1918 that he could deliver such a peace.

In September, 1917, a new party emerged in Germany, the Fatherland party. Many conservative and a few liberal churchmen joined it because it advocated a continuation of the war to a victorious end and it opposed political reform. A few liberal churchmen wanted a negotiated peace, men like Martin Rade, editor of *Die Christliche Welt*. Rade was deeply disturbed that the churches seemed to promote hatred rather than peace, a condition that to him spelled the bankruptcy of Christendom. Conservatives knew that political reform would probably lead to the disestablishment of the Lutheran *Volkskirche*, since this is often a normal consequence of the establishment of democracy. It would lead also to a loss of control of confessional education in the public schools.[1]

Some conservative clergymen resorted to a sharp separation of public and private morality in opposing the Reichstag peace resolution. They fell back on a double morality whereby pastors should not meddle in politics, asserting that Christianity could have no bearing upon specific state policies. Christians were told not to sit in moral judgment over the actions of the state. This dangerous double morality absolutized the nation and weakened Christian responsibility for passing moral judgment on the nation or its governing regime.[2]

The Armistice of November 11, 1918, psychologically crushed most Christian nationalists in Germany. It is difficult to accept defeat when you have preached or listened to a "gospel of nationalism" for four years. Defeat is enough to make you lose your faith. Hermann Lahusen saw the changes coming and wrote to his son: "Prussia is gone, Germany is gone, utopians rule us. The Kaiser lies sick in bed. And God? And divine justice? We are living through Golgotha. . . . We are under the judgment of God and will submit ourselves to it.'' He advised his son that it would be preferable to hope for death than to go into unbelief.[3] On the day of the Armistice he wrote: "The Kaiser in Holland! Now even honor is gone. The end of the Hohenzollerns. One wants to cry tears of blood. Our poor people. We did not deserve this. True, we were an immature nation, we were unworthy before God, but we were without leadership, that was our cruel fate and in vain we stand here: God give us a man! We will clasp hands and go our way in the dark until God sends us light again.''[4]

War theology has a strange inertia. Its premises keep on working, even after defeat and armistice. If you have preached for four years that God will not fail the German *Volk* then the only consistent hypothesis to explain defeat is to say that the German *Volk* failed God. That was the essence of the *Dolchstosslegende*, the "stab-in-the-back legend,'' which claimed that the military forces of the Reich, while betrayed from within, were *im Felde unbesiegt*—undefeated in the field. This theory seemed to bring coherence into a confusing picture, because Germany ended the war occupying thousands of square miles of enemy territory in both east and west. The only key to the paradox was treachery, treason. Unpatriotic groups like communists, socialists, liberals, and Jews had fallen on the nation and stabbed it in the back. They had fomented unrest, caused strikes, and preached defeatism. As far as we can tell the first occurrence of the *Dolchstosslegende* was in a sermon by the eminent pastor, Bruno Doehring, February 3, 1918. He called those on the home front "venal and cowardly creatures'' who had "treacherously desecrated the altar of the fatherland'' with the blood of brothers and had "put the murder weapon'' into the hands of those who attacked their brothers at the front.[5]

Gerhard Tolzien asked why it was that the allied superiority, which had been evident from the first, should suddenly break Germany now? He concluded that it must have been a sort of "spiritual influenza'' that went through the national brain. It would have been better to die suddenly like an oak tree struck down by lightning, than to be hit from within, from behind. What happened to the "spirit of 1914''?

We do not have that spirit any more. Another spirit has come upon us. An evil spirit that rolls like a cloud of gas through the homeland right up to the front. What can we complain about now? As long as the old spirit remained, God allowed us to win. But a nation with the spirit that pervades the land nowadays can never win. We could weep tears of blood; however, one good thing has come of this: our guilt is obvious and we have no reason to grumble and to ask, "Why have you forsaken us?''[6]

Yet, like many clerics, Tolzien could hope for the future. He recalled that defeat of Prussia in 1806 had turned that nation around and allowed it to recover its faith and finally defeat Napoleon I. God purified Israel by defeat, first by the Assyrians and then by the Babylonians. In a sermon delivered Christmas Day, 1918, Tolzien looked cheerfully to the next chapter in German history:

Germanness and Christianity will again harmonize! Germanness and Christianity have already harmonized well. May our German-Christian Christmas festival testify to that. Germanness and Christianity also harmonize in our one hundred year old song. And one hundred years from now nothing will be lost or spoiled. At Christmas 2018 our descendants will sing again, with more joy, more freedom, and more piety than we, in a German and Christian fatherland that has been thoroughly redeemed.[7]

But a few preachers had deep misgivings about the future of the German fatherland and church. Earlier in the war Samuel Keller had warned that if the church did not keep patriotism enriched with religion "then after the war we will experience not only religious but also patriotic and moral and national bankruptcy. Then this war will prove to be a bridge to the Antichrist and God must reject us."[8] In a memorial service, November 24, Ernst Dryander observed, "Today it is a matter of the question of whether our *Volk* will still remain a Christian *Volk* or not, or whether a new heathenism will appear, a heathenism that is worse than the old heathenism, because the old was religious whereas the new will be an enemy of religion."[9]

THE END OF THE WAR IN BRITAIN

Meanwhile, across the Channel the end of the war took a different course, inasmuch as Britain was going to be one of the victors and determine the shape of things to come. On the day of the Armistice, Parliament adjourned for a service of thanksgiving in Saint Margaret's Church, Westminster. Members of the London Stock Exchange stopped their trading momentarily to sing the doxology, "Praise God from whom all blessings flow." King George confessed that he thanked God. All this, as Marwick said, was "a genuine expression of the religious element ever present in the war fever."[10] Many preachers used Revelation 18:2 as their text that Sunday: "Fallen, fallen is Babylon the great." In a sermon called "God's Verdict," J. A. Carnegie told his flock that Germany

has been beaten to the dust because she estranged herself from God and set herself upon the side of the powers of sin and darkness; because she set her might against right; because she embraced the gospel of bloodshed and the sword against the Gospel of Peace; because she set the forces of materialism against the power of Christ. . . . God, through our arms, and the arms of our Allies, has beaten to the dust again an Empire which defied him. And great is the fall of her; a lesson to the whole world: an example to the heathen; a mighty monument to the power of Christianity. . . . Babylon is fallen and bound. The reek of her pestilence is blowing away. The air is purer already. The sun of a great peace is rising and gilding the hilltops with a golden glory.[11]

With the German fleet in Scapa Flow, concluded Winnington-Ingram, we British can truly exult, with Paul, "We have fought a good fight!" Matthew Arnold had proved right: there *is* an eternal law in the universe that makes for righteousness. Solomon was correct when he said that "the ungodly shall be rooted out at last" (Prov. 2:22). Surely the British will continue to fear God, he said, after such a demonstration of divine justice. But, if not, "we are the most ungrateful, purblind set of people whom God has ever deigned to use, and we shall certainly be disowned by Him later on." If the British did not see God after what He did in the war it would be to "trample the Son of God and put Him to an open shame."[17]

Just as in Germany, British war theology had a definite inertia about it, a thrust that kept on working right down to the Armistice and beyond. All during the conflict certain preachers had advocated a hard line against Germany for all her sins, an unforgiving policy that would demand vengeance against the Germans after victory. Weston described German brutality in her African colonies and then concluded, "The Peace Conference that shall allow him to try again will be guilty of the wilful betrayal of liberty, and of the rights of the weakest people of the earth."[13] "A nation, like a man, must pay the price of its own crimes," said Drummond, "and we confer no benefit upon it by trying to conceal our deep abhorrence of its guilt."[14] Dawson warned that the sword of Christ that felled Germany must not be allowed to fall back into its scabbard "until righteousness stands once more as Lord of the world."[15] Carnegie warned about a "mistaken magnanimity" toward Germany that would stop short of just punishment: "We should be untrue to our children yet unborn if we agreed to any terms of peace which left to them the heritage of a renewed ordeal."[16] Muir maintained that "there should be no peace, until an outraged humanity has compelled her [Germany] to realize her crime and make such atonement possible."[17] A complete end must be sought to German militarism, said Worsey: "If not, our children and our children's children may have reason to curse our memories in the days to come."[18]

Cecil Chesterton, brother of G. K. Chesterton, railed against the liberals and pacifists who would not want the kaiser to be humiliated, who insisted that we must crush militarism everywhere, in Britain as well as in Germany. The difference between British and German militarism was so great in degree, he argued, that one could make a special case for the utter destruction of Prussian-German militarism. This war paradoxically was not to end war but to end a certain kind of peace, "the peace of Prussia that passeth all abhorrence." This was no time for stupid sentimentality—Carthage must be destroyed! We must drive a stake through the vampire's heart![19]

Such purple rhetoric was really out of place. All these absolutists and hardliners indubitably contributed to the disastrous "Khaki Election" of December 14, 1918, which John M. Keynes called the most unfortunate election in modern British history. Lloyd George took to the stump promising to make Britain a "fit country for heroes to live in." To get the money to keep this pledge he had to promise that he would go to Versailles and "squeeze the Germans until the pips squeak." One of the most popular slogans in this election was "Hang the Kaiser!" Several internationalists were defeated, despite all the talk about a League of Nations and collective security.[20]

The clergy sowed the wind and then the diplomats reaped the whirlwind. For four years clerics had painted the conflict in absolute terms: God versus Satan, Christianity versus neopaganism, freedom versus despotism, love versus Social Darwinism. But when the war is over you find that you are dealing at the peace conference with Satan and you do not compromise with Satan. As McDougall said, "We cannot hate the Germans right up to the end of the war, and then find ourselves generous and sympathetic, able to resume our old ways of working together, and quick to realize our common bonds of religion and origin and our common task."[21]

Nietzsche observed in 1873 that "a great victory is a great danger." Many Britons realized in 1919 that they were standing at a crucial turning-point in European history. "Never in history," wrote historian Seton-Watson, "will the statesmen, in whose hands the control of Foreign Policy lies, have been faced by so great a responsibility as in those months of negotiation which must inevitably separate the conclusions of hostilities and the final establishment of peace."[22] The trouble was that many intellectuals, like H. G. Wells, had a fantastically naive view of how to solve some European problems. "Let us redraw the map of Europe boldly," declared Wells, "as we mean it to be redrawn—and let us replan society as we mean it to be reconstructed. Now is the opportunity to do fundamental things that will not otherwise get done for hundreds of years."[23] Woods said he wanted to see "the new Europe divided into its natural divisions of race and nation, no country to be coerced by a foreign tyranny, but each free to arrange itself under its natural authority."[24] If you look at an (accurate!) ethnic map of Europe, you will agree with Willis that this is a case of "criminal utopianism."[25]

Point Fourteen of Woodrow Wilson's peace program was the League of Nations. Seldom in history has a nation's clergy showed such enthusiasm for a project as the British clergy did for the League of Nations. In February, 1918, the Upper House of Canterbury Convocation passed this resolution:

That this house notes with especial satisfaction the prominent place recently given by prominent statesmen among the Allies to the proposal of a League of Nations. We desire to welcome in the name of the Prince of Peace the idea of such a League as shall promote the brotherhood of man, and shall have power at the last resort to constrain by economic pressure or armed force any nation which should refuse to submit to an international tribunal any dispute with another nation. Further, we desire that such a League of Nations should not merely be regarded as a more or less remote consequence of peace, but that provision for its organization should be included in the conditions of a settlement.[26]

The clerical imagination was suddenly seized by the idea of a supranational agency empowered to keep the peace. As Marrin observed, "Men were moved as if by a vision of the Beyond."[27] They treated the coming of Woodrow Wilson with almost as much reverence as the coming of Christ; Wilson was bringing a "New Deal" in diplomacy; the old diplomacy had obviously failed to prevent the near-suicide of western civilization. In a book called *God and the Allies: A View of the Grande Entente*, Rosslyn Bruce, Vicar of Saint Augustine's in Edgbaston, urged that the alliance was not an accident of history but "a practical link in the chain of Divine purposes, working through the human means of friendly nations, to the establishment of an international understanding throughout the whole of civilized society."[28] The league would spell the end of *Realpolitik* for all time to come, so it seemed.

But . . . *given the nature of man*—the cynic always starts his objection with that phrase—how could such a league ever succeed? Is it not the quintessence of utopianism? Many preachers reacted sharply to this pessimism and launched a frontal attack on it. Some quoted Lord Asquith to the effect that our choice at this juncture of history is between utopia or hell. It is either the league or utter destruction! This sounded very much like the faulty dilemma of the Germans: *Weltmacht oder Niedergang*!

The pessimists stood condemned from the mouth of the Lord Jesus himself—"O ye of little faith!" Lenwood exclaimed, "Brotherhood is only waiting for those who have the courage to believe it possible."[29] Barry cited Nietzsche's admonition to "live dangerously" and insisted that "all things are possible with God," even the end of diplomatic quarrels; to say human nature is hopelessly corrupt is the only real form of atheism, the refusal to believe in goodness, the deliberate acquiescence of our lower nature, the abdication of our manhood.[30] The trouble with politicians, noted Oman, is that they are seldom prophets; they disbelieve in utopias; we must see visions and dream dreams of future brotherhood.[31] To say that war is species-predictable or biologically necessary is to talk like Bernhardi. War can be abolished now, just like slavery, dueling, and polygamy were abolished in history. People once thought slavery was endemic but then bold believers in righteousness summoned the courage to abolish it by law. People of the twentieth century must simply have the kind of faith that moves mountains. "One thing is clear," concluded Newton, "the future of the world is democratic and nothing can stop it. Tokens could not be plainer, and far-seeing religious leaders, who divine the curve of destiny, will seek to leaven the future now in the making with the spirit of the Gospel."[32]

Many churchmen insisted that the League of Nations was a logical long-range outcome of Christian ethics working in western history. Bishop Gore affirmed that everyone had become a socialist during the war, not in the Marxist sense, but in the Christian sense. We have learned, he said, to care for the whole body now, to be suspicious of Adam Smith, Social Darwinism, and all forms of individualism and competition. The church had failed to apply Christian love to the realms of industry and diplomacy and this constituted "one of the most remarkable instances of moral blindness which history presents to us."[33] The League of Nations would replace the old notion of national competition. The league comes from the spirit of God because "it will rest upon the idea of fellowship and humanity, supreme in its interests over all separate national claims, a fellowship based on justice and the rights of the weaker as well as the stronger nations—an idea which has mainly had its origin in Christian thought or imagination, and which is the product of a civilisation at least deeply leavened by Christianity and to which the name of Christ is still the name above every name."[34]

There were many British clergymen who dared to hope for the success of a League of Nations, but they expressed their hope with a clear proviso: we must have a new heart, a new spirit, a *new man* to accomplish it. The Wilsonian New Deal required a new human type, just as the Marxist revolution required a new kind of man. As Roberts expressed it: "The only real security against war is international goodwill; and the establishment of international goodwill involves a 'transvaluation of values' on a stupendous scale."[35] Orchard concurred: "Nothing less than the conversion of Europe, including ourselves, to Christianity, is the task set before us."[36] "A League of Nations must be no mere theory of statesmen," said Archbishop Davidson; "It is to be the peoples' pact. So far as in us lies, we are answerable before God and man that it live and grow."[37] "We must firmly believe," said Mackarness, "that some day the vast world-empire built upon force . . . will crumble to pieces; and an empire of truth and justice and freedom, in which Christ Himself rules, will dominate the hearts and consciences of mankind."[38]

William Temple complained of the lack of unity in Christendom at this fateful hour. "What we need," he claimed, "is an international society, actually and perceptibly one, bound together by devotion to Christ." He suggested that they add a new clause to the creed: "I believe in the Holy Catholic Church and regret that it does not exist."[39]

At the end of the Second World War the British people accepted the argument, embodied in the Beveridge Report, that a nation could maintain full employment in peacetime if it could do it in wartime. All that was lacking was the determination. Curiously, a similar argument was used at the end of the Great War in connection with the League of Nations and collective security. Woods argued: "If the white heat of enthusiasm can fuse the Empire in a few day's notice, what could be done if the white heat of the love of Christ were brought to bear upon the nations of the world?"[40] Burroughs declared that we must have the "spirit of the trenches," the spirit of sacrifice and selflessness to achieve the postwar ideal of a better world. The method is there and we need only try it, for if we do not, "the whole future will curse our generation for letting itself be overcome of evil when it might have overcome evil with good."[41]

It was felt that war would never again be so popular as before. "Our men will come back," said Patten, "hating war with a great hatred."[42] Henson predicted that "nevermore shall we be cheated by the pageantry and purple rhetoric of war. Henceforth we shall see it in the light of this monstrous conflict, and know it for what it is—the masterpiece of Satan."[43]

Many churchmen, however, could not shake that uneasy feeling that the Great War would not end war but would be merely the prelude to a more terrible war. Burroughs admitted the choice was between utopia and hell but conceded that the odds seemed to be in favor of hell.[44] Barry confessed that he was looking for a "vision splendid" but it seemed to vanish in the light of actual day.[45] Roberts saw the future correctly when he predicted that, "Whenever the war ends it will be followed by a settlement on the basis of political expediency which will start the same old cycle of international suspicion, hate, and ill will, and lead to the same deadly consummation in another generation."[46] Dudden confessed that he was reduced to "blank despair" thinking about the unreality of a League of Nations. His forecast of the next war was disturbingly accurate:

As you look into the future, can you discern any brighter prospect than that of kingdoms arrayed against kingdoms and continents against continents—gigantic armies grappling with gigantic armies; airships by the thousand raining bombs upon doomed cities, whose inhabitants burrow like rats underground to escape destruction; all the resources of science taxed to the uttermost to furnish effective instruments for this diabolical work of devastation; and the last relics of conventional chivalry and generosity and magnanimity rent in rags and torn to tatters?[47]

This is a sad note on which to end—the pessimists were right. It would take a new kind of European, nay, a new kind of man, to end war and make the League of Nations work. Europe labored but produced nothing new in the years to come.

NOTES

1. See Borg, *Old-Prussian Church*, 40ff; Fischer, *Germany's War Aims*, 95ff; Hans Gatzke, *Germany's Drive to the West* (Baltimore, 1950); Arthur Rosenberg, *Imperial Germany* (Boston, 1964), 73ff; Mehnert, *Evangelische Kirche*, 69-72.

2. Borg, *Old-Prussian Church*, 44.

3. Friedrich Lahusen to Hermann Lahusen, October 11, 1918, in Hermann Lahusen, D. Friedrich *Lahusen Vater und Seelsorger: Briefe an seinen Sohn* (Gütersloh, 1929), 146.

4. November 11, 1918, ibid., 149.

5. Pressel, *Kriegspredigt*, 305-6.

6. *Kriegspredigten*, VII, 63, 69. Harnack observed during this difficult time: "We have not only sinned in Mammonism, we have not understood the signs of the times. The overestimation of our power and might was worse than a false calculation or deception." Zahn-Harnack, *Harnack*, 374.

7. *Kriegspredigten*, VII, 96.

8. *Ist Gott neutral?*, 10-11.

9. *Evangelische Reden*, XVII, 22.

10. *The Deluge*, 260.

11. "God's Verdict," *Sermons for the Peace Celebration*, 15, 115.

12. *Victory and After*, 57, 90.

13. *Black Slaves of Prussia*, 18.
14. *Soul of a Nation*, 127.
15. *Christ and the Sword*, 27.
16. *Sermons on Subjects*, 17, 19.
17. *War and Christian Duty*, 213.
18. *Under the War Cloud*, xi; see also Mathews, *Three Years' War*, 86; Benett, *England's Mission*, 16-17; Woods, *Christianity and War*, 8; Hügel, *The German Soul*, 198.
19. All this comes in ch. 7, "Thou shalt not suffer a witch to live," in *The Prussian Hath Said in His Heart*, 206-210.
20. See Marwick, *The Deluge*, 262; Marrin, *Last Crusade*, 232ff.; one must in fairness mention the warning voices concerning conducting the peace conference in an atmosphere of hate. See Moberly, *Christian Conduct in War Time*, 13; Sclater, *Eve of Battle*, 86; Henson, *War-Time Sermons*, 49; Maclennan, *Price of Blood*, 13; Clutton-Brock, *Are We To Punish Germany?*, 12-13; Davidson, *Testing of a Nation*, 180; Lenwood, *Chariots of Fire*, 5.
21. *Germany and Germans*, 16.
22. *What Is At Stake*, 3.
23. Willis, *England's Holy War*, 262.
24. *War Watchwords*, 81.
25. *England's Holy War*, 262.
26. Bell, *Randall Davidson*, 891.
27. *Last Crusade*, 240.
28. (Birmingham, 1915), vii.
29. *Chariots of Fire*, 15.
30. *Religion and the War*, 27-28.
31. *War and Its Issues*, 104.
32. *Sword of the Spirit*, xvi; see also Cairns, *Answer to Bernhardi*, 14; Paget, *In the Day of Battle*, 54, 140; Ryle, *Attitude of Church towards War*, 31; Winnington-Ingram, *Christ and the World at War* (Mathews), 58, 156.
33. *League of Nations*, 17.
34. Ibid., 43-44; see also Macnutt, *Reproach of War*, 40; Offer, *C*, XXXI (1917), 742; Ivens, *Sermons for Peace Celebrations*, 27; Snell, *Supreme Duty*, 15; Barry, *Religion and the War*, 34-36; Holland, *So as by Fire*, 107; Mackarness, *Faith and Duty*, 100.
35. "Quest of Christian Duty," 39.
36. *The Real War*, 10.
37. *Testing of a Nation*, 203.
38. *Faith and Duty*, 63.
39. *Christianity and War*, 14; see also Brent, *Commonwealth of Mankind*, 14.
40. *War Watchwords*, 65.
41. *End of It All*, 5.
42. *Decoration of the Cross*, 38.
43. *War-Time Sermons*, 105.
44. *Fight for the Future*, 17.
45. *Religion and the War*, 59.
46. "Quest of Christian Duty," 33.
47. *Delayed Victory*, 163, 172.

9

Afterword: Abusing Religion

The first casualty in a war, they say, is truth. This is especially true if the war is a holy war, an ideological struggle, a *Kulturkampf*, or "struggle between civilizations." When powers strive for mere territory the truth does not suffer as much as when they pose as vicars of righteousness, as representatives of God or absolute Truth. A holy war tempts people to demonize the enemy and call for his complete destruction. It makes peace talks sound like treason or the sin against the Holy Ghost. It makes rational diplomacy very difficult.

Nietzsche observed that bad music and bad arguments all seem to sound good in wartime; one might add to this list bad sermons, bad scripture selection, bad exegesis. Preachers are often embarrassed when they look back at their wartime sermons and wartime behavior. Charles L. Warr, Minister of Saint Giles Cathedral, Edinburgh, confessed:

The Church, to an unfortunate degree, had become an instrument of the State and in too many pulpits the preacher had assumed the role of a recruiting sergeant. Almost every place of worship throughout the length and breadth of the land displayed the Union Jack, generally placed above the Holy Table, while some had great shields carrying the flags of all the allied nations. The first thing I did myself when I went to St. Paul's was to have a huge Union Jack and the national flag of Scotland displayed upon the east wall of the chancel. Being young, and owing to the inflamed feelings of the times, I said many things from my pulpit during the first six months of my ministry that I deeply regret. It is no excuse to say that many preachers were doing the same thing. I still feel ashamed when I recall declaiming on one occasion—about the time of Haig's "Our backs are to the Wall" message—that anyone who talked of initiating peace negotiations with the rulers of Germany was a moral and spiritual leper who ought to be shunned and cut by every decent-minded and honest man! . . . This was the muddled, fuddled atmosphere we were living in during the last years of the war. Those people who had remained capable of calm dispassionate thinking had for years been under a dreadful strain. It is not easy at this length of time to appreciate how heavy the strain had been. To such the war had been a great shock, a great burden and a bitter humiliation.[1]

If we are ever to learn from this "muddled, fuddled" atmosphere of war, we need to review some of the myths, errors, and illusions that were proclaimed on both sides during the Great War.

MYTHS, ERRORS, AND ILLUSIONS

Both Germany and Britain saw each other through special filters. Both committed the fallacy of special pleading by selecting the features of the enemy they wished to debunk and ignoring many other features.

The Germans were blinded by three myths: race, religion, and the British empire. Any serious attempt to explain the war as a racial struggle was based on an illusion. Germans pictured the war as a struggle between Teutons and Slavs and thus berated England for betraying the white race by fighting in alliance with Gallic France, Slavic Russia, and Mongolian Japan. But Germany was allied with Asiatic Turkey and Slavic Bulgaria, so there must not have been anything inherently unworthy in Slavic and Oriental allies.

German churchmen blasted the British for betraying Protestantism by fighting with Roman Catholic France, Orthodox Russia, and Buddhist Japan, but Protestant Germany fought with Roman Catholic Austria-Hungary, Muslim Turkey, and Orthodox Bulgaria. The sad fact was that religion had long since ceased to be a determining factor in diplomatic and military alliances. As far back as the Thirty Years War, Catholic France sent money to Protestant Germany to fight Catholic Austria. One is reminded of the principle given by an Englishman to his inquiring son: "England has no eternal allies, only eternal interests."

The great myth that hoodwinked the Germans the most was the British empire, that immense Satanic fraud, based on imperialism, greed, and tyranny. They predicted it would collapse like a house of cards when war came. They said India would rise in revolt, Ireland would rush into civil war, the Boers would strike to avenge their recent defeat, Canada would remain neutral, and America would opt for German culture. None of these things happened. It is true that the British empire was not quite the happy family depicted by the Anglican divines, but neither was it the ramshackle league portrayed by the German clerics. It held together and played a crucial role in saving the mother country from defeat in 1918.

It was a bit too neat for the German preachers to beat their breasts in lamentation and talk about British hypocrisy and how it had been concealed until 1914. If hypocrisy were such a basic British trait it surely would have been discovered long before 1914. To say the British had tricked everyone since the empire started would be an embarrassing admission of one's own ignorance or naïveté. Trietschke had long berated the British for being tricky and hypocritical and getting people to fight their wars for them.

The British were not quite as blind as the Germans but they too were misled by some of their own abstractions, especially militarism and the unholy trinity. It was one thing to point to German militarism as a problem in the stability of Europe (it was), but it caused great confusion in the search for a more stable order to picture it as an abstract entity with a life and will of its own, uncontrolled by its creators. The Germans made a good point when they noted that British navalism was just a special form of militarism, adapted to the peculiar needs of an island nation. If the British had made a greater effort to understand German history they might have discovered why the Germans prized their land army as much as the British prized their navy.

British churchmen found a convenient scapegoat in the unholy trinity—Bernhardi, Nietzsche, and Treitschke. They exaggerated the extent to which these three thinkers dominated the intellectual life of the Second Reich. By demonizing the German enemy many Britons made a negotiated peace virtually impossible. Chaplain Studdert-Kennedy, for example, asserted blatantly that the cause of the war was "the calm untroubled rejection by a whole people of the Christian basis of civilization, and all ideas of international law."[2] Preachers like this should have recalled the sage advice of Edmund Burke: "I do not know the method of drawing up an indictment against a whole people."

As Willis argued, it probably would have turned out better for all concerned if all the powers had just agreed with George Bernard Shaw and said that the war was a balance-of-power struggle instead of a holy war.[3] That way we might have avoided the unfortunate "Khaki Election" of December, 1918, when the British electorate became obsessed with the idea of reparations. Edwyn Bevan admitted a grave error here on the part of the British.

England had a chance at the end of last year of splendid action which will perhaps never recur in our history. If our object was not so much to recoup ourselves for our material losses as to restore to its place in the moral fellowship of the world a nation which had gone astray after false gods, we might at that moment have done practically anything we liked with Germany. Instead of that, we were convulsively yelling to election candidates: "Make Germany pay," and whilst the German children were dying or becoming stunted in mind and body for want of food, we tightened our blockade. Is it the true God whom *we* follow?[4]

When opponents in a holy war struggle with each other, they usually absolutize the issues that separate them and finally end up uttering some ridiculous faulty dilemma. The Germans said the war was a matter of "world power or downfall," while the British insisted that the choice for the world in 1919 was "utopia or hell." the Germans got neither world power nor downfall and the British got neither utopia nor hell. But both would probably have gotten a better third alternative between the horns if they had not stated the choices in such stark unrealistic terms.

Both nations, to a degree, were misled by the charge of materialism and mechanism. The British accused the Germans of blindly following the teachings of Social Darwinism while the Germans accused the British of being a nation of petty shopkeepers. Both sides were wrong, because the differences between them on the matter of materialism were negligible. They were both modern, secular, industrial, affluent, hedonistic peoples—German idealism to the contrary notwithstanding. The British clergy seemed more aware of the fact that all European nations had been corrupted by materialism.

As for mechanism, it sounded like a convenient escape from responsibility to blame the war on this principle. It contradicted the emphasis on free will found in many sermons on theodicy. Just before he died, Kaiser William II said farewell to some British guests: "Come back and see me again next summer if you can." Then he added, "but you won't be able to because the machine is running away with *him* [Hitler] as it ran away with *me*."[5] This remark sounds wise but falls to pieces under historical analysis. As a matter of fact, neither world war was started with excessive military pressure on the ruler. Indeed, Hitler had to lash his army forward; the reluctance of the generals to unleash the dogs of war caused him to refer contemptuously to "mastiffs who had forgotten how to bite."

We recall that L. P. Jacks and Henri Bergson had blamed the war on mechanism, charging, of course, that the principle was stronger in Germany. Jacks claimed that the war broke out when the military machine reached a certain stage of development. But this is an untenable determinism. Human beings caused the Great War, not machines. Machines have no power by themselves to declare war or make peace. They simply do as they are told. They cannot operate without human direction. Man was responsible for the Great War.

THE DANGERS OF RELIGIOUS NATIONALISM

At the end of a study like this, the historian has a certain obligation to philosophize. By now it should be apparent that there are certain pitfalls to Christian nationalism, whether German or British. These pitfalls may conveniently be summarized under the heading of four "temptations."

First, religious nationalism tempts the patriot to forget the cardinal doctrine of the unity of the human race. The patriot becomes so busy extolling the virtues of his own particular people that he neglects the crucial truth that "all men are men." Saint Paul said that God made every nation of men from the same source (Acts 17:26). He told the Galatians that no ethnic distinctions could exist in the Body of Christ (Gal. 3:28). In the parable of the Good Samaritan Christ taught that a neighbor is anyone who needs our help, regardless of his nationality (Luke 15:11-32).

In 1537 Roman pontiff Paul III sent out an official statement reassuring European Christians about the status of natives they had encountered in the New World. He declared that only Satan would want anyone to believe that these people were animals, "dumb brutes created for our services." On the contrary, he asserted, "the Indians are truly men" and "they are not only capable of understanding the Catholic faith, but, according to our information, they desire exceedingly to receive it."[6] Perhaps such a statement needs to be issued at frequent intervals to counteract the centrifugal effects of uncritical nationalism.

Second, religious nationalism tempts the patriot to distort the scripture. In his zeal to encourage patriotism or stimulate a fighting spirit he rummages through the Bible irresponsibly, tearing passages from their contexts, wresting statements to the destruction of a sound hermeneutic.

There were many examples of this, on both sides, but surely the most egregious came from German clergymen, who infused most cardinal doctrines with German nationalism. As Pressel shows in his masterful study, grace became God's promise of national renewal; faith became trust in God's providential guidance of the German nation through history; the communion of the saints became the community of the *Volk*; God's covenant became a special bond with the German nation; law became obedience to national values; and sin became neglect of national duties.[7]

The most striking example was the misuse of the biblical doctrine of the Holy Spirit. In fact, one could argue that the abuse of this doctrine is the key to when nationalism goes wrong. Many German preachers made the Spirit into a *Volksgeist*, an impersonal entity that fills members of the *Volk*, rather than the divine person who unites all believers, regardless of nationality (1 Cor. 12:13). Making the Holy Spirit into a *Volksgeist* was a gross distortion of biblical teaching.[8]

Third, religious nationalism tempts the patriot to see his nation's history as *Heilsgeschichte*, as a sacred story of God's guidance and blessing on a chosen people. As noted many times in this study, both the British and the Germans felt that God had prepared their nation for a great mission in world history. There is nothing necessarily wrong in this view, since the Bible clearly teaches that God prepares and uses nations in history to bring about his plans (Dan. 4:32; Acts 17:26; Ex. 9:16; Rom. 9:17). The belief becomes wrong when the person preaching it loses his perspective and concludes that God's use justifies anything the nation might want to do. This was the mistake made by the Briton who quipped, "God has given us the British Empire so let us enjoy it!" The fact that God has developed a nation in history to accomplish a certain task does not mean that he excuses its sins; God used the Assyrians for a special job and then destroyed them because of their sins (Isa. 10:12).

German pastors in the Franco-Prussian War and the First World War engaged in a dangerous eulogy of militarism. They claimed it was a gift of God to the German people, a divine instrument to protect the true gospel, the Protestant faith. Maybe so, maybe not. But Ludendorff and Hitler used that same army to conquer Europe. Did God intend the first use of the army but not the second? One must be very careful in identifying any movement in history as necessarily the revelation of God. The great mistake of the religious patriot is to uncritically identify anything that promotes the national interest as the will of God.

A few preachers on both sides (too few!) issued this warning in the Great War but it was probably lost on most Christians. Wace's words bear repeating to every generation: "If God has given us wealth, and strength, and prosperity, and imperial power, we may be sure it is in order that we may be His instruments for the spread of the kingdom, for bringing the knowledge of Christ and of Christ's salvation to the ends of the earth. . . . Do not let us suppose that there is any other object whatever in God's dispensations."[9]

Finally, religious nationalism tempts the patriot to overlook the faults of his government and his nation. Religious patriotism tends to destroy that critical distance the Christian should keep from the powers that be. Many Christians attempt to whitewash everything their government does, especially if it claims to rule in the interests of the church or of morality and is fighting an "evil" opponent.

It has been said that Christianity's main contribution to western political thought was the doctrine of the two cities—the city of God and the city of man. Christian theology relates man not only to an earthly commonwealth but also to an eternal end, a transcendent commonwealth. Christianity thus broke open the one-world view of the classical world with its incipient totalitarianism. By belonging to a city above all earthly commonwealths, man cannot be reduced to a mere citizen of an earthly state. "In Christian political theory," writes Ramsey, "the mere fact that a man is a citizen elsewhere keeps him from being only a citizen here. By distinguishing two cities, Christianity corrected the implicit absolutism of loyalty to earthly kingdoms."[10]

It is here that we see the dangers of pantheism or immanentialism, the theology that blurs the distinction between the two cities. By making historical process the locus of God's revelation and by identifying the human culture as the Kingdom of God, immanental theology practically erases the distinction between the two cities. If the doctrine of the two cities was a safeguard against totalitarianism, then we may consider immanentalism as an invitation to its resurgence. Not surprisingly, some of the strongest statements of immanentalism come from religious spokesmen of the Third Reich.[11]

The Christian patriot will not likely deify any mundane commonwealth if he will remember the doctrine of the two cities and a verse from Saint Paul: "Our citizenship is in heaven. And we eagerly await a Savior from there, the Lord Jesus Christ" (Phil. 3:20).

A FINAL WORD ON GERMANY

The Great War and its aftermath helped bring the Third Reich into being. Was there a causal connection between the German Christian nationalism of 1914-18 and Nazi ideology? Yes, to a certain extent. We are not saying that the pastors of World War I would have all voted for Hitler or implemented the Final Solution. We are simply saying that some key religious ideas of the war helped create a climate of opinion that made the Third Reich possible. One could develop a case for the thesis that the first "German Christians" were not the pro-Nazi Protestants of the Third Reich but the religious patriots of the Great War.

In the main, German Protestant churchmen were just too eager to blend nationalism and Christianity, to harmonize kaiser and Christ. They almost destroyed the universal, international quality of the Gospel by constantly affirming the uniqueness of the *Volk* with its peculiar *Volksgeist*. Most of them claimed to be true to the reformed faith, but as Hammer remarks, "These arbitrary and romantic combinations of German and Christian, Platonic and idealistic ideas could hardly make the claim to even half way reproduce the biblical and Reformed faith."[12] Saint Paul and Saint Augustine and Martin Luther would have had great difficulty in finding the Gospel they preached in the "Gospel of Nationalism."

As noted earlier, a strong element in the German mind was the principle of idealism, the belief in *Geist* and its superiority over mass, matter, and numbers. German pastors carried this principle to an absurd extreme. Even Christ warned that one had to consider the physical factors that might frustrate the exertions of the will: "What king, going to encounter another king in war, will not sit down and take counsel whether he is able with ten thousand to meet him who comes against him with twenty thousand?" (Luke 14:31). There will always be a grain of truth in Napoleon's quip that "God is on the side of the strongest batallions."

Once the Great War bogged down in the trenches, any objective observer should have been able to discern that it was becoming a war of attrition, the kind of struggle that Germany, outnumbered as she was, could not win. That would have been an ideal (!) time for a strong attack of realism, but the German intellectuals, among them the Protestant churchmen, clung to the steady message of idealism—spirit is more potent than matter, willpower can defeat all opponents, all things are possible to the obstinate. The German people discovered too late that when the British blockade kept out food, that they could not eat sermons and ideals. They had been misled by their spiritual leaders. But the idealists did not repent; when Hitler took on the Soviet Union in 1941 he was illustrating the same naïve idealism.

It is but a short step from the romantic-religious nationalism of the Great War to the volkish-romantic Pangermanism of the Third Reich. All you need to do is add racism and deepen the immanental thrust of the theology until you have God revealing himself directly through national events like the movement of National Socialism.[13] God had already revealed himself in August 4, 1914, had he not? God made all the nations radically different and charged them to cultivate their diversity, did he not? With all these doctrines you can easily prepare a people to accept *Gleichschaltung*, or "coordination." People already had a firm notion of the national essence, backed up with theological sanctions; all you need to do is add blood and race to define the *Volk* and you are close to Nazi racism.

Such a view fosters a spirit of intolerance. It implies that pluralism is a sin against God, that a nation must be monolithic culturally. If a certain group does not fit the national "style" then it must be removed, because it is *gemeinschaftsfremd*—"community strange." German Christian war theology played right into the hands of radical nationalists when it put God behind such an ethnic monism.

German Christian nationalism was at the crossroads in 1919. Defeat should have destroyed the war theology of the religious patriots but it did not. Most of them joined the unrepentant patriots in pushing the stab-in-the-back legend, which said that Germany lost the war on the home front, not the battlefield. The Christian church could have helped to shepherd the nation through this crisis and point it in a direction that would have led to sanity, moderation, and recovery, but it did not. It was a fateful missed opportunity.

To speak candidly, by the twentieth century German nationalism had become a menace to civilization. It was born in the Napoleonic era and carried the birthmark of romanticism from then on. It matured in that strange period called the Second Reich with its sundry illusions about racism, imperialism, eugenics, and Social Darwinism. In its first century, it picked up some rather unpleasant traits. By 1914 it was narrow, petty, racist, arrogant, immature, hypersensitive, paranoid, and resentful. In other words—sick. The Christian clergy gave a religious justification, a theological underpinning, to a sick nationalism.

Let us hope the church, in all nations, has learned a lesson. Christian clergymen should be careful never to give unconditional support to *any* nationalism, but certainly not to a sick nationalism.

NOTES

1. *The Glimmering Landscape* (London, 1960), 118-19.
2. *Rough Talks*, 58.
3. *England's Holy War*, 177.
4. "The Problem of the New Germany," *CQR*, LXXXVIII (July, 1919), 270.
5. Cowles, *The Kaiser*, 428.
6. Lewis Hanke, *The Spanish Struggle for Justice in the Conquest of America* (Boston, 1965), 72.
7. *Kriegspredigt, passim.*
8. See Marsch, "Politische Predigt zum Kriegsbeginn," 529. This abuse of the Holy Spirit occurred also in the War of Liberation and the Franco-Prussian War. See Hoover, *Gospel of Nationalism*, 75ff.
9. *War and the Gospel*, 167.
10. *War and the Christian Conscience*, xxi.
11. For example, the first article of the creed for the radical German Christians affirmed: "In Hitler, Christ, God, the Helper and Redeemer, has become mighty amongst us." See A. L. Drummond, *German Protestantism Since Luther* (London, 1951), 164-65.

12. *Kriegstheologie*, 157.

13. Brakelmann shows this development in regard to Seeberg in his *Kriegstheologie*, 105. See also Marsch, "Politische Predigt zum Kriegsbeginn," 534.

Bibliography

PRIMARY SOURCES: BRITISH

Adams, W. G. S. *International Control*. London: Oxford University Press, 1915.

Allison, J. M. *Raemaeker's Cartoon History of the War*. London: John Lane, 1919.

An Appeal to Christians. N. p., May 20, 1916.

Anglicanus. *The Problem of Evil*. London: Stock, 1916.

Archer, Williams. *501 Gems of German Thought*. London: N. p., 1917.

Ballard, Frank. *Britain Justified: The War from the Christian Standpoint*. London: Kelley, 1914.

_____. *The Mistakes of Pacifism or Why a Christian Can Have Anything to Do With War*. London: Kelley, 1915.

_____. *Plain Truth versus German Lies*. London: Kelley, 1915.

Barry, F. R. *Religion and the War*. London: Methuen, 1915.

Beck, James. *Germany's Case Tried in Court*. London: N. p., 1916.

Bedier, Joseph. *German Atrocities from German Evidence*. Trans. Bernhard Harrison. Paris: N. p., n.d.

Begbie, Harold. *On the Side of the Angels*. London: N. p., 1915.

Bennet, W. *England's Mission*. London: Oxford University Press, n.d.

Bergson, Henri. *The Meaning of the War: Life and Matter in Conflict*. London: Unwin, 1915.

Bernard, John Henry. *In War Time*. London: Mowbray, 1917.

Bevan, Edwyn. *Brothers All: The War and the Race Question*. London: Oxford University Press, 1914.

Black, James. *Around the Guns: Sundays in Camp*. London: Clarke, 1915.

Blackburne, Harry. *This Also Happened on the Western Front: The Padre's Story*. London: N. p., 1932.

Brent, C. H. *The Commonwealth of Mankind*. London: Mowbray, 1917.

Brown, William A. *The Allies of Faith*. Oxford: Blackwell, 1914.

Bruce, Rosslyn. *God and the Allies: A View of the Grande Entente*. Birmingham: N. p., 1915.

Bull, Paul. *Christianity and War: An Appeal to Conscientious Objectors.* London: SPCK (Society for Propagation of Christian Knowledge), 1918.

_____. *Peace and War: Notes of Sermons and Addresses.* London: N. p., 1917.

Burne, C. S. *"Might Makes Right?" The New Gospel of Germany.* London: N. p., 1914.

Burroughs, E. A. *The End of It All: Thoughts on War Aims and Their Attainment.* London: N. p., 1918.

_____. *The Eternal Goal: Three Letters to the Times on the Spiritual Issues of the Present Situation.* London: Longmans, 1915.

_____. *A Faith for the Firing Line.* London: Nisbet, 1915.

_____. *The Fight for the Future.* London: Nisbet, 1916.

_____. *The Patience of God: Some Thoughts in Preparation for the National Mission of Repentance and Hope.* London: Longmans, 1916.

_____. *The Valley of Decision: A Plea for Wholeness in Thought and Life.* London: N. p., 1916.

Bury, Herbert. *Here and There in the War Area.* London: N. p., 1916.

Cairns, D. S. *An Answer to Bernhardi.* London: Oxford University Press, 1914.

Call of the War to the Clergy. London: N. p., 1916.

Carnegie, W. H. *Sermons on Subjects Suggested by the War.* London: Macmillan, 1915.

Carpenter, J. E. (ed.). *Ethical and Religious Problems of the War: Fourteen Addresses.* London: Lindsey, 1916.

Chesterton, Cecil. *The Prussian Hath Said in His Heart.* London: N. p., 1914.

Chesterton, G. K. *The Barbarism of Berlin.* London: N. p., 1914.

_____. *The Crimes of England.* London: N. p., 1915.

Chirol, Valentine. *Germany and the Fear of Russia.* London: Oxford University Press, 1914.

Clarke, C. H. *The Ravings of a Renegade: Being the War Essays of H. S. Chamberlain.* London: N. p., 1915.

Clifford, John. *The War and the Churches.* London: Clarke, 1914.

Clutton-Brock. *Are We to Punish Germany, If We Can?* London: Oxford University Press, 1915.

_____. *Bernhardism in England.* London: Oxford University Press, 1915.

_____. *The Cure for War.* London: Oxford University Press, 1915.

Cook, Edward. *Why Britain Is at War: The Causes and the Issues.* London: Macmillan, 1914.

Cook, T. A., ed. *The Crimes of Germany.* London: N. p., n.d.

_____. *Kaiser, Krupp and Culture.* London: Murray, 1915.

Coulton, G. G. *Pacifist Illusions: A Criticism of the Union of Democratic Control.* Cambridge: Bowes, 1915.

Crafer, T. W. *A Prophet's Vision and the War.* London: Skeffington, 1916.

_____. *Soldiers of Holy Writ.* London: Skeffington, 1915.

Cram, Ralph A. *The Significance of the Great War.* Boston: Victorian Club, 1914.

Cramb, J. A. *Germany and England.* London: Murray, 1914.

Davidson, Randall T. *Quit You Like Men! Sermons in Time of War.* London: SPCK, 1915.

_____. *The Testing of a Nation.* London: Macmillan, 1919.

Dawson, Joseph. *Christ and the Sword: Words for the War-Perplexed.* London: Kelley, 1916.

Dearmer, Percy. *Patriotism*. London: Oxford University Press, 1915.

Denison, Henry P. *Some Spiritual Lessons of the War: Five Sermons*. London: Scott, 1915.

Drawbridge, C. L. *The War and Religious Ideals*. London: N. p., 1915.

Drummond, William H. *The Soul of the Nation: Essays on Religion, Patriotism, and National Duty*. London: Lindsey, 1917.

Dudden, F. Holmes. *The Delayed Victory and Other Sermons*. London: Longmans, 1918.

_____. *The Problem of Human Suffering and the War*. London: Longmans, 1919.

Durkheim, Emile. *"Germany Above All"*: *The German Mental Attitude and the War*. Paris: N. p., 1915.

Ethics of War. Ramsgate: N. p., 1915.

Faith and War: Guidance and Comfort for Anxious Times from Great Preachers. London: Smith, 1916.

Fisher, H. A. L. *The War: Its Causes and Issues*. London: Longmans, 1914.

Forbes, Avary H. *Salvation by Science*. London: N. p., n.d.

Formby, C. Wykeham. *Why Did God Allow the War?* London: Gardner, 1917.

Forsyth, P. T. *The Justification of God: Lectures for War-Time on a Christian Theodicy*. London: N. p., 1916.

Fry, Joan M. (ed.). *Christ and Peace: A Discussion of Some Fundamental Issues Raised by the War*. London: Headley, 1915.

"G". *The End Is Not Yet: Five War Sermons by "G"*. London: Hunter and Longhurst, 1914.

Germany's Two Gospels: Being an Answer to the Appeal of the German Evangelicals. London: Buck and Wootoon, n.d.

Gore, Charles. *Crisis in Church and Nation*. London: Mowbray, 1916.

_____. *The League of Nations: The Opportunity of the Church*. London: Hodder and Stoughton, 1919.

_____. *Patriotism in the Bible*. London: Mowbray, 1915.

_____. *The War and the Church and Other Addresses*. London: Mowbray, 1914.

Gough, A. W. *God's Strong People*. London: N. p., 1915.

Gray, A. Herbert. *The Only Alternative to War*. London: Oxford University Press, 1914.

_____. *The War Spirit in our National Life*. London: Oxford University Press, 1914.

Handcock, John. *God's Dealings with the British Empire*. Cambridge: Deighton, 1916.

Hankey, Donald. *The Beloved Captain: Selected Chapters from "A Student in Arms."* London: Melrose, 1917.

Harrison, Austin. *The Kaiser's War*. London: Allen and Unwin, 1914.

Headlam, James W. *England, Germany, and Europe*. London: Macmillan, 1914.

Henson, H. H. *War-Time Sermons*. London: Macmillan, 1915.

Hogg, A. G. *Christianity and Force*. London: Oxford University Press, 1915.

Holland, Henry S. *So as by Fire: Notes on the War*. 2 vols. London: Wells, 1915-16.

Holmes, E. E. *The Colours of the King: Red, White, and Blue*. London: Longmans, 1914.

Hope, Anthony. *The New (German) Testament*. London: N. p., 1914.

Hubbard, Elbert. *Who Lifted the Lid off of Hell?* N. p., 1914.

Hudson, William. *Wilhelm and His God and Other War Sonnets.* London: N. p., n.d.

Hunt, W. H. *Two Plain Sermons on the European War.* London: Skeffington, 1914.

Image, Selwyn. *Art, Morals, and the War.* London: Oxford University Press, 1914.

Ivens, C. L. *Intercession During: Two Plain Sermons.* London: Skeffington, 1914.

Jones, Dennis. *The Diary of a Padre.* Manchester: N. p., n.d.

Kaiser or Christ? The War and Its Issues. London: Clarke, n.d.

Kelman, John. *Salted with Fire.* London: Hodder and Stoughton, 1915.

_____. *The War and Preaching.* London: Hodder and Stoughton, 1919.

Lang, Cosmo G. *The Church and the Clergy at This Time of War.* London, 1916.

Lenwood, Frank. *Chariots of Fire.* London: Oxford University Press, 1915.

_____. *Pharisaism and War.* London: Oxford University Press, 1915.

Leonard, George H. *Love Came Down at Christmas.* London: Oxford University Press, 1914.

Lyttelton, Edward. *Britain's Duty To-day.* London: N. p., n.d.

_____. *What Are We Fighting For?* London: Longmans, 1914.

Mackarness, Charles C. *Faith and Duty in Time of War.* London: Mowbray, 1916.

Maclean, Norman. *God and the Soldier.* London: Hodder and Stoughton, 1917.

Maclennan, Kenneth. *The Price of Blood.* London: Oxford University Press, 1915.

Macnutt, Frederic B. *The Reproach of War: Addresses Given in St. Saviour's Cathedral, Southwark.* London: Scott, 1914.

Mathews, Basil, ed. *Christ and the World at War: Sermons Preached in War-Time.* London: Clarke, 1916.

_____. *Three Years' War for Peace.* London: Hodder and Stoughton, 1917.

McCurdy, C. A. *Freedom's Call and Duty.* London: Smith, 1918.

McDougall, Eleanor. *Germany and the Germans.* London: Oxford University Press, 1915.

McEntyre, John E. *The Christian's Perplexity: Christ and the War.* London: N. p., 1915.

Mellor, Stanley. *Which Gospel Do You Accept?* Liverpool: N. p., 1914.

M'Fadyen, John E. *The Bible and the War.* London: N. p., 1916.

Millard, F. L. H. *Short War Sermons for Good Friday and Easter.* London: Skeffington, 1916.

Mitchell, P. Chalmers. *Evolution and the War.* London: Murray, 1915.

Moberly, W. H. *Christian Conduct in War Time.* London: Oxford University Press, 1914.

Morgan, G. Campbell. *God, Humanity and the War.* London: Clarke, 1915.

Moulton, James H. *British and German Scholarship.* London: Oxford University Press, 1915.

Mozley, J. B. *War: A Sermon Preached Before the University of Oxford.* London: Longmans, 1915.

Muir, John. *War and Christian Duty.* Paisley: Gardner, 1916.

Murray, Marr. *The Christian's War Book.* London: Hodder and Stoughton, 1914.

Mursell, Walter A. *The Bruising of Belgium.* Paisley: Gardner, 1915.

Newton, Joseph F. *The Sword of the Spirit: Britain and America in the Great War.* London: Nisbet, 1918.

Oldham, J. H. *The Church the Hope of the Future.* London: Oxford University Press, 1915.

_____. *The Decisive Hour: Is it Lost?* London: Oxford University Press, 1914.

Oman, John. *The War and Its Issues: An Attempt at a Christian Judgment.* Cambridge: University Press, 1915.

Orchard, W. E. *The Real War.* London: Oxford University Press, 1914.

Paganism or Christ? Letchworth: Garden City Press, 1915.

Paget, H. L. *In the Day of Battle.* London: Longmans, 1915.

Paterson-Smyth, J. *God and the War: Some Lessons of the Present Crisis.* London: Hodder and Stoughton, 1915.

_____. *The Men Who Died in Battle.* London: Hodder and Stoughton, 1915.

Patten, John A. *The Decoration of the Cross and Other Papers from France.* London: Clarke, 1918.

Plowden-Wardlaw, James. *The Test of War: War Addresses Given at Cambridge.* London: Scott, 1916.

Potter, J. Hasloch. *The Discipline of War.* London: Skeffington, 1915.

_____. *The Judgment of War.* London: Skeffington, 1915.

Preston, E. A. *War and the Task of the Church.* London: N. p., 1914.

Raleigh, Walter. *The War of Ideas.* Oxford: Clarendon, 1917.

Removing of Mountains. London: Oxford University Press, 1915.

Renshaw, W. Heaton. *Christ and the War: Very Simple Talks.* London: Allen and Unwin, 1916.

Roberts, Richard. *Are We Worth Fighting For?* London: Oxford University Press, 1914.

Robinson, J. Armitage. *Holy Ground: Sermons Preached in Time of War.* London: Macmillan, 1914.

Ryle, Herbert E. *The Attitude of the Church towards War.* London: Longmans, 1915.

Sanday, William. *The Deeper Causes of the War.* London: Oxford University Press, 1914.

_____. *The Meaning of the War for Germany and Great Britain: An Attempt at Synthesis.* Oxford: Clarendon, 1915.

Sclater, J. R. P. *The Eve of Battle: Addresses at Church Parade.* London: Hodder and Stoughton, 1915.

Selbig, W. B. *The War and Theology.* London: Oxford University Press, 1915.

Sermons for the Peace Celebrations by Various Writers. London: Skeffington, 1919.

Seton-Watson, R. W. *What Is at Stake in the War.* London: Oxford University Press, 1915.

Sinker, John. *The War, Its Deeds and Lessons.* London: Skeffington, 1916.

Smith, A. L. *The Christian Attitude to War.* London: Oxford University Press, 1915.

Smith, George Adam. *The War, the Nation, and the Church.* London: Hodder and Stoughton, 1916.

Smuts, Jan Christian. *The British Commonwealth of Nations.* London: Hodder and Stoughton, 1917.

Snell, Barnard J. *How Are We to Love Our Enemies?* London: N. p., 1915.

_____. *The Supreme Duty of Us Englishmen.* London: N. p., 1917.

Solano, E. J. *The Pacifist Lie: A Book for Sailors and Soldiers.* London: N. p., 1918.

Streeter, B. H. *War, This War and the Sermon on the Mount.* London: Oxford University Press, 1915.

Studdert-Kennedy, G. A. *Rough Talks by a Padre.* London: Hodder and Stoughton, n.d.

"Temporary Chaplain." *The Padre*. London: N. p., n.d.

Temple, William. *Christianity and War*. London: Oxford University Press, 1914.

_____. *Church and Nation*. London: Macmillan, 1915.

_____. *Our Need for a Catholic Church*. London: Oxford University Press, 1915.

Thomas, J. M. Floyd. *The Immorality of Non-Resistance*. Birmingham: Cornish Brothers, 1915.

Thompson, Alex M. *Prussia's Devilish Creed*. London: Clarion, n.d.

Thomson, J. Arthur. *Biology and War*. London: Oxford University Press, 1915.

To the Christian Scholars of Europe and America: A Reply from Oxford to the German Address to Evangelical Christians. London: Oxford University Press, 1914.

Ussher, R. *Christianity and the War*. Buckingham: Walford, n.d.

Velimirovic, Nicolai. *The Religious Spirit of the Slavs*. London: Macmillan, 1916.

Wace, Henry. *The War and the Gospel: Sermons and Addresses during the Present War*. London: Thynne, 1917.

Walters, E. W. *The Souls of the Brave*. London: Kelley, 1916.

Ward. *Thoughts in War Time*. London: Catholic Truth Society, 1915.

Warr, Charles L. *The Glimmering Landscape*. London: N. p., 1960.

Weston, Frank. *The Black Slaves of Prussia: An Open Letter Addressed to General Smuts*. London: N. p., 1918.

Whittingham, George N. *Who Is to Blame?* London: Richards, 1916.

Winnington-Ingram, Arthur F. W. *The Church in Time of War*. London: Wells, 1915.

_____. *A Day of God: Being Five Addresses on the Subject of the Present War*. London: Wells, 1914.

_____. *Drinking the Cup*. London: Wells, 1914.

_____. *The Potter and the Clay*. London: Wells, 1917.

_____. *Victory and After*. London: Wells, 1919.

Winton, E. *The Spiritual Sanctions of a League of Nations*. London: Oxford University Press, 1919.

_____. *The Visions of Youth*. London: Oxford University Press, 1915.

Witness of the Church in the Present Crisis. London: Oxford University Press, 1914.

Woodford, J. J. *Divine Providence and War: A Sermon*. London: New Church Press, 1916.

Woods, F. T. *War Watchwords from Bradford Parish Church*. Leeds: Jackson, 1914.

Woods, H. G. *Christianity and War: Preached at the Temple Church*. London: Scott, 1916.

_____. *The Two Swords*. Birmingham: Cornish Brothers, 1916.

Worsey, F. W. *Under the War-Cloud*. London: Skeffington, 1914.

_____. *War and the Easter Hope: Four Addresses*. London: Skeffington, 1915.

PRIMARY SOURCES: GERMAN

Althaus-Göttingen, Paul. *Kommt, lasst uns anbeten! Acht Kreigspredigten in Russisch-Polen*. Berlin: Vaterlandischen Verlag, 1915.

Aner, Karl. *Hammer oder Kreuz? Eine Abwehr alldeutscher Denkart im Namen des deutschen Christentums*. Jena: Diederichs, 1917.

_____. *Kriegsbilder aus der Bibel*. Berlin: Curtius, n.d.

Arper, Karl. *Agende für Kriegszeiten*. Göttingen: Vandenhoeck and Ruprecht, 1915.

Axenfeld, Karl. *Germany's Battle for the Freedom of the Christian Missions.* Berlin-Steglitz, 1919.

_____. *Unter Gottes gewaltiger Hand. Gedanken über das Erlebnis der deutschen Mission im Weltkrieg.* Berlin, 1917.

Bauke, Hermann. *Im deutschen Lüttich: Vier Reden.* Berlin: Warneck, 1916.

Bendix, Reinhard. *Max Weber: An Intellectual Portrait.* New York: Doubleday, 1960.

Besier, Gerhard. *Die protestantischen Kirchen Europas im Ersten Weltkrieg.* Göttingen: Vandenhoeck and Ruprecht, 1984.

Bezzel, Hermann von. *Sendlinger Predigten: Eine Auswahl Predigten aus den Jahren 1914 bis 1916.* 2 vols. Munich: Müller and Fröhligh, 1919.

Blume, Wilhelm von. *Der deutsche Militarismus.* Tübingen: Kloeres, 1915.

Blumhardt, Christoph. *Gottes Reich kommt! Predigten und Andachten aus den Jahren 1907 bis 1917.* Erlenback-Zürich: Rotapfel, 1932.

Bonne, Georg. *Unser Helden fallen sterben aber nicht!* Munich: Reinhardt, 1918.

Brauns, Heinrich. *Der gerechte Krieg.* Kempten-Munich, 1915.

Broecker, D. von. *Der Erlöser Israels.* Hamburg: Rauhen Haus, 1914.

_____. *Habt Glauben an Gott.* Hamburg: Rauhen Haus, 1914.

Buchholz. *Glaube ist Kraft!* Stuttgart: N. p., 1917.

Buder, Walther. *In Gottes Heerdienst: Fünfzehn Feldpredigten 1917-1918.* Stuttgart: Steinkopf, 1918.

Bürckstümmer, Christian. *Ein feste Burg ist unser Gott: Sammlung von Kriegspredigten.* Munich: Beck, 1915.

Conrad. *Festhalten bis ans Ende: Andachten für die Kriegszeit.* Berlin: Warneck, 1916.

Cordes, D. *Kriegsbrot: Predigten und Ansprachen aus dem ersten Kriegsjahr August 1914 bis Juli 1915.* Leipzig: Eger, 1916.

Deissmann, Adolf. *Deutscher Schwertsegen: Kräfte der Heimat fürs reisige Heer.* Stuttgart and Berlin: Deutsche Verlags-Anstalt, 1915.

_____. *Innerest Aufgebot: Deutsche Worte im Weltkrieg.* Berlin: Scherl, 1915.

Deutsche Theologen über den Krieg—Stimmen aus schwerer Zeit. Ed. Wilhelm Laible. Leipzig, 1915.

Dibelius, Otto. *Gottes Ruf in Deutschlands Schicksalstunde.* Berlin-Lichterfelde: Runge, 1915.

Dieterich, Reinhold. *Gott mit uns: Zwölf Predigten und Ansprachen aus den Kriegsmonaten August, September, und Oktober 1914.* Ulm: Kerler, 1914.

Doehring, Bruno. *Ein feste Burg: Predigten und Reden aus eherner Zeit. Zum Bester der Nationalstiftung für die Hinterbliebenen der im Kriege Gefallenen.* 2 vols. Berlin: Hobbing, n.d.

_____. *Gott und wir Deutsche: Gedanken zur Gegenwart.* Berlin: Zillessen, 1916.

_____. *Gott und wir Deutsche: Gedanker zur Gegenwart: Neue Folge.* Berlin: Zillessen, 1917.

_____. *Ihr habt nicht gewollt.* Berlin: Zillessen, 1919.

_____. *Und wenn die Welt voll Teufel wär!* Berlin: Zillessen, 1916.

Dryander, Ernst. *Evangelische Reden in schwerer Zeit.* 24 vols. Berlin: Mittler, 1915-21.

Dunkmann, Karl. *Der Katechismus des Feldgrauen.* Vilna: Verlag Armeezeitung, 1916.

Dunkmann-Greifswald, D. *Krieg und Weltanschauung.* Dresden: Ungelenk, 1914.

Eck, Samuel. *Wir glauben, darum bleiben wir.* Giessen, 1914.

Eger, Karl. *Sechs Predigten aus dem ersten Kriegsjahre.* Halle: Niemeyer, 1915.

Eissfeldt, Otto. *Krieg und Bibel.* Tübingen: Mohr, 1915.

Evers, Edwin. *1870 und 1914: Gedanken und Erinnerungen eines Kriegesveteranen von 1870.* Berlin: N. p., n.d.

Faulhaber, Michael von. *Das Schwert des Geistes: Feldpredigten im Weltkrieg.* Freiburg/Breisgau: Herder, 1917.

Findet uns gross die grosse Zeit? Sechs Predigten und Ansprachen gehalten in Leipzig im September 1914. Leipzig: Eger, 1914.

Foerster, Erich. *Heldentod—Seliger Tod!* Heidelberg: Evangelischer Verlag, 1914.

Füllkrug, Gerhard. *Unter Christi Fahnen: Fünfzehn Kriegspredigten aus Kleinstand und Grosstadt.* Schwerin: Bahn, 1916.

Gerecke, K. *Wir Deutschen im Kampfe um die Ideale.* Braunschweig: Wollermann, 1916.

Geyer, Christian. *Die Stimme des Christus im Krieg: Predigten aus dem dritten Kriegsjahr.* Munich: Kaiser, 1917.

Glage-Hamburg, Max. *Der Krieg und der Christ: Glaubensworte in ernster Zeit.* Hamburg: Rauhen Haus, 1914.

Gott strafe England! Munich: Simplicissimus, n.d.

Gottes Frage an unser deutschen Volk. Stuttgart: N. p., 1915.

Guertler, Martin. *Gott unser Schutz! Den Feinden Trutz! Kriegspredigten und Kriegslieder.* Marienburg: Grossnich, 1914.

Haecker, Johannes. *Von Krieg und Kreuz und Ewigkeit! Predigten.* Berlin-Lichterfelde: Runge, 1915.

Haering, D. *Drei Predigten aus ernster Zeit.* Stuttgart: Steinkopf, 1918.

Hättenschwiller, Otto. *Aus blutgetränkter Erde: 300 Kriegsbeispiele für Prediger, Kathecheten und Erzieher.* Regensburg: Pustet, 1916.

Haller, J. *Warum und wofür wir kämpfen.* Tübingen: Kloeres, 1914.

Harnack, Adolf von. *Aus der Friedens- und Kriegsarbeit: Reden und Aufsätze.* Vol. 3, new edition. Giessen: Töpelmann, 1916.

_____. *Erforschtes und Erlebtes: Reden und Aufsätze.* Vol. 4, new edition. Giessen: Töpelmann, 1923.

Hasse, Else. *Der grosse Krieg und die deutsche Seele.* Munich: Kösel, 1917.

Hennig, Martin. *Fromm und Deutsch.* Hamburg: Rauhen Haus, n.d.

Hilbert, Gerhard. *Krieg und Kreuz: Zwei Vorträge.* Schwerin: Bahn, 1915.

_____. *Weltkrieg und Gottes Weltregierung.* Schwerin: Bahn, 1916.

Hintze, Otto. *Die englischen Weltherrschaftspläne und der gegenwärtige Krieg.* Berlin, 1915.

_____. *Deutschland und der Weltkrieg.* Leipzig and Berlin: Teubner, 1915.

Hoberg, Gottfried. *Der Krieg Deutschlands gegen Frankreich und die katolische Religion.* Freiburg/Breisgau: Herder, 1915.

Horn. *Gott—unser Zuflucht.* N.p., n.d.

_____. *Heiligen Zorn!* N.p., n.d.

_____. *Im Zeichen des Kreuzes.* N.p., n.d.

Hüssel, L. *Der Tod kein Ende.* Wiesbaden: Abigt, n.d.

Humburg, P. *Drei Kriegsandachten gehalten in der Neuen reformierten Kirche zu Elberfeld im September 1914.* Cassel: N.p., n.d.

Ihmels, Ludwig. *Aufwärts die Herzen: 21 Predigten aus dem Kirchenjahr 1915/16.* Leipzig: Hinrichs, 1918.

_____. *Darum auch wir: 7 Predigten während der Kriegszeit*. Leipzig: Hinrichs, 1914.

_____. *Das Evangelium von Jesus Christus in schwerer Zeit*. Leipzig: Hinrichs, 1916.

Jaeger, Paul. *Kreigs-Pfingsten 1915*. Heidelberg: Evangelischer Verlag, 1915.

Kattenbusch, F. *Über Feindesliebe im Sinne des Christentums*. Gotha: Perthes, 1916.

Keller, Samuel. *Ist Gott Neutral?* Freiburg/Breisgau: Momber, n.d.

Kern, P. *Warum dieser Weltkrieg? Die Antwort der Bibel auf diese Frage*. Zwickau, 1916.

Kessler, J. *Durch Gott zum Sieg*. Dresden: Ungelenk, 1914.

_____. *Furchtlos und Treu*. Dresden: Ungelenk, 1914.

_____. *Unser Glaube ist Sieg*. Dresden: Ungelenk, 1915.

Kirchner, P. *Kriegszweifel*. Kaiserlautern: N.p., n.d.

Kirmss, Paul. *Fürchte dich nicht, denn ich bin mit dir*. Berlin: N.p., 1915.

_____. *Eine gute Wehr und Waffen*. Berlin: N.p., 1915.

_____. *Kriegspredigten*. Berlin: N.p., 1914.

_____. *Das Reich muss uns doch bleiben*. Berlin: N.p., 1916.

Kirn, Bernhard. *Acht Dorf-Kriegspredigten*. Reutlingen: Ensslin and Laiblin, n.d.

Klein, Paul. *Du bist mein Hammer meine Kriegswaffe*. Mannheim: Hahn, 1914.

Koehler, Franz. *Die deutsch-protestantische Kriegspredigt der Gegenwart dargestellt in ihren religiös-sittlichen Problemen und in ihrer homiletischen Eigenart*. Giessen: Töpelmann, 1915.

König, Karl. *Kriegspredigten*. Jena: Diederichs, 1915.

_____. *Neue Kriegspredigten*. Jena: Diederichs, 1915.

_____. *Staat und Kirche: Der Deutsche Weg zur Zukunft*. Jena: Diederichs, 1912.

Kramer. *Patriotische sowie Kriegs- und Friedens-Predigten*. Leipzig: Krüger, 1914.

Kremers, Herman. *Deutscher Glaube, deutscher Gott!* Bonn: Georgi, 1914.

Kriegsvorträge in der Heimat. Gladbach: N.p., 1917.

Kritizinger, Johannes. *Mit Schmerzen gesucht*. Berlin: Evangelischer Trostbund, n.d.

_____. *Vertrauen und Geduld*. Berlin: Evangelischer Trostbund, 1916.

Kröber, Max. *Gottes Saat im Kriegsjahr: Kriegspredigten*. Berlin: N.p., 1915.

Kuhaupt, W. *Gibt es eine sittliche Weltordnung?* Stuttgart: Greiner, 1920.

Lahusen, Friedrich. *Christbaum und Schwert: Weihnachtsbuch für Feld und Heimat*. Berlin: N.p., 1915.

_____. *Die fünfte Bitte des Vaterlands und England*. Berlin: Warneck, 1915.

Lahusen, Hermann. *D. Friedrich Lahusen Vater und Seelsorger: Briefe an seinen Sohn*. Gütersloh: Bertelsmann, 1929.

Lehmann, Walter, ed. *Deutsche Frömmigkeit: Stimmen deutscher Gottesfreunde*. Jena: Diederichs, 1917.

_____. *Vom deutscher Gott: Vierzehn Predigten aus den Kriegsmonaten August, September, und Oktober 1914*. Ulm: Kerler, 1914.

Le Seur, Paul. *Frohbotschaft in Feindesland: Predigten*. Berlin: Warneck, 1915.

_____. *Vom werdenden Deutschland: Eine Kriegspredigt*. Berlin: Warneck, 1916.

Löber, Georg. *Christentum und Krieg?* Leipzig: Strauch, 1915.

Lorenz, Albert. *Warum blüht der Hohenzollern Krone?* Bonn: Georgi, 1915.

Meinhof, Carl. *Sittlichkeit und Krieg*. Hamburg, 1914.

Meyer, Wilhelm. *Nach der Bewährung die Verklärung: Bibelworte an Kriegergräbern*. Marburg: Elwert, 1916.

_____. *Vom ehrlichen Krieg: Ein Büchlein von Gott und uns Deutschen.* Marburg: Elwert, n.d.

Mulert, Hermann. *Der Christ und das Vaterland.* Leipzig: Hinrichs, 1915.

Naumann, Gottfried. *Stark in Gott: Predigten aus der Kriegszeit.* Leipzig: Hinrichs, 1915.

Nowak, G. *Stark und getrost im Herrn: Predigten aus ernster Zeit gehalten im Grossen Hauptquartier.* Berlin: Warneck, 1917.

Ott, Emil. *Religion, Krieg, und Vaterland.* Munich: Beck, 1915.

Pfennigsdorf, Emil. *Wie predigten wir heute Evangelium? Die Lebensfrage der christlichen Verkündigung in entschneidender Zeit.* Leipzig: Scholl, 1917.

Philippi, Fritz. *An der Front: Feldpredigten.* Wiesbaden: Staadt, 1916.

Pott, August. *Vom Feld fürs Feld: Predigten.* Marburg: Elwert, 1915.

Rade, Martin. *Dieser Krieg und das Christentum.* Stuttgart and Berlin: Deutsche Verlags-Anstalt, 1915.

Reetz. *An meine Soldaten: Ansprachen und Predigten während des ersten Kriegsjahres.* Leipzig: N.p., 1916.

Rendtorff, Franz. *Aus dem dritten Kriegswinter: Fünf Predigten.* Leipzig: Hinrichs, 1917.

Rhode, Franz. *Kriegspredigten.* Karlsruhe: Braun, 1914.

Risch, Adolf. *Mit Gott wollen wir Taten tun! Kriegspredigten, Andachten und Gebete.* Kaiserlautern: N.p., 1914.

Rittelmeyer, Friedrich. *Christ und Krieg: Predigten aus der Kriegszeit.* Munich: Kaiser, n.d.

_____. *Deutschlands religiöser Weltberuf.* Nuremberg: N.p., 1916.

_____. *Von der religiösen Zukunft des deutsches Geistes: Zwei Vorträge.* Nuremberg: N.p., n.d.

Roethe, Gustav. *Vom Tode fürs Vaterland.* Berlin: N.p., 1914.

Rolffs, Ernst, ed. *Evangelian-Predigten aus der Kriegszeit.* Göttingen: Vandenhoeck and Ruprecht, 1916.

_____. *Der heilige Krieg wider den inneren Feind: Elf Predigten aus dem dritten Kriegsjahr.* Göttingen: Vandenhoeck and Ruprecht, 1918.

Rump, J. *Berliner Kriegs-Betstunden, Soldatenpredigten, Kriegspredigten, und Gedächnisfeiern zu Ehren Gefallener.* Leipzig: Krüger, 1915.

_____. *Kriegspredigten für die festlose Hälfte des Kirchenjahres.* Leipzig: Krüger, 1915.

Sardemann, D. *Das Reich Gottes und der Krieg.* Cassel: Billardy and Augustin, n.d.

Schian, Martin. *Die deutsche evangelische Kirche im Weltkriege.* Berlin: Mittler, 1921.

Schneller, Ludwig. *Drei Kriegspredigten in der Kirche in Cöln (Marienburg) gehalten.* Cologne: Palästinahaus, 1914.

Schowalter, August. *Der Krieg in Predigten.* Barmen: Biermann, 1915.

Schubert, Hans von. *Die Erziehung unseres Volkes zum Welt zum Weltvolk.* Berlin: N.p., 1916.

_____. *Die Weihe des Kriegs.* Berlin: N.p., n.d.

Seeberg, E. *Religion im Feld.* Berlin-Lichterfelde: Runge, 1918.

Seeberg, Reinhold. *Geschichte, Krieg, und Seele: Reden und Aufsätze aus den Tagen des Weltkrieges.* Leipzig: Poelle and Meyer, 1916.

Spanuth, H. *Der Weltkrieg im Unterricht.* Gotha: Perthes, 1915.

Stahl, Emil. *Deutsches Kriegs ABC.* Munich: N.p., 1915.

Steltz, Theodor. *Krieg und Christentum.* Schwetzingen: Moch, 1915.

Stock, August. *Gott nimmt von uns alles weh! Drei Festpredigten zu Weihnacht und Neujahr im Kriegsjahr 1914/15.* Berlin-Lichterfelde: Runge, 1915.

Suderow, L. *Aus ernsten Tagen: Predigten aus der Kriegszeit, gehalten in der evangelischen Kirche zu Gnesen.* Gnesen: Baenisch, n.d.

Titius, Arthur. *Unser Krieg: Ethische Betrachtungen.* Tübingen: Mohr, 1915.

_____. *Worin gleicht unsere Gegenwart der Zeit der Freiheitskriege?* Hanover: Hahn, 1915.

Tolzien, Gerhard. *Die Kreuzworte im Kriege.* Schwerin: Bahn, 1916.

_____. *Kriegspredigten im Dom zu Schwerin gehalten.* 7 vols. Schwerin: Bahn, 1914-19.

_____. *Die Tragik in des Kaisers Leben.* Berlin, 1915.

Troeltsch, Ernst. *Deutscher Geist und Westeuropa: Gesammelte kulturphilosophische Aufsätze und Reden.* Tübingen: Mohr, 1925.

_____. *Deutscher Glaube und Deutsche Sitte in unserem grossen Kriege.* Berlin: N.p., n.d.

Völker, Karl. *Der Weltkrieg als Wendepunkt der Kirchengeschichte.* Vienna: N.p., 1915.

Vorwerk, Dietrich. *Was sagt der Weltkrieg den deutschen Christen?* Schwerin: Bahn, 1915.

Werner, Julius. *Deutschtum und Christentum: Gedenkreden.* Heidelberg: Winter, 1906.

Windisch, Hans. *Totenfest im Kriegsjahr.* Leipzig: N.p., 1914.

Wurster, Paul. *Das english Christenvolk und wir.* Tübingen: Kloeres, 1915.

_____. *Kriegspredigten aus dem grossen Krieg 1915 und 1916 von verschiedenen Verfassern.* Stuttgart: N.p., 1915.

Zurhellen, Otto. *Kriegspredigten.* Tübingen: Mohr, 1915.

SECONDARY WORKS

Bainton, Roland H. *Christian Attitudes toward War and Peace.* New York, 1960.

Balfour, Michael. *The Kaiser and His Times.* New York: Norton, 1972.

Baron, Salo W. *Modern Nationalism and Religion.* New York: Harper, 1947.

Bedborough, George. *Arms and the Clergy.* London: Pioneer, 1934.

Bell, G. K. A. *Randall Davidson: Archbishop of Canterbury.* Oxford: Oxford University Press, 1952.

Bigler, Robert M. "The Rise of Political Protestantism in Nineteenth Century Germany." *Church History.* Vol. XXXIV, No. 4 (December, 1965), 423-44.

Borg, Daniel R. *The Old-Prussian Church and the Weimar Republic: A Study in Political Adjustment, 1917-1927.* Hanover and London, NH: University Press of New England, 1984.

Bossenbrook, William J. *The German Mind.* Detroit: Wayne State University Press, 1961.

Brakelmann, Günter. *Der deutsche Protestantismus im Epochenjahr 1917.* Witten: Luther-Verlag, 1974.

_____. *Protestantische Kriegstheologie im Ersten Weltkrieg: Reinhold Seeberg al Theologe des deutschen Imperialismus.* Bielefeld: Luther-Verlag, 1974.

Brinton, Crane. *A History of Western Morals.* New York: Harcourt, Brace, and Co., 1959.

Cassirer, Ernst. *The Myth of the State.* New Haven: Yale University Press, 1946.

Chadwick, Owen. *The Victorian Church.* London, 1966.

Chambers, F. P. *The War behind the War, 1914-1918.* London: Faber, 1939.

Churchill, Winston. *The World Crisis.* London: N.p., 1929.

Conway, John S. "The Political Theology of Martin Niemöller." *German Studies Review.* Vol. 9, No. 3 (October, 1986), pp. 521-46.

Cowles, Virginia. *The Kaiser.* New York: Harper, 1963.

Cruttwell, C. R. M. F. *A History of the Great War.* Oxford, 1964.

Drummond, Andrew. *German Protestantism Since Luther.* London: Epworth, 1951.

Ericksen, Robert P. "The Political Theology of Paul Althaus: Nazi Supporter." *German Studies Review.* Vol. 9, No. 3 (October, 1986), 547-68.

Eyck, Erich. *Das persönliche Regiment Wilhelm II.* Zürich, 1948.

Fischer, Fritz. *Germany's Aims in the First World War.* New York: Norton, 1967.

Hammer, Karl. *Deutsche Kriegstheologie, 1870-1918.* Munich: Kösel-Verlag, 1971.

Hayes, Carlton J. H. *Essays on Nationalism.* New York: Macmillan, 1926.

_____. *The Historical Evolution of Modern Nationalism.* New York: Macmillan, 1931.

_____. *Nationalism: A Religion.* New York: Macmillan, 1960.

Heger, Adolf. *Evangelische Verkündigung und deutsches Nationalbewusstsein: Zur Geschichte der Predigt von 1806-1848.* Berlin: Junker and Dünnhaupt, 1939.

Hertz, Frederick. *Nationality in History and Politics: A Study of the Psychology and Sociology of National Sentiment and Character.* New York: Oxford University Press, 1944.

Hoover, Arlie J. "The Dangers of Religious Patriotism: A German Example." *Restoration Quarterly.* Vol. 29, No. 2 (1987), 87-96.

_____. "God and German Unification: Protestant Patriotic Preaching During the Franco-Prussian War, 1870-71." *Fides et Historia.* Vol. 18, No. 2 (June, 1986), 20-32.

_____. "God and Germany in the Great War." *Canadian Review of Studies in Nationalism.* Vol. 14, No. 1 (Spring, 1987), 65-82.

_____. *The Gospel of Nationalism: German Patriotic Preaching from Napoleon to Versailles.* Stuttgart: Steiner, 1986.

_____. "Religion and National Stereotypes: A German Protestant Example." *History of European Ideas.* Vol. 8, No. 3 (1987), 297-307.

Huber, Wolfgang. "Evangelische Theologie und Kirche beim Ausbruch des Ersten Weltkrieges." *Historische Beiträge zur Friedensforderung.* Stuttgart-Munich, 1970.

James, William. *Varieties of Religious Experience.* New York: Longmans, Green, and Co., 1941.

Kohn, Hans. *The Idea of Nationalism: A Study in Its Origins and Background.* New York: Macmillan, 1948.

_____. *The Mind of Germany: The Education of a Nation.* New York: Scribners, 1960.

_____. "Romanticism and the Rise of German Nationalism." *The Review of Politics.* Vol. 12, No. 4 (October, 1950), 443-72.

Krieger, Leonard. *The German Idea of Freedom.* Boston: Beacon Press, 1957.

Lasswell, Harold D. *Propaganda Technique in the World War.* London, 1927.

Lemberg, Eugen. *Nationalismus.* 2 vols. Reinbeck/Hamburg, 1964.

Lenz, Max. "Nationalität und Religion." *Preussische Jahrbücher.* Vol. 137 (January-March, 1907), 385-408.

Liddel-Hart, B. H. *A History of the World War, 1914-1918.* London, 1934.

Lübbe, Hermann. *Politische Philosophie in Deutschland: Studien zu ihrer Geschichte.* Basel and Stuttgart: Schwage, 1963.

Marrin, Albert. *The Last Crusade: The Church of England in the First World War.* Durham, N.C.: Duke University Press, 1974.

Marsch, Wolf-Dieter. "Politische Predigt zum Kriegsbeginn, 1914/15." *Evangelische Theologie.* Vol. 24 (1964), 513-38.

Marwick, Arthur. *The Deluge: British Society and the First World War.* London: Macmillan, 1965.

Mehnert, Gottfried. *Evangelische Kirche und Politik 1917-1919. Die politische Strömungen im deutschen Protestantismus von der Julikrise 1917 bis zum Herbst 1919.* Düsseldorf: Droste, 1959.

Messerschmidt, Manfred. *Deutschland in Englisher Sicht. Der wandlungendes Deutschlandsbildes in der Englischen Geschichts-Schreibung.* Düsseldorf: Trilsch, 1955.

Mosse, George. *The Crisis of German Ideology.* New York: Grosset and Dunlap, 1964.

Mowat, C. L. *The New Cambridge Modern History.* Vol. 12, *The Shifting Balance of World Forces, 1898-1945.* Cambridge: Cambridge University Press, 1968.

Muir, Ramsay. *Nationalism and Internationalism: The Culmination of Modern History.* Boston: Houghton Mifflin, 1977.

Piechowski, Paul. *Die Kriegspredigt von 1870/71.* Leipzig: Scholl, 1916.

Pinson, Koppel S. *Pietism as a Factor in the Rise of German Nationalism.* New York: Columbia University Press, 1934.

Pressel, Wilhelm. *Die Kriegspredigt 1914-1918 in der evangelische Kirche Deutschlands.* Göttingen: Vandenhoeck and Ruprecht, 1967.

Schwabe, Klaus. "Zur Politischen Haltung der Deutschen Professoren im Ersten Weltkrieg." *Historische Zeitschrift.* Vol. 193 (1961), 601-34.

Shafer, Boyd. *Nationalism: Myth and Reality.* New York: Harcourt, Brace, and Co., 1955.

Snyder, Louis L. *The Meaning of Nationalism.* New Brunswick, NJ: Rutgers University Press, 1954.

Taylor, A. J. P. *The Struggle for Mastery in Europe.* Oxford: Clarendon, 1954.

Thatcher, David S. *Nietzsche in England, 1890-1914: The Growth of a Reputation.* Toronto: University Press, 1970.

Tuchman, Barbara. *The Guns of August.* New York: Macmillan, 1962.

_____. *The Proud Tower: A Portrait of the World Before the War, 1890-1914.* New York: Macmillan, 1966.

Viereck, Peter. *Metapolitics: From the Romantics to Hitler.* New York: Knopf, 1941.

Wilkinson, Alan. *The Church of England and the First World War.* London: SPCK, 1978.

Willis, Irene C. *England's Holy War: A Study of English Liberal Idealism During the Great War.* New York: Knopf, 1928.

Wittram, Reinhard. *Nationalismus und Säkularisation: Beiträge zur Geschichte und Problematik des Nationalgeistes.* Lüneburg, 1949.

Woodward, E. L. *Great Britain and the German Navy.* Oxford, 1935.

Zahn-Harnack, Agnes von. *Adolf von Harnack.* Berlin: Gruyter, 1951.

Index

ABOUT THE AUTHOR

ARLIE J. HOOVER is professor of history at Abilene Christian University in Abilene, Texas. Formerly professor of history and philosophy at Pepperdine University in Malibu, California, he received his M.A. and Ph.D. from the University of Texas at Austin. He has lived in Europe for several years and has done research at the universities of Berlin, Heidelberg, Marburg, Oxford, and Cambridge. His first publication on the topic of clerical nationalism was *The Gospel of Nationalism* (1986).